Consequences of
Child Abuse

Consequences of
Child Abuse

Margaret A. Lynch
Senior Lecturer in Community Paediatrics,
Guy's Hospital,
London

and

Jacqueline Roberts
Research Social Worker,
Park Hospital for Children,
Oxford

1982   ACADEMIC PRESS
A Subsidiary of Harcourt Brace Jovanovich, Publishers
London   New York
Paris   San Diego   San Francisco   São Paulo
Sydney   Tokyo   Toronto

ACADEMIC PRESS INC. (LONDON) LTD
24–28 Oval Road,
London NW1

U.S. Edition published by
ACADEMIC PRESS INC.
111 Fifth Avenue,
New York, New York 10003

British Library Cataloguing in Publication Data

Lynch, M.
    Consequences of child abuse.
    1. Child abuse
    I. Title   II. Roberts, J.C.
    362.7′044   HV713

ISBN 0 12 4605702

LCCCN 82 71014

Phototypesetting by Permanent Typesetters,
Hong Kong and printed in Great Britain
by Galliard (Printers) Ltd, Great Yarmouth

Foreword

In novel clinical practice, research and service are indivisible. Neither is possible (nor ethical) without the other. In 1962, Henry Kempe forced a reluctant medical world to face the fact that many of our child patients were the victims of physical abuse. A few months later, we found ourselves having a facility for the treatment of whole families as in-patients: hospital based family medicine, a new and, hence, a daunting prospect.

I was flooded with guilt-ridden memories. In 1948 the National Health Service began. Oxygen was now free. We could give our tiny blue premature babies as much as we liked. We did. And we did not monitor such obviously good practice. The babies we blinded with retrolental fibroplasia haunt all childrens' doctors of my generation.

In this book Margaret Lynch and Jacquie Roberts examine in great depth the outcome of a novel form of in-patient treatment for families in whom cataclysmic breakdown of intrafamilial bonds had occurred. I have found their honest and penetrating analyses a most helpful corrective to complacency.

All those who have professional responsibilities for children will benefit if they read and ponder on the thoughts and findings here reported. These families were treated as wholes, often over several weeks, as in-patients and several years as out-patients — yet, when we look at the results, we are forced, I believe, to agree with the authors that prevention is the only true final goal.

Christopher Ounsted, M.A., D.M., F.R.C.P.,
F.R.C. Psych., D.P.M., D.C.H.

June, 1982

Preface

It is no coincidence that the title of this book, "Consequences of Child Abuse", evokes memories of the well known parlour game where participants add a new episode to a story in total ignorance of the earlier sections. Over the years we have watched a similar game being played with the lives of some abused children: magistrates, senior social workers and paediatricians have made major decisions concerning a child's life which seem to have had little connection with earlier events. The disjointed biographies of some of the children known to us have produced disturbed and confused teenagers who themselves will face great difficulties in becoming adequate parents. From the mid-1960s abused children, together with their parents and siblings, were being admitted to the family unit at the Park Hospital for Children, Oxford. The follow-up study reported in this book is the result of the staff's curiosity about what, in the long-term, was happening to the children and their families. From a previous study (Lynch and Ounsted, 1976) we knew the short-term outcome to be good with high rates of rehabilitation and little recurrent abuse. However, we did not know in detail what had happened to all the children and their families in the years following discharge. Where were they? What problems, if any, did they have now? By answering these questions we hoped to provide some of the much needed information required to ensure more effective long-term planning for all abused children. Our study was designed primarily to identify the problems experienced by the children and their parents, not to evaluate the intervention they received, though of course our findings do enable us to comment on some aspects of management.

For the purpose of our study we identified all the physically abused children who had been admitted to the Park Hospital with their families from the time the family unit was opened until the beginning of 1975. During this period of time there were 42 such children from 40 families who had received residential therapy for the problem of child abuse. In 1977 the children from 38 of these families together with their current caretakers participated in our comprehensive follow-up study. Our findings form the basis of this book. It is not written for any one professional group and we hope practitioners, academics and social policy makers will all find something of relevance.

Firstly we put our study in the context of other follow-up studies and give the background details of the admission of the families to the Park Hospital following identification of the abuse. Then the legal proceedings taken to protect the children both immediately and during the follow-up interval are described. This is followed by the results of our assessments of the children's growth, health and intellectual development with a discussion of their behaviour and emotional problems. We consider the number and type of placements outside the family experienced by the children. Then we give detailed accounts of the parents and current caretakers together with subjective reports from the parents on life in the family home at the time of follow-up. Finally we describe the children who by our criteria could be said to be doing well. We try to work out why these children had survived the abusive environment and describe them in some detail.

Each of the chapters describing our findings contains a review of the relevant literature. The book concludes with a general discussion of what we feel the implications of our small study are for those who work with abused children. Overall our main aim is to provide as full a picture as possible of the consequences of child abuse for a small group of families whom we came to know very well.

March 1982   Margaret A. Lynch
                                                        Jacqueline Roberts

Contents

Acknowledgements

We first and foremost thank Dr Christopher Ounsted without whom this study would have been impossible. All the staff at the Park Hospital are thanked for their enthusiastic co-operation with the project. We are indebted to the parents and children who agreed to participate in this study, many with the intention of helping other families who might face a similar predicament. The authors received funding from Action Research for the Crippled Child and Oxford University Medical Research Fund. Jacqueline Roberts was seconded by Oxfordshire Social Services Department.

Sue Gretton, Occupational Therapist, Doreen Baxter and John Richer, Clinical Psychologists at the Park Hospital, helped us directly with the assessments. The neurological classification was devised with the help of Dr Jennifer Dennis. The Oxfordshire School Psychological Service helped us with the distribution of questionnaires to the children's teachers. We could not have completed our assessments of children living at a distance from the hospital without the help of social workers, local educational psychologists and, for two families, the B.A.O.R.

We thank the staff of the residental establishments, day nurseries and playgroups for welcoming us and answering our questions. We thank all the teachers, doctors, health visitors and social workers who completed our questionnaires. We were helped in the collection of our data from schools by Pam Duff, social work student. Veronica Stogdon, research assistant, helped prepare data for computer analysis which was kindly carried out by the Oxfordshire Regional Health Authority.

We are grateful to the following for reading manuscripts and making constructive comments: Professor Roger Robinson, Roger Smith, Professor Olive Stevenson, Richard White and Pat Yudkin. Our excellent secretary, Mrs Jean Warland, typed our never-ending drafts with skill and patience.

Finally we would like to acknowledge our own families, without whom the book would have been completed sooner!

This book is dedicated to Christopher Ounsted and all
members of staff, past, present and future at the Park
Hospital for Children.

1. What can we learn from follow-up studies?

Any review of the literature describing the outcome of child abuse soon reveals the difficulties both of following up samples of abused children and of interpreting the results obtained. In this chapter we explore the problems encountered and describe our attempts to overcome them when planning our own project.

A. Identification of sample

The sample of children studied will depend on the definition of abuse used and the population available. Research on child abuse is relatively new and there is no internationally agreed definition. Indeed, the criteria for including children in a follow-up study are almost as numerous as the studies themselves. For example, Elmer and Gregg (1967) originally studied only children who had multiple skeletal injuries, whereas Martin *et al.* (1974) included all inflicted injuries however mild. Both these authors excluded uninjured children with neglect or failure to thrive whereas McRae *et al.* (1973) included poisoning, hypothermia and failure to thrive in the definition of their sample. Several other authors have included neglect without physical injuries (Morse *et al.*, 1970; Birrell and Birrell, 1968).

Another drawback is seldom mentioned: when collecting samples, researchers often depend on other people's diagnoses and judgements. For example, for Martin's 1974 study "names of potential study subjects were obtained through hospital charts. . ." Such retrospectively identified samples are at the mercy of the idiosyncracies of the initial data collection and retrieval system available. Undoubtedly some early studies relied on staff's memories. For instance, Birrell and

1

Birrell (1968) wrote that "The memories of all ward sisters were taxed back for 2½ years..."! Given the understandable reluctance to diagnose child abuse (Ounsted, 1975), it is very likely that any retrospective identification will miss cases. To avoid these problems, Green *et al.* (1974) chose as their criteria for abuse "that it be of an on-going or recurrent nature and confirmed by investigation of protective services." This makes for a more certain diagnosis but it provides a very limited sample of abused children. The only thing all the reported studies have in common is that someone somewhere in his considered and professional opinion recorded that the child had been abused.

The actual location of the sample studied could also limit the range of abuse considered and thereby influence the outcome. A paediatrician identifying cases in the accident department will study a far different sample from that seen by an educational welfare officer in schools. It is also possible that the characteristics of the general population from which the sample is drawn may be of greater determining influence on the results than the occurrence of child abuse. For example, Elmer (1977) followed up a group of 'traumatized' infants. She compared them 8 years later with controls matched for age, race, sex and socio-economic status. She looked at multiple variables and found few differences. She concluded that "the use of matched comparison groups to evaluate the outcome for abused children does offer a means to *correct* conclusions based on the study of abused children alone". But another interpretation of these findings is that the equally high incidence of family and neighbourhood violence in both index and control groups, together with the underlying problems of severe poverty affecting all the families, overpowered any specific effect of abuse.

It would be rash to claim that we have been able to overcome all these difficulties in setting up our own follow-up study. We restricted the sample to children with definite physical abuse who were admitted to the residential unit at the Park Hospital over a defined period of time. As the hospital has no accident and emergency department, all cases were referrals from other medical or social work agencies and included a wide range of injuries from the life-threatening to minor bruising. While we do not know how the referral system and the hospital's reputation biased the sample available for study, we can at least be confident of the diagnosis. We did not have to rely on others to collect the index cases and in many instances we personally received the parent's admission of inflicting abuse.

B. Data collection

The amount of data gathered in a follow-up study will be limited by the time, money and expertise available. The larger the number of cases followed up, the less comprehensive the assessment and the more the researcher will depend on distant and unknown people to collect the data. The wider and the more impersonal the study becomes, the less reliable the results. For example, the results of an American nation-wide survey (Gil, 1969) of "legally reported incidents" of child abuse can only uncover part of the whole problem of child abuse and neglect, and probably reveals as much about "legal reporting" as it does about child abuse. As Gil himself writes: "Since abuse incidents tend to occur in the privacy of a family's home, not all of them do come to the attention of individuals or institutions who are required to report and not all such incidents that are known . . . are actually reported." Many large or detailed research projects collect information by sending out questionnaires to professionals involved with the families. Unless such questionnaires are short and explicit, they are very unlikely to be filled in accurately, if at all (Freeman, 1977). The natural response to receiving a long and complicated questionnaire is either to throw it in the bin or leave it at the bottom of the in-tray.

Because of the difficulties of obtaining a consistent definition of "child abuse", it is probably too soon to attempt large-scale epidemio-logical follow-up studies. At present, small comprehensive studies of a clearly defined sample of children — like our own — will probably provide a better quality of information. The results of such enquiries may well then determine the key questions to be asked in large-scale projects. However, the great danger of using small samples is that people will use the results to make sweeping statements about whole populations. For example, it was unfortunate that five children who died in Preston, Lancashire in the three years 1970-1972 (Hall, 1975) led to the emotive, much quoted and misleading statement that about two children are battered to death every day in the U.K. (Howells, 1974; Sunday Times, 1977).

Whatever the size of a sample, one is inevitably dependent on the co-operation of the professionals who are providing services to the child and his family. It is therefore relevant to consider here the attitude these individuals might have towards the researcher and the project. Service personnel who see themselves as hard-working and underpaid, often understandably resent "research workers". From the outside,

their lives seem relaxed and far away from the constant demands of
clients. Therefore, it is essential that time is allowed for explaining the
purpose and implications of the research to those expected to deliver
services to the families in the sample. The co-operation of a professional already involved with a family is invaluable when trying to
recruit them for a project. If the worker whom the family trusts feels
positively towards the research team, then it is likely that the parents
will agree to be seen or allow information to be passed on. Without the
backing of such professionals, one is liable to receive a letter that
reads: "I explained your project to Mr. and Mrs. X. Their initial
reaction was to agree to participate but, after discussing it with me,
they decided it would not be in their best interests." It must also be
remembered that many workers feel very uncomfortable when dealing
with child abuse. Their aversion to the problem may produce denial. If
they cannot believe a child was ever abused, they are unlikely to want
to take part in a long-term follow-up of his abuse. Added to this is the
professional's suspicion of any project that might be interpreted as
monitoring professional practice. Throughout our research studies
we have made a point of always trying to meet any professional
working with a family. This entailed a lot of time and travelling, but
the enthusiasm with which many helped us made it very worthwhile.

When reviewing the literature we were alarmed by the number of
children in other researchers' original samples that were unavailable
for follow-up assessment. For example, Martin et al. (1974) lost 25% of
his identified sample of 159 abused children, and a further 40% were
not assessed for various reasons, including unco-operative parents,
too great a distance for children to travel, and adoption. He finally
assessed only 58 out of the original sample of 159. His experience is
not exceptional: Birrell and Birrell (1968) had lost contact with 33% of
a sample of 42 children; Friedman and Morse (1974) were unable to
assess 25% of 54 injured children and McRae et al. (1973) located and
examined only 34 out of 88 children (39%). Of the rest, 16 were
completely lost, 8 had died, 4 were in institutions and a further 26
either refused to participate, lived too far away or failed to attend the
arranged assessment.

Obviously, results which reflect the assessments of less than half the
original samples are open to serious criticism as there could be an
enormous difference between those families who attend for follow-up
assessment and those who do not. For all we know, it could be a very
positive sign for the family to refuse to co-operate in research. On the
other hand, some of the lost children could be dead.

We were particularly fortunate to locate eventually 39 families in the
original sample of 40 and assess the children from 38; only one family

refused totally to participate. Our success was partly because of the Park Hospital's policy not to terminate formally contact with families. Some were still attending the hospital's out-patient service and others were still open social work cases, which naturally made tracing much easier. Nevertheless, the search took a great deal of persistence, time, detective work and luck, with one or two families only being discovered 18 months after the beginning of the search.

C. Control groups

The problem of finding a group of children who can be compared meaningfully with a sample of abused children remains unsolved. A case/control format is the conventional way of conducting a clinical study but its use is only legitimate when it is possible to isolate and keep constant the factors under analysis. In studies of the outcome of child abuse, such an approach proves difficult, if not impossible. For example, to look at factors influencing the outcome of child abuse in a given geographical area, the type and extent of injury and the age of child would have to be kept constant. Given the variety of cases we have seen, it would take more than a professional life-time to collect such a sample. If an attempt were made to match for all factors, apart from confirmed inflicted injuries, as Elmer did in her study (1977), one might simply obtain a control group of children who were abused but not actually identified as such. Other researchers have suggested comparing abused children with those who have been subject to ideal child-rearing techniques, but who is in a position to identify such "super parents"? One possible future solution may be the use of a longitudinal study of a large birth cohort. If the abused children were reliably identified, their development could be compared with that of the rest of the study population. Our way of tackling the control group problem was to assess all the unharmed brothers and sisters as well as the abused children. In this way we could keep reasonably constant the environmental influences. Even so, this comparison does not account for age difference, different birth order or the all-important individual differences in each child. Any parent who has several children can report how variably their offspring reacted to very similar care and circumstances.

D. Interpretation of data

A major weakness of all follow-up studies that claim to assess the effect of abuse on a child's development is the lack of comparable medical and developmental data for the period prior to the injury.

Even something as seemingly straightforward as neurological handicap in an abused child is not always easy to blame on the abuse incident. We know several severely mentally handicapped children who were abused but, from parents' and others' subjective reports we feel that they were probably handicapped before the injury occurred.

As abuse is often combined with neglect and failure to thrive (Elmer and Gregg, 1967; Ebbin *et al.*, 1969; Morse *et al.*, 1970; Martin, 1972; Martin *et al.*, 1974) the follow-up outcome in some cases could be the result of neglect and malnutrition rather than the injuries. Even if we were to restrict ourselves to isolated incidents of physical abuse, the range of injuries is enormous; it is common sense that a badly beaten head will have different results from a lacerated and bruised backside! Furthermore, if a child is assessed say, 10 years after an abuse incident, many other extraneous influences on his life such as accidents, family changes, different schools, household moves, and simply the passage of time, could all affect his developmental progress. Consequently, any follow-up study of abused children really only gives a picture of a heterogeneous group of children who have suffered perhaps one thing in common: physical injury inflicted by their parents. Nevertheless, because of therapeutic implications, it is important to attempt to find out what effect the type and severity of the injury may have on the long-term outcome.

When the follow-up data have been collected there are then problems with interpretation. Even what would appear to be a straight-forward mortality rate can produce uncertainty. Does the mortality rate include all children who die as a direct result of abuse? Suspicious child deaths discovered on post-mortem will not always be notified to the person concerned with collecting the names of abused children. Then the mortality rates made after identification will include deaths from re-injury, deaths from the long-term complications of injuries, and deaths from unrelated causes as well as deaths as a direct result of the identified abuse.

Subsequent injury rates are often used to assess outcome and the effect of intervention, as was done in the NSPCC Surveys (1972, 1975). Does abuse follow abuse, even after professional help? But reports of subsequent injuries are open to misinterpretation. Even the tiniest bruise may be detected by a zealous therapist working with an abusing family, whereas only the more serious abuse which requires medical attention will be recorded for families who are not receiving child protection services. Moreover, subsequent injury rates should not be the only criterion used to judge the quality of a child's life or the effectiveness of intervention. Recent literature, such as the study by the

NSPCC Research Team (Baher *et al.*, 1976) has hinted that there may be for some children more destructive influences in their lives apart from inflicted injuries:

> "Whether the child is removed from home or remains with his family, it is likely that specific and intensive therapeutic intervention will be required if there is to be any chance of undoing long-term distortion in a child's relationship with the mother."

The medical follow-up literature has mainly concentrated on the subsequent physical and intellectual status of the abused child, less attention being paid to the development and well-being of other members of the family and the effect this has on the emotional health of the child. Documentation of permanent physical handicap will give no better picture of outcome than will subsequent injury rates. While it is impossible to reverse neurological damage, its impact on an individual child's later life can be greatly modified by the care and attention he receives. On the other hand, a child can survive physical abuse neurologically intact, to become an emotional cripple because of repeated parental rejection. For example, a girl with a mild hemiplegia and poor vision, living in a stable and caring family, could well have a qualitatively far better life than a highly intelligent, beautiful blonde whose divorced mother hates her and whose absent father rarely visits. It therefore seems important to make a follow-up enquiry of abused children as comprehensive and wide-ranging as possible.

In the end we felt that a follow-up study can only really ask a very general question: "What is the outcome of being identified as an abused child?" To answer this and understand the world of the abused child, it would seem appropriate to adopt a developmental viewpoint, enabling us to look at the unfolding biography of the child and his family. In every case a series of interrelated adverse social and medical events have led up to the physical abuse. The inflicted injury should never be thought of as a chance happening in an otherwise normal, happy child. The characteristics of abusing parents, their diffuse social problems and the high prevalence of ill-health in the family are all associated with children's developmental problems. Abusing parents' typical attitudes towards child-rearing, especially their rigidity, intolerance and unrealistic expectations, are all destined to produce further developmental and behavioural problems. Even the effects of intervention can be detrimental to a child's development: prolonged stays in hospital, uncertainties while case conferences are convened and legal action is considered, massive attention given to the parents, "trials" back at home and multiple visits from social workers and health-care professionals.

II. OUTLINE OF OUR STUDY

Our own study was greatly influenced by the need for a developmental approach. The practical limitations of time and manpower gave us further strong reasons for deciding to carry out a personal, detailed study of a small number of families who had all spent some time in the Park Hospital family unit. Base-line data were therefore available in the hospital records and for some children assessments had been carried out at intervals throughout the follow-up period. Thus, for example, it was possible to study most children's growth patterns since the abuse incident.

At the research follow-up assessment, each child had a detailed physical and neurological examination. All those children under 5 years had a Mary Sheridan developmental assessment. Those over 3 years were tested by a psychologist and IQ scores were obtained. All the children were observed alone in a period of free play. The length of the assessment meant that all the families spent at least one afternoon with us at the hospital. We tried to make the experience as much fun as possible for the children and made sure that each child received an explanation of the assessment appropriate to his age and circumstances. The families varied greatly in their reaction to the visit and we obtained much extra interesting information simply from spending so much time with them.

Following the hospital assessments, the families were visited at home and an interview with the parents tape-recorded. There was a set interview schedule which usually lasted between 1 and 2 hours. A questionnaire was later filled in from listening to the tapes — they were not transcribed in full. When planning this interview schedule we asked the advice of several parents and piloted it on families currently staying in the family unit because of child abuse. This proved very valuable. For those children not currently living with their parents, we tried to interview both the caretakers and the natural parents but, as expected, not all these natural parents agreed to be seen.

Information about the family's use of health and social services was obtained firstly from the parents and then, with their permission, checked against the relevant records. Brief questionnaires were sent to social workers and family doctors to obtain a few well-defined facts and, if they wished to give it, their current opinion of the family. We had a 100% response rate. Child care proceedings were checked against official sources, but we relied on parents (and the occasional press report) to tell us of their other brushes with the law.

Teachers of all school-age children were interviewed and they also completed questionnaires about the children's behaviour in school. Nursery schools, playgroups and residential homes were also visited and information obtained from the staff at all these establishments.

The project involved us in a considerable amount of travelling: over 8000 miles were travelled by us or the families still living in the U.K. before the information gathering was complete. We were impressed by the distance some parents were prepared to come to see us. One mother brought her three boisterous sons on buses and trains from the other side of central London. Three families were seen and assessed abroad: one in the United States and two in Germany.

Without our close association with the diagnostic and therapeutic services of the Park Hospital, our research would have been impossible. Many of the families, including those where legal action had been taken, had very positive feelings towards the hospital and its staff. Those with negative feelings seemed to welcome the opportunity to tell us what they thought of the place. A few ghosts were laid and constructive suggestions for improving facilities were put forward by some parents and children. Our own previous experiences of working with abusing families undoubtedly influenced our research design and our method of approaching the families. It is difficult to know how we would have coped with the project without this experience. Families in crisis — and some abusing families always seem to be in one — are not going to distinguish between researchers and therapists. If such a family asks for help, one must at least make sure they get it. It is, we believe, unethical in such circumstances to make one's observations and disappear. Such action will simply confirm the families' feelings of distrust and resentment towards authority. Back-up facilities are always required by researchers intending to see and evaluate abusing families. Any medical, developmental or emotional problem revealed in the course of our investigation was referred for assessment and treatment. Time was allowed for discussing findings with parents and, where appropriate, with the families' medical and social work advisers.

In conclusion, we have amassed a mound of facts and impressions and have been granted privileged glimpses into the lives of families where a child had been diagnosed as abused. We hope to share many of these with our readers, although our prime concern is to report the more formal data. The emotions the families have revealed to us could never be measured or put on computer tape, but this does not diminish their painful significance. For example, how does one code the anguish of an intelligent and caring young mother watching her two children playing in the garden? One, a 3-year old, is a bright, boisterous, well-grown young boy; the other, a girl and 8 years old, is visually, physically and neurologically handicapped as the direct result of injuries inflicted by that same mother when she was very young and living in a totally different world.

As the Park Hospital service for abused children and their families is almost unique, it would be unrealistic to claim that general conclusions should be drawn from our study. However, it must be stressed that this has never been our aim. Rather we hope to draw as true and detailed a picture as possible of a small number of abused children and their families in order to guide others in their understanding of the full implications of child abuse and its importance in the lives of all the family members. We are not claiming to measure the outcome of abuse — rather to capture a true picture of the lives of abused children and their families, albeit for one fleeting moment. What actually happens to a small group of abused children could be just as enlightening as the estimate of statistical probabilities for a whole population. The reader must judge for himself.

II. The Park Hospital and our sample

I. THERAPEUTIC BACKGROUND

The families in this study have all participated in the residential family therapy that is available at the Park Hospital for Children, Oxford. By considering the hospital's philosophy and the range of facilities available there, it is easy to understand how the therapy for families evolved and how child abuse came to be a major concern.

The Park Hospital for Children is a National Health Service Hospital which began in 1958 with Dr Christopher Ounsted as its Medical Director. The hospital deals with children's neurological and psychiatric disorders and is a National Centre for Epilepsy. There are beds for 30 children in-patients. From the time the hospital opened, the assessment and treatment of a wide range of disorders has always included evaluation and therapy of the associated family problems.

The hospital's main building is an early Victorian red brick house which looks more like a large, rambling, family home than a hospital. It is surrounded by very pleasant park-like grounds. In 1964 a bungalow with accommodation for three families was added to the hospital along with a number of schoolrooms and playrooms. When the bungalow (the family unit) was built, it was envisaged that the main need would be for the psychotherapy of parents and siblings of irreversibly handicapped children, but the late 1960s and early 1970s brought a dramatic increase in the referrals to the hospital of cases of actual or threatened child abuse and neglect. Thus, in 1971 − 1973, child abuse cases represented about half the admissions to the unit. In 1975 a peak was reached: 28 out of the 30 families admitted for that year (85%) were admitted because of actual or threatened child abuse. Since then, the rate has gone right down to approximately 30%, with only one case of actual abuse admitted in 1979.

A. The family unit

The bungalow where the families stay is just a few yards from the main door of the hospital. Each family has a small bed-sitting room and shares the main sitting room, dining area, kitchen, bathroom and laundry facilities. Meals are provided from the hospital kitchen or, if they choose, the parents can cook for themselves. Sometimes whole families eat alongside the children and staff in the main hospital dining room. The parents are responsible for cleaning their own rooms and communal areas in the unit, a task performed at variable levels of efficiency and co-operation. The parents have their own front door key and, as long as appointments are kept, are free to come and go as they wish. A telephone is available in the unit, both for outside calls and as a link with the main hospital building. All the facilities in the main hospital which include several playrooms and a well equipped occupational/play therapy department can be used by the families in the unit. Often, at least initially, an abused child will be expected to sleep in the night nursery in the main building and be looked after some of the time in the day nursery which is staffed by experienced and qualified nursery nurses.

The architecture of the unit and its close links with the main hospital facilities are themselves essential aspects of the therapy. The building is planned to combine privacy for each family along with quick and easy access to the hospital staff. For example, at night, the nursing and medical staff provide on-call care for the unit. The aim is for the parents to feel secure and cared for without feeling watched. This is not always believed initially, as one mother told us during the follow-up study that she was convinced that her room was "bugged" and that we were constantly watching her through hidden cameras! In fact, we have been asked occasionally by professional visitors why we do not have closed circuit television. It has been our experience that the parents need to feel trusted and not under suspicion, before they can begin to trust the hospital staff in a way which we feel is necessary, before therapy can begin.

B. The hospital staff

Although the Park Hospital is small, with provision for only 30 in-patients, it provides a wide-ranging out-patient service which requires a large number of staff from different professions. Any of these staff can be available to the families in the unit if necessary. Because the staff are part of a wider organization, working in the emotionally stressful and exhausting sphere of child abuse need be only a small part of their day. They can find relief by working in another area of the hospital and on another type of problem.

The aim at the Park Hospital is to contain the whole range of paediatric, psychiatric, social, medical and legal problems within the scope of an integrated, multi-disciplinary team with a common sense of commitment. Comprehensive services can then be given to these families who have closely interrelated emotional, practical and medical problems. Too often the diversity of facilities needed by these families is provided by services which are both geographically and ideologically widely separated. The staff available to the families resident in the unit are as follows:

(1) *Nurses.* Some nurses have trained as paediatric nurses and others as psychiatric nurses; occasionally they have both qualifications. Others have had no formal training, but have often worked in the hospital for many years and are parents themselves. They provide a stable background of well-tried ideas and common sense. A key member of the team is a nurse who spends most of the day working with the parents and the children who are resident in the unit.

(2) *The medical personnel* in the hospital have either paediatric or psychiatric qualifications and some have both. There are four consultants and their junior staff. A family planning specialist visits the hospital regularly. There is a busy electroencephalography unit in the hospital grounds.

(3) *A social work department* is based in the hospital. The social workers work as therapists in the hospital, and provide essential links with the community services.

(4) *The occupational therapists* have their own department where the staff have developed special skills in the assessment and treatment of handicapped and disturbed children. They have also developed therapy for parents and children who have a serious relationship problem. Each child is seen in this department and usually parent/child interaction is assessed and treated there.

(5) *A clinical psychology department* provides detailed assessment and treatment of the psychological problems in all the patients. Often behaviour therapy programmes are devised there.

(6) *The hospital school* is staffed by four full-time and one part-time teacher and a headmaster. All school-age children resident at the hospital attend the school. A few children attend as day cases and observations and assessments are made of the children's educa-

tional ability and requirements. Special help is provided for
children with particular learning difficulties.

(7) *A physiotherapist* is available for the treatment of handicapped
children.

(8) *A speech therapist* also regularly visits the hospital for assessment and treatment of language disorders; this is a much needed
recent innovation.

There are therefore many members of staff with wide and varying
responsibilities and interest, any one of whom could be called upon to
help a family in the unit. In addition to all this, there is a research unit
in the grounds where research studies include long-term follow-up
studies of children with neonatal convulsions and children with
temporal lobe epilepsy, an assessment of the educational problems of
children with epilepsy and the research project which began in
February 1975 into the prediction, prevention and treatment of child
abuse and neglect.

It is important to understand fully the philosophy at the hospital
where the families are resident. No-one wears uniform and there is an
informal, family-like atmosphere. There are very regular meetings to
discuss in-patients, to plan forthcoming admissions and to discuss
general policy. In addition, there is a weekly seminar open to all staff
and visitors. All treatment for families in the unit is planned at regular
weekly meetings. The families are aware of these meetings, to which
community helpers such as social workers, health visitors and family
doctors are invited.

C. Therapy of child abuse at the Park Hospital

The families who are admitted to the family unit form a small proportion of all the referred cases of actual or threatened child abuse.
Often cases are managed as out-patients with varying types of attendance to different departments of the hospital. Some families will be
expected to spend several days a week at the hospital; others may
attend, for example, the play therapy department for just an hour a
week. Increasingly staff have become involved in treating cases in the
community. Several health centres, with the Park Hospital providing
a back-up service, have now developed their own strategies for dealing
with cases of actual and threatened abuse (Beswick *et al.*, 1976) and
are providing group therapy for a number of mothers and young
children (Roberts *et al.*, 1977). Since July 1978, the Park Hospital has
also provided a preventive service at the local maternity hospital.
Regular, twice-weekly ward-rounds are held there for the midwives to

refer and discuss families where they are concerned that there could be future bonding difficulties. Occasionally such families are admitted to the family unit straight from the maternity hospital (Ounsted *et al.*, 1982).

Some abused children are admitted to the hospital without their families. This includes the rare cases where the parents are considered so disturbed that the abused child needs to be protected from them while they undergo long-term individual therapy. Families do not usually stay very long in the unit; the length of stay depends on the families' needs and the ability to set up supportive services in the community when they return home. Most families stay between 3–6 weeks.

Obviously, with such a wide range of facilities, therapy will vary according to each family's need, but there are general principles and guidelines that are followed in all cases. Firstly, every family will have a full medical, psychiatric and social assessment. When taking a family history it is commonly found that hostility and violence have ruled for generations. A full understanding of the complex family relationships must be attained and this is greatly facilitated when the family is in a residential setting where the whole assessment can be a continuous process. The incidence of medical illness in these families is high. Frequently it is found that the abused child has been ill since conception (Lynch, 1975) and that the mothers often have minor debilitating complaints (Lynch and Ounsted, 1976) such as iron deficiency anaemia and migraine headaches. Some mothers have been found with serious, undiagnosed illness, examples being chronic renal disease, thyrotoxicosis, tuberculosis and multiple sclerosis.

Siblings must not be omitted from the assessment. It has been known that illness or problems in the sibling can lead to the abuse of the proband. In addition to a medical examination, all the children are now given full developmental and psychological assessments. We have come to realize that it is important to include the siblings in this assessment as the proband must be understood in the context of his family: it may be the difference between him and his siblings that singles him out for abuse (Lynch, 1976).

Both parents are usually given a thorough psychiatric assessment. Serious mental illness is rarely found but depression, immature personalities and so-called "personality disorders" are often ascribed to the parents. Pathological jealousy in the fathers is quite common. Many of the mothers are taking prescribed tranquillizers or antidepressants, usually benzodiazepines or tricyclics. It is an irony that these drugs, which are meant to relieve the parents' problems, may

precipitate a battering episode (Lynch *et al.*, 1975; Gray, 1977). One of
the first steps of our therapy is to try to stop all drugs and reduce
dependency on both alcohol and cigarettes.

Almost invariably, the parents need help with marital and sexual
problems. The social problems which beset the family are likely to be
very diffuse, with the parents experiencing difficulties in almost every
area of their lives. Before one can start unravelling these complex
problems, careful assessment and planning are needed. Finally, it may
be that the child will have to be detained in the hospital on a legal order
and a continuous collaboration with police and social services will be
needed to provide legal protection for the child.

The aim of the residential therapy is to provide total family care. The
whole family is brought into a safe place where the abused child is
protected from the parents and the parents are protected from com-
mitting a crime. They are given a chance to escape from the pressures
that have been closing in on them at home. Without having to ask,
the family is provided with food, warmth, privacy and an unde-
manding routine. All therapy is given against a background of
warmth and caring from adults whom the families can trust. The
therapy has to be flexible but a cardinal rule for everyone at the
hospital is to be punctual and predictable — the surest way of gaining
trust from these parents. If the family does not establish trust in the
therapists, then a proper assessment would be impossible as the
parents would not admit to all their problems or reveal their true
feelings.

The involvement of the father in the residential therapy has to be
varied to fit in with his work schedule, but his willing participation in
the treatment is one of the conditions of admission. He is encouraged
to spend time off from work at the family unit and will be expected to
attend psychotherapy, marital therapy and play therapy as required.
The more fathers have been encouraged and expected to be involved
with their children, the more they have responded. After initial dif-
fidence, most fathers are both willing and interested.

Each family admitted to the unit is assigned a doctor and a social
worker with whom they have regular appointments. Psychotherapy is
available according to need but mostly sessions will concentrate on
improving the disturbed family relationships. The parents have some
choice about the person with whom they make their main therapeutic
relationship. Much of the therapy is in the form of practical help in
child care. The aim is that the family should become part of a group of
people who care, who are predictable, trustworthy and consistent, and

it is hoped that the family will form a bond with the whole institution rather than with individual members of staff.

Group therapy is run in the family unit to help the parents learn how to get on with other adults. Often the other families in the unit will be there for different reasons and this can be of great benefit to abusive parents who then put their own problems into perspective. For example, a mother who is disappointed and complaining about a clumsy and difficult child may be confronted by another whose mentally retarded child is having recurrent seizures. It is very often that parents will learn from other parents that which they are reluctant to accept from those in authority.

Play therapy for the abused child, both alone and with his parents, is a crucial part of the residential therapy. Often the parents have to learn for the first time how to play with and talk to their children. The children, too, need to learn how to have fun. Having talked about the problems they have in their relationships with their children, the parents then need to learn how to react positively towards them. Eventually the aim is to get parents and children to develop a normal parent/child relationship and to enjoy each other's company — something they have seldom done in the past. Where the therapy is successful, both parents and children become more secure and independent. They are able to establish "open relationships" (Ounsted *et al.*, 1974), instead of staying trapped in their small closed system, each member feeling more free to look outwards from the family and look to the future with hope.

The aims are not achieved in all cases. If, after a while in the unit, it is found that there is no chance of a healthy bond being formed between parents and child, action is taken as quickly as possible to find a suitable placement for the child. An important part of the treatment then becomes helping the parents adjust to the fact that they will not be caring for that particular child.

Therapy, of course, does not end the day the family leaves the hospital. In some cases, families need years of continuous support. They may return regularly as day-patients or members of the family may attend various out-patient sessions. Follow-up services are shared with community workers and domiciliary visits are made by all members of staff. Families are encouraged to use the telephone to the nursing staff as a 24-hour lifeline in times of crisis. Involvement is not terminated formally as it is hoped that the family will not break the bond they have formed with the hospital.

II. THE STUDY SAMPLE ON ADMISSION

The 40 study families received residential therapy at the family unit between the years 1966 and 1974. The therapy was evolving over these years and the study families attended at different stages during this development. As can be seen in Table 1, the number of abusive families admitted increased steadily up to 1974.

Table 1 Year of admission

1966	1968	1969	1970	1971	1972	1973	1974	1975
1	1	2	1	4	7	8	15	1[a]

[a]This family were admitted just outside our study period but are included because the referral and arrangements for admission all occurred in 1974.

A. The abused children

There were 42 abused children from the 40 families as two sets of twins were included. The ages of the abused children at the time of admission ranged from 1 month to 3½ years, as seen in Table 2.

Table 2 Age on admission

	0-6 months	6-12 months	1-3 years	3-5 years	5-8 years	8 years
Abused $n = 42$	18	10	10	4	0	0
Siblings $n = 25$	0	4	11	6	3	1

Half the abused children were boys and half were girls.

Twenty-three of the children had been seriously abused and 19 moderately. Our definition of severity of abuse is similar to that used by the NSPCC in their reports since 1969. Thus the serious group includes all intracranial injuries, fractures, severe burns and attempts at poisoning or asphyxiation, if the child lost consciousness. Most of the moderate injuries were bruises and lacerations or attempts at asphyxiation where there was no evidence of the child losing consciousness. The injuries that initiated referral are summarized in Table 3.

Table 3   Main injury — 42 children

Type of injury	Number of incidents
Intracranial bleed	7
Fractures (including 4 skull fractures)	12
Soft tissue injury	17
Burn	1
Attempted poisoning	2
Attempted drowning	1
Attempted suffocation/strangulation	2

Where a child had more than one injury around the time of referral — which was a common occurrence — only the most serious is shown in Table 3. For example, one boy categorized as having a broken leg, also had a superficial burn and multiple bruising. Another child entered under "attempted poisoning" also had a minor head injury and her mother gave a history of attempting suffocation a few days earlier.

In addition to multiple injuries at the time of referral, there was evidence that 17 children had suffered previous abuse and a further six had histories suggestive of inflicted injuries. The great majority of all these previous injuries were very minor and in retrospect could be seen to be examples of Ounsted's "open warnings" (1975); for example, 2 weeks before a 10-week old girl arrived in hospital, moribund with bilateral subdural haematomata, her mother had caused minor bruising to the baby's buttocks during a feeding battle. She had demonstrated the injury to the family doctor who, not realizing the significance of this "open warning", reassured the mother that she had done no serious damage and prescribed tranquillizers to calm her down!

Some of the less severely injured children were referred directly by family doctors, psychiatrists and social workers. The more severely injured children, because there is neither an accident and emergency department nor an acute paediatric ward at the Park Hospital, were most likely to have been referred by paediatricians who had cared for them when acutely ill. The length of time that the children were separated from their parents immediately prior to the Park Hospital admission varied: 19 had experienced no separation, 5 had been separated for under 1 week, 12 children for between 1 week and 1 month and only

six had been separated for more than 1 month. For all but two of them
the reason for separation had been hospital in-patient treatment. Of
the other two, one was in a children's home and the other in a
convalescent home.

B. The siblings

At the time of admission, the 40 families had a total of 69 children
living with them. All but two of these were admitted to the family unit.
The ages of the siblings ranged from 6 months to 8 years, as seen in
Table 2. Twenty-one of the abused children had no siblings (including
one set of twins). Eleven families had two children, seven families had
three children (including one set of twins) and only one family had four
children. Over half the abused children were under 12 months at the
time of admission whereas only 16% of the siblings were that young.
In 12 families the abused child was the youngest (including one set of
twins) and in only seven families (18%) did an abused child have a
younger sibling at the time of abuse.

At the time of admission there was no evidence that any of the
siblings were currently being subjected to physical abuse. While in the
past there had been some concern about the emotional care of a few of
the siblings, none had been identified as physically abused children. As
we shall see in later chapters, this lack of physical injury did not
necessarily protect against developmental and behavioural problems.

C. The parents

At the time of admission there were nine families with no male head of
the household, including two families where the father was in gaol.
Table 4 shows that the rest of the families belonged to all socio-
economic groups.

Table 4   Social class on admission

I+II	IIIm +n.m.	IV	V	Unemp.	Unsupp. mothers	Forces	Gaol
5	8	10	2	1	7	5	2

$n = 40$

There is less of a bias towards the lower social classes than there is in other British studies. For example, only 2.5% of the parents studied by Smith *et al.* (1973) were in social class II and there were no fathers in the professions. In the NSPCC research study (Baher *et al.*, 1976) there were no professional fathers and only one out of the 25 families was in social class II. Baldwin and Oliver (1975) report that at least two out of three families of their retrospective series were social class V. Only one father in our sample was unemployed at the time of admission, which is a much lower rate than reported in the above-mentioned studies. The fathers of five families were in the Armed Forces (three American, two British).

The majority of parents were Caucasians. There was one Chinese family and there were five mixed marriages, including two Pakistani fathers, one West Indian father, one West Indian mother and one black American father. There were language problems for the staff in only two families — the Chinese family and the family where a Pakistani father was married to an Italian.

The age of the parents at the time of admission is shown in Table 5.

Table 5   Parents' ages on admission

	Under 21 years	21-25 years	26-30 years	31-35 years	36 years and above	Not known
Mothers $n = 40$	12	20	3	3	2	—
Fathers $n = 33$	4	15	6	5	2	1

The ages ranged from 16½ years to 36½ years. The mean age of the mothers was 23.7 years and of the fathers, 26.4 years. This relatively young age is similar to that of the sample studied by Smith *et al.* (1973) where the mean age of the mothers was 23.5 years and of the fathers, 27 years. At the time of the abuse incident 30% of our sample of mothers were under 21 years. Furthermore, 25 mothers (62.5%) were under 20 years at the time of the birth of their first child.

Twenty-three (57.5%) of the mothers were known to have suffered from psychiatric or emotional ill-health since the birth of the abused child and even more of the mothers had evidence of earlier emotional problems, often having a history of suicidal gestures. This impression of a high rate of "attempted suicide" among abusing parents has recently been confirmed (Roberts and Hawton, 1980). Of the fathers, only two admitted to a formal psychiatric history. However, when it came to admission to the Park Hospital, several more fathers were found to have disturbed personalities.

Nearly one-third of the mothers had suffered from problems of physical ill-health since the birth of the abused child, with a high incidence of gynaecological problems. Even at the Park Hospital, problems of ill-health in the fathers were seldom reported at the time of admission. However, on detailed questioning on follow-up, it became apparent that a number of them had long-term psycho-somatic complaints such as migraine, backache and fainting attacks. As already reported, (Lynch, 1975), physical ill-health seems to be a contributing factor leading up to child abuse and, as described by Steele and Pollock (1974), the parents do not fall into any one of the usual psychiatric diagnostic categories, but suffer from a wide range of psycho-somatic illnesses.

All the families lived within a 50-mile radius of the Park Hospital and came from both urban and rural districts. The majority (80%) lived in adequate housing. However, three families were in seriously sub-standard living conditions including two in caravans. One family was in a homeless families unit, one mother was in a mother and baby unit and three families were in severely overcrowded conditions, sharing accommodation with relatives. The rate of poor, overcrowded or inadequate housing (20%) is high for the Oxford area but not as high as the sample studied by the NSPCC research team in London (Baher et al., 1976) where 17 out of 25 (68%) families lived in overcrowded conditions.

In the main, the social and demographic characteristics of the parents of these 40 families differ from other British samples of families of abused children. This probably is a reflection of the population from which the sample is drawn, which is very different from those in large metropolitan areas studied by the NSPCC and Smith et al. (1973). Furthermore, the NSPCC traditionally deals with the underprivileged.

D. Outcome of admission

The aim of our service is to rehabilitate the family so that the child may return home safely without prolonged separation. The majority of these 40 families stayed in the unit for at least 3 weeks (Table 6) but only 15% needed to stay longer than 9 weeks.

Table 6   Length of stay in family unit

	Under 7 days	1-3 weeks	3-6 weeks	6-9 weeks	9 weeks+
Families n = 40	2	7	14	11	6

As can be seen from Table 7, 34 (81%) of the abused children went home with their natural parents following the admission. A further three children (including one set of twins) went to stay with close relatives together with their natural mothers. Only five abused children (and none of the siblings) were separated from their natural parents on discharge. As can be seen in Chapter VIII, these placements were not all maintained throughout the follow-up period.

The arrangements for follow-up vary for each family and, as we have already stated, the arrangements are most often shared with workers in the community. There are times, however, especially when a Care Order is made, when the statutory agencies take over the management of the case completely and advice from the Park Hospital is not always heeded. It was particularly this group of cases which created a gap in our knowledge about the later development of abused children.

Table 7   Placement on discharge from hospital

	With 2 parents	With 1 parent only	Foster home	Children's home	With Mother and relatives
Abused n = 42	25[a]	9[b]	4	1	3
Siblings n = 25	16	9[b]	0	0	0

[a] One abused child was with mother + step-father.
[b] An abused child + sibling were with their father only.

In order to give a more vivid picture of the families and the circumstances of the admission, we have chosen three case examples. The
first is a case where we feel the aims of rehabilitating the child with the
family were achieved:

Caroline was an 8-month old baby girl who was admitted to the paediatric
ward in a stuporous state, having had a series of fits, with retinal haemorrhages and a series of bruises on her forehead and chin. She was malnou-
rished and on recovery of consciousness, was described as an introverted
and very unresponsive baby. She had suffered a series of fits over approximately a week but the parents had not sought medical help. They
claimed they thought babies had convulsions when they were teething.
The father was an intelligent though angry young man who, in his
opinion, had failed to achieve his potential and was working as a
milkman. The mother was very young, having conceived Caroline when
she was only 15 years old. The parents were living in a cramped, small
and damp caravan. Caroline had already been seriously ill. When she was
6 weeks old she started vomiting and dropped to below her birth weight
but the parents delayed seeking medical advice. She was eventually
operated on for pyloric stenosis.
    The abuse occurred 6 months following Caroline's return home from
hospital. After the second admission and the diagnosis of child abuse,
Caroline was transferred to the Park Hospital. Initially no explanation
was given for the baby's injuries and the parents were very angry and
mistrustful, constantly asking whether their child would be taken away
from them. After initial refusal they finally agreed to admission to the
family unit and eventually participated in the therapy. During their stay
the parents confessed to many difficulties in looking after Caroline. She
would not sleep, she had been thrown on to the bed by her dad in exasper-
ation, they had many marital rows and dad was jealous of the baby.
Caroline's mother also revealed that she was terrified of being left alone
with Caroline in the caravan. The intervention consisted of prolonged
marital therapy with the parents and intensive therapy with mother and
baby together. At the beginning of admission there was no bond at all
between mother and baby and Caroline did not discriminate between her
mother and strangers. After 2 months the family were discharged home
under close supervision from both the Park Hospital and the social
services. The police were informed of the injuries but decided not to
prosecute. Since then the family have been rehoused, have had a second
child and are a normal, happy family with no current contact with the
social services department.

The second case is one where separation of the child from the parents
seemed imperative after the assessment made at the Park Hospital.
The child went initially to a children's home and was then fostered
successfully. Although rehabilitation with the parents was not
achieved, the actual outcome for the child was successful:

Philip was admitted to the Park Hospital following several incidents or so-called "accidents" and the final one was when he vomited up tablets which his mother had put in his cereal. Philip's mother was a 19-year old woman who was separated from her husband. She had had a violent and unhappy childhood and had simply decided that she was going to get married at 18 years. This she did, to an abusive, incontinent and impotent young man whom she had known for 6 weeks. While escaping from her husband, the mother was raped and conceived Philip. On admission the mother confessed to the abuse and showed herself to be very disturbed, at times aggressive and prone to sudden mood changes. She had no patience at all with the baby and often slapped him for no reason. She herself agreed that the best for Philip would be for him to be received into care. She said that she had hurt Philip because she felt impelled to hurt people who did not love her. She had, in fact, almost strangled her sister when she was only 8 years old! Philip was eventually fostered with his maternal aunt which initially caused family friction. However, on follow-up, he was shown to be a happy, confident and integrated young boy of normal intelligence.

The third case is an example where an attempt was made to rehabilitate the family, but it failed. The abused child returned home with the parents but soon, after continuous monitoring, the necessity for permanent separation became clear:

Ruth was an 8-month old baby girl when admitted to the Park Hospital with her 2½-year old sister. Ruth had previously suffered multiple bruising on the head, several fractures of the skull and a spiral facture of the left humerus. Both she and her sister were extremely retarded in their development and the family were finally referred to the Park Hospital when their mother walked out of the home, leaving the children for hours and declaring that she was going to commit suicide. The children were admitted to the Park Hospital. Their mother, after a short period of in-patient treatment at the adjoining psychiatric hospital, joined them in the family unit.

During her admission to the Park Hospital, the mother showed herself to have totally unrealistic expectations of her children and very little idea of normal development. She was very easily upset and had a violent temper which she could not control. The father showed himself to be very concerned about his children's health and development, but totally impatient of and angry with his wife.

The children were helped a great deal by intensive play therapy and made rapid progress in their development. It was felt that neither children had ever played in their lives before. Despite a vast amount of effort by the staff, by the time of discharge it was felt that the mother's relationship with both children still remained disturbed. However, elaborate plans were made to continue therapy following discharge. Ruth was officially discharged to her parents, but on the condition that she should spend most of the week with foster parents. Her sister spent most of the day with a child-minder. These arrangements broke down as the mother failed to make any improvement in her ability to care for the children and the father opted out of the family problems. Both children were then admitted to a small children's home and were still living there when we saw them on follow-up.

We felt that this placement in a children's home was a very successful one in that, although both the children were extremely disturbed on admission, the excellent staff there provided such good care and intensive therapy that at the time of follow-up the children were getting to know a couple with whom they are now fostered extremely successfully. Not only did the staff manage to heal serious emotional damage in these children, but they also dealt very effectively with the disruptive and potentially dangerous behaviour of the parents who visited regularly.

These three cases demonstrate the varied types of families admitted and the varying treatment they receive. They show that "success" in our therapy does not always mean rehabilitation of the abused child with the family. For some abused children the right decision was found to be permanent separation from their abusing parents and an effective placement with a substitute family. The decision is not always made at the time of discharge: the third example represents those cases where no final decision about placement could be made until after a closely supervised trial at home.

III. LOCATION OF SAMPLE ON FOLLOW-UP

As stated in the previous chapter, 39 out of the original 40 families were eventually traced. We therefore failed to locate only one of the 42 abused children. This was a seriously abused child from an American Air Force family who had returned with only her mother to the States. At the time of follow-up a letter to the mother brought no reply and our attempts to trace the father via the American Air Force Welfare Organization also failed.

Two abused children from a further two families were not available for assessment on follow-up. One was dead. He had suffered a subdural haematoma at the age of 10 weeks then developed a hydrocephalus requiring neurosurgical intervention with the insertion of a valve. There was no doubt that he was going to be neurologically handicapped. He was found unexpectedly dead at home at the age of 18 months. A post-mortem examination gave the cause of death as meningitis. His parents and younger sibling willingly participated in the study.

The other child not assessed had recently been placed for adoption and access was refused. Therefore we were able to assess 39 out of the original 42 abused children (21 of these had suffered serious injuries and 18 moderate).

It was our intention to include all the siblings and half-siblings born to these families by the time of follow-up. We knew of 47 such siblings, of whom 20 had been born after the family's discharge from the Park Hospital. We were able to assess 41 of these children. The reasons for not assessing the other six varied: one sibling was adopted soon after the family's discharge from hospital and, in spite of considerable help from the social services, we were unable to locate him because his adoptive family had moved house. One sibling was born later to the two natural parents of an abused child who had been taken into care. The parents allowed us to have up-to-date information on this child but refused to let us see him. Three other children were born to the natural father and stepmother of an abused child who had been in care for many years. The father again allowed us to have basic information about his children, but refused to see us at his home. The last sibling not assessed was a child born later to the parents of the abused child placed for adoption.

The omission of the only two adopted children in the series is regrettable, especially in the light of current policies for the adoption of so-called "hard-to-place" children. Most abused children would fit into such a category. Therefore, research of the later adoption of these children is crucial to help the agencies placing children to work out which placements are more likely to be successful. From our point of view it would have been interesting to compare the adopted children with those in long-term foster placements.

In the case of the abused child who had been placed for adoption recently, we approached the social services department and the natural mother, asking them to participate in the study. The natural mother seriously considered co-operating, but in the end felt that she was unable to do so as it would be too stressful for her personally. The social services department were extremely reluctant to approach the abused child's adoptive parents and refused to allow us to do so independently. It seemed that we were being kept away from the adoptive parents because it was feared we would upset the child's placement. We wondered how secure the placement would be if it were so vulnerable.

The mean length of time between discharge and follow-up assessment was 4 years and varied from 1 year 1 month to 10 years 4 months.

The placements of the 80 children participating are summarized in Table 8.

Table 8   Placements of 80 children

	With 2 parents	With 1 parent only	Foster home	Children's home	Hospital
Abused n = 39	23	7	4	4	1
Siblings n = 41	35	5	0	1	0

The rest of this book describes the detailed findings of the follow-up assessments made of the 39 abused children alive on follow-up, the 41 siblings and their families. Information will also be given on the interval since their discharge from the Park Hospital and, wherever possible, we will try to relate the outcome on follow-up to earlier experiences.

SUMMARY OF FINDINGS

(1)   The 42 index abused children and their families (n = 40) had all spent some time in the family unit at the Park Hospital between 1966 and 1974.

(2)   Sixty-seven per cent of the abused children were under the age of 1 year at the time of admission. (Age range one month to 3½ years.)

(3)   Twenty three (55%) of the children had been seriously injured and 19 (45%) moderately. At least 17 of the children had evidence of previous "open warnings".

(4)   The 42 abused children had a total of 27 siblings; all but two of these were admitted to the unit.

(5)   The families came from a wide range of socio-economic backgrounds. Nine families had no male head, including two where the father was in gaol.

(6)   The mean age of the mothers was 23.7 years and of the fathers 26.4 years. Thirty per cent of the mothers were under 21 years at the time of the abuse.

(7)   Over half the mothers had a history of emotional problems and nearly one third had suffered physical ill-health since the birth of

the index child. The information on the fathers' medical histories was incomplete, but there was suggestion of a high incidence of psycho-somatic disorder.

(8)   Twenty per cent of the families were living in unsatisfactory accommodation.

(9)   The majority of families spent at least 3 weeks in the unit (range under 1 week to over 9), and at discharge only five children (all abused) were placed away from their parents.

(10) At follow-up 39 of the original 40 families were located. Thirty-nine of the 42 abused children and 41 of the 47 siblings were comprehensively assessed. The mean follow-up interval was 4 years.

III. Legal action and reception into care

In all cases of child abuse our first consideration must be the future safety of the child. Often this has to be guaranteed by legal action and reception into care. For this reason it seems appropriate to consider at an early stage in the book the legal orders and processes that were used as part of the management of our sample of abused children and their siblings. Only the 80 children actually seen in follow-up will be considered and our discussion will be limited to the legal processes actually used for our sample. Before presenting the data relating to the 80 children, a brief definition and explanation will be given of each piece of legislation being considered. For further discussion of the application of child care legislation for abused children, the authors would recommend Brenda Hoggett's book "Parents and Children" (1977) in a series about social work and law. We will also be discussing the problems surrounding court appearances and the involvement of the police with our families.

I. EMERGENCY POWERS OF REMOVAL

In this country, Place of Safety Orders are designed to allow emergency action to be taken to remove a child from a dangerous environment or to prevent his removal from a safe place — usually a hospital. There are several ways in which this can be done. Under section 28(1) of the Children and Young Persons Act 1969, any person (usually a hospital or social services social worker) may apply for an order to a single magistrate at any time and in any place. Nothing has to be proved by the applicant, but the magistrate must be satisfied that the applicant has reasonable cause to believe that one of the grounds for instituting and granting a Care Order exists. Physically injured children can be covered by one of the three conditions:

(1) "his proper development is being avoidably prevented or neglected",
(2) "his health is being avoidably impaired or neglected", or
(3) "he is being ill-treated."

Siblings are covered by a condition which extends the grounds for an order to children living in a household where there has already been abuse. The magistrate can authorize the applicant to take the child (or children) to a place of safety and detain them for up to 28 days or a shorter specified period. The parents do not have to be informed before the order is taken, but the detainer is expected to tell them as soon as possible afterwards and explain the reasons for the action (1969 Act, section 28(3)). The parents have no right of appeal (except to the High Court on a point of law), nor can the order be renewed at the end of the specified period. An interim order can be granted before expiry (once again for 28 days only, if heard by a single justice). If such an order is not obtained, the care and custody of the child return to his parents when the Place of Safety Order expires.

The police are also able to detain a child (section 2(2) of the 1969 Act). In such cases the detention lasts for up to 8 days only. The grounds are the same as those required for detention by a magistrate but the parents can apply immediately to a magistrate for release (Section 28(4) and (5)). If the child has to be detained for longer than 8 days, an interim order is necessary before care proceedings can be started (section 28(6)).

If abuse is suspected and access cannot be gained to premises to find the child, it is possible to apply to a justice for a warrant under section 40 of the Children and Young Persons Act 1933, which will authorize the police to enter and search. If the suspicions are found to be justified, the child can be removed on a Place of Safety Order that lasts for up to 28 days (Children and Young Persons Act 1963, section 23(1)). In addition to the Acts already mentioned, it is possible to remove private foster children and "protected" children using the 1958 Children Act and 1958 Adoption Act respectively.

In the literature, discussions of emergency powers for immediate removal of children from homes, or their retention in a safe place reveal an understandable ambivalence. It is seen by some as a necessary but possibly dangerous legal tool (Sussman and Cohen, 1975; Wilford et al., 1979). Firstly, although one cannot deny the necessity of having efficient emergency powers of removal of children in serious danger, there is a risk that the relative ease with which an order can be obtained encourages workers to play safe and separate parents and child without exploring other options. As Hallett and Stevenson (1980) report, there was a dramatic increase in the number of Place of Safety Orders granted during the years 1972–1976. Table 9 is a reproduction of theirs, demonstrating this increase and relating it in time to the Maria Colwell Inquiry and Report.

Table 9

Date	No. of Place of Safety Orders[a]
March 1972	204
March 1973	214
Maria Colwell Inquiry Sitting	
March 1974	353
Publication of Maria Colwell Report	
March 1975	596
March 1976	759

[a] In force to local authorities at 31st March 1972 - 1976.

From Hallett and Stevenson, 1980 "Child Abuse: Aspects of Interprofessional Co-operation". London, George Allen and Unwin.

They discuss several possible explanations for this increase, including greater recognition of child abuse, the emphasis put on the need to consider seeking a Place of Safety Order in the DHSS Local Authority Social Services Letter (1974), as well as the increases in professional anxiety with a tendency to "play safe". The large NSPCC study (1977) (Creighton and Owtram) also gives details of numbers of children who were subjects of Place of Safety Orders. Of the 778 children included in the study, 102 (13%) had such an order made. It was the order used most often in the sample as a whole and the majority were later converted into more permanent orders (Care Orders or Supervision Orders). Significantly more of the seriously injured children than the moderately injured children had been on Place of Safety Orders ($p < 0.01$).

Another anxiety expressed is that the power to remove a child could destroy any trust the parents might have in the worker and threaten the therapeutic relationship. It has certainly not been our experience that the need to take legal action to retain a child in a therapeutic setting prevents effective work with the parents, or robs the person who initiated the action of credibility. More frequently at the Park Hospital the effect seems to be the reverse. The parents agree that further injuries must be prevented and both therapists and parents know that it would be dangerous to return the child home. However, it is natural that often the parents, when confronted with the fact that their child has been deliberately injured, will react angrily and demand to go and take their child home with them. A father in a family where a Place of Safety Order was taken, later described to us his feelings when he was told that his baby's fractured skull was a result of abuse. He had been colluding with his wife's battering of the child for some time and knew that she must have caused the injuries. However, he felt that as head of the household he must deny the implication and demand to take his wife and child home. It was with relief that he accepted the legal intervention, thereafter encouraging his wife to stay and frequently attending the hospital himself. A young single mother provides another example of how a Place of Safety Order helped initiate therapy. The child was transferred to the Park Hospital when her fracture was healing and the mother was invited to stay. Initially she accepted but subsequently, in the course of the first afternoon, sought out the admitting doctor on several occasions, threatening to discharge herself and her child. Each time she agreed to stay. However, finally, towards evening, she made yet another demand and this time would not be dissuaded. A Place of Safety Order was immediately sought and granted. The mother, instead of being angry, came and thanked the doctor for relieving her of the decision whether or not to leave the child in hospital. She had been eager to appear a good mother, she explained, and had argued with herself that a good mother would deny abuse and take the child home.

Demands by the parents to take a child home, or outbursts of anger resulting in a Place of Safety Order, should not be seen as negative indicators of the success of subsequent therapy. Indeed, it has often seemed to us an encouraging sign that the parents may well become motivated when therapy starts. In contrast, we have found that those parents who passively agree with everything can subsequently show little interest in modifying their child-rearing practices. However, when comparing our experiences with those of others, it must be recognized that when an order is taken out in connection with an admission to the Park Hospital, as well as ensuring a child's safety, we are able to offer therapy to the whole family.

We were unable to find any rates in the literature for the use of emergency orders to remove unharmed siblings, but the impression gained from observations of practice in this country is that all too frequently siblings are removed almost automatically when a child has been severely abused. This stems from a natural concern about the danger to other children in the household. It is felt that the abuse of one child may imply the mistreatment of others (Reinhart and Elmer, 1964). This fear can lead to the extension of temporary removal and of legal proceedings to the siblings of the abused child. Sussman and Cohen (1975) give the example of one typical case where a judge in a New York family court removed two siblings of an abused child from the care of their mother. Relying on the "imminent danger" doctrine, the judge explained: "Experience teaches" that if a parent abuses one child, he will abuse them all. Our experience has been that while a few parents will abuse any child, most abuse only one. This is most likely to be true when the abused child has predisposing factors not shared by the siblings (Lynch, 1975). Thus, before inflicting unnecessary separation, there is a need for rapid assessment of both parents and all children.

A. Place of Safety Orders in the sample

Among the children seen by us in follow-up, five had been made subjects of Place of Safety Orders before admission to the Park Hospital. All had been admitted initially to acute paediatric wards, three (which included a pair of twins) with severe injuries. Place of Safety Orders were taken out on a further five abused children at the time of admission to the Park Hospital, or within the first few days. These orders were taken out in direct response to parental threats to remove the child from the hospital. All these children had suffered severe injuries. Only one sibling was placed on an order during admission. Although uninjured, there was considerable concern about her emotional well-being.

In four out of the 11 Place of Safety Orders taken out before or during the children's admission to the Park Hospital, no further legal action was taken. A Supervision Order was sought and granted on one boy, and six others (including the sibling) were placed on Care Orders. However, only one of the 11 children was not initially discharged home with one or both parents.

During the follow-up interval, nine children (six abused) from four families were made the subject of Place of Safety Orders. One family of four had all been on Supervision Orders at the time of admission to the Park. A crisis in the family resulted in the taking of Place of Safety

Orders, temporary removal of the children from the home and a conversion of the Supervision Orders into Care Orders. Also included in the nine children were a pair of twins, allowed home with their mother under close supervision. As feared, arrangements quickly broke down and Place of Safety Orders were taken to remove the children from her care. Care Orders were subsequently granted. The three other children were placed on Place of Safety Orders because of incidents thought to be due to abuse. For one child this happened twice: once at the age of 9 months, when she was reabused by her mother, and again 8 years later when assaulted by her stepmother.

Thus 26% of the abused children were on Place of Safety Orders during their admission to the Park, and another 15% were made subject of such orders during the follow-up interval. Only 10% of the siblings were ever placed on a Safety Order. Interestingly, the total rate of 41% of the abused children on Place of Safety Orders is very similar to the 36% reported by the NSPCC research study (1976) which is another example of intensive therapeutic intervention.

II. CARE PROCEEDINGS

Care proceedings in cases of child abuse are brought before the juvenile court under section I of the Children and Young Persons Act 1969. This legislation was not specifically designed for the protection of abused and neglected children. Also covered by the section are children in moral danger, those beyond the control of parent or guardian, those not receiving efficient full-time education and delinquent children. For an order to be granted for an abused child, the Act requires that it be shown that the child is in need of care or control which he will not receive unless the court makes an order. It is the child himself who is the respondent and if he is over 5 years of age, he must be physically brought before the court. Those with a legitimate interest in the proceedings, i.e. parents, must be notified of them. A recent provision extends this to include any foster parent or other person with whom the child has had his home for not less than 6 weeks ending not more than 6 months before the application (Magistrate's Courts (Children and Young Persons) Rules, 1970, Rule 14(3)).

Before the implementation of the 1975 Act, the rules allowed the parent to conduct the case in court on the child's behalf (Rule 17). This was clearly ludicrous in child abuse cases. When a solicitor was appointed on legal aid, though often briefed by the parents, he was representing the child and this led to further confusion. Two sections of the Children Act 1975 are designed to remove these ambiguities. The court may now order that a parent is not treated as representing the child (section 32A (1)), and appoint a guardian *ad litem* for the child (section 32B (1)). When the Act is fully implemented the parent will be able to make separate applications for legal aid in order to take part (Children Act 1975, section 65) and thereby meet any allegations against himself. Once the grounds for an order have been proved, the Court is directed to consider the child's "general conduct, home surroundings, school record and medical history" (Rule 20) before deciding which order, if any, should be granted. In practice, in child abuse cases, the choice is usually between a Care Order and a Supervision Order. These were the only orders to have been granted for children in our sample.

A Care Order places the child in the care of the local authority until the age of 18 (or 19 if he was 16 when the order was made), unless the court decides to discharge the order earlier. The authority will decide where the child will live and this can include the parental home. In England and Wales, approximately 30% of all children on Care Orders are home "on trial" (Thoburn, 1979). Applications to discharge a Care Order can be made to the juvenile court by the local authority or the child or by the child's parent or guardian (section 70 (2)) acting on his behalf. Where the application is not opposed, the court is empowered to appoint a guardian *ad litem* under the Children Act, 1975. Appeals against the making of an order or against the dismissal of an application to discharge an order can be brought by the child or local authority and are heard by the Crown court. Appeals, except on pure points of law, are not allowed against the refusal of an order or the granting of a discharge.

When a Supervision Order is made on a child, he normally stays in his current home, but is under the supervision of the local authority for a specified period of up to 3 years. The protection offered by such an order is limited and the duties of the supervisor and obligations of the parents undefined. There is no legal obligation upon the parents to allow the supervisor into the house to see the child. If serious concern develops, a Place of Safety Order or warrant would have to be sought. Lack of co-operation by the parents can only be overcome by applying for the Supervision Order to be discharged and replaced by a Care Order. For the above reasons it is felt that Supervision Orders have a limited part to play in the management of child abuse. It can be argued that if a child is to be allowed home only with the guarantee of regular surveillance, this is better achieved with the security of a Care Order which gives the local authority well-defined rights.

In the literature it is difficult to obtain comparable data for rates of care proceedings for abused children. Speight *et al.* (1979) give a figure for "legal sanctions" which includes both Care Orders and section 2 resolutions.

Two of the NSPCC Reports (1969 and 1975) do give comparable rates. Of the 78 children described in the 1969 study, 40% were on Care Orders by at least 6 months after registration. Of the 34 cases registered in Manchester in 1973 (NSPCC, 1975), 23.5% were placed on Care Orders by 3 months after notification. Finally, of the 25 battered children studied by the NSPCC research team (Baher *et al.*, 1976), 32% were placed on Care Orders at some time during the team's contact with the families.

A. Care Orders and Supervision Orders in the sample

One child was already on a Care Order at the time of his admission to the Park Hospital. Seven abused children (18%) were made subjects of Care Orders as a direct result of decisions made during their admission. Five of these had been subjects of Place of Safety Orders. Only one sibling was placed on a Care Order during admission and she too had been the subject of a Place of Safety Order.

During the follow-up interval, five more abused children were made the subjects of Care Orders, all following Place of Safety Orders. For one child already referred to, this happened twice as the original Fit Person Order (the equivalent of a Care Order prior to the 1969 Act) had been revoked. One child was placed on a Place of Safety Order, but following admission to the Park Hospital, it was felt that the injury was the result of a genuine accident. Social services continued with care proceedings but no order was granted. Three siblings from one family, along with their abused brother, were placed on Care Orders during the follow-up interval. They had all been on Supervision Orders.

Overall a total of 13 abused children (33%) were made subjects of Care Orders at some time after identification of abuse. A total of four siblings were also placed on Care Orders. Only one of the 17 Care Orders had been discharged at the time we followed up the families. Ten of these 17 children on Care Orders had been subject to Interim Orders prior to full Care Orders being granted. In fact, only five families were involved in repeat court hearings as the family of four children and two sets of twins were all initially on Interim Care Orders. Thus, for most parents, the legal proceedings were resolved relatively soon after it was decided that legal action should be taken. Delays were often avoided because the comprehensive assessment that followed the family's admission enabled the necessary reports and evidence to be collected rapidly. It is our impression that it was considerably easier in Oxfordshire to avoid Interim Care Orders than it is in a busy metropolitan area.

One abused child and three siblings were on Supervision Orders at the time of the family's admission to the Park. Later, as we have already mentioned, all these children were placed on Care Orders during follow-up. One child who was put on a Place of Safety Order at the beginning of his admission to the Park Hospital, subsequently went home on a Supervision Order. This had been discharged by the time the family was seen by us for the follow-up study. Another two children, an abused child and his sibling, were both put on Matrimonial Proceedings Supervision Orders by a divorce court judge during the follow-up period.

B. Court appearances

Those cases where care proceedings were taken, involved court appearances for parents and staff. While we cannot claim complete absence of bad experiences and unpleasant court room scenes, the hearings were not universally traumatic. Indeed, we often felt that an appearance in court had been therapeutic for all concerned, strengthening bonds between the parents and staff. This was more likely to be true if the hearing came towards the end of the family's stay in the Park Hospital and when a long-term management plan had been worked out and agreed with the parents. Under such circumstances the proceedings often passed off smoothly without the application for a Care Order being challenged — the parents agreeing with the need for legal protection for their child and themselves. Before the hearing, care was taken to ensure that the parents were aware of the evidence that was going to be given by the Park staff, including details of the injuries. If X-rays were to be presented, the parents would already have seen them. Efforts were also made to include in the statements to the court evidence of any strengths the parents might have, together with comments about the progress the family had made during the admission. Throughout the hospital's contact with the family, the staff would have been honest about the possibility of care proceedings and the parents would have been advised about getting legal representation for their child. For some families an appearance in court acted as a catharsis — parents admitting their guilt openly and looking forward to a fresh start. The subsequent feeling of relief in such circumstances can be enormous. One mother illustrates well the need to admit guilt openly. So convincing had been her outward appearance of "the perfect housewife and mother" that her family doctor gave notice of his intention to attend court and give evidence to the effect that this mother could not possibly have harmed her baby. It was the mother herself who telephoned the doctor, asking him not to attend as she intended to admit openly to the battering.

These experiences of legal proceedings and court appearances seem to have been less distressing than those described by the NSPCC team (1976). Their approach was initially very different from ours. Basing their ideas on those expressed by Kempe and colleagues (1968), they attempted to separate therapeutic and legal roles. The way they had planned to achieve this was for the NSPCC worker to remain the "good" therapist while the Social Services social worker took any necessary legal action, thereby being identified by the parents as "bad". When this proved impossible, because of the Social Services social worker's understandable reluctance to be seen as wholly "bad" and the need for the NSPCC worker to give evidence in court, conflicts and feelings of betrayal resulted. By being open and honest with parents about the need for legal action, the staff at the Park Hospital are able to avoid much of this confusion and reduce the feelings of conflict that inevitably surround court appearance. Rather than separate the therapeutic from the legal role, the aim is to demonstrate that care and control can be shown by one person. In addition to this, the fact that the Park Hospital is a children's hospital makes it easier for parents and staff to remember that protection of the child must come first when planning future family therapy. Another advantage experienced by the Park Hospital team is that medical evidence can usually be given by a member of the team, which avoids the difficulties described by the NSPCC of persuading an outside doctor to attend court and give evidence.

It is clear from our own experience and the accounts given by the NSPCC research team (Baher et al., 1976) that giving evidence in court in cases of child abuse can be one of the most personally difficult tasks in a professional career. At the Park Hospital this is fully acknowledged and much support is given at the time of the court appearance and specific skills in giving evidence are clearly taught. Prior to attending court, discussions are held with the county solicitors who are encouraged to join case conferences.

III. RECEPTION INTO CARE

Children can be received into care at the request of their parents under section 1 of the Children Act, 1948 (Now section 2 of Child Care Act 1980). In practice this is often the result of a parent being advised to agree to reception of their child into care, but this section does not allow the removal of the child from his parents without their full consent. Under the 1948 Act, the receiving authority does not have the right to keep the child, should a parent or guardian wish to take over his care (Section 1 (3)): indeed, the authorities have a positive duty to encourage them to do so. Problems inevitably arise when it is not in the child's best interests to be returned to the parents. Such circumstances are likely to occur with abused children or where the parents have been persuaded to allow them to be taken into care. Not infrequently such parents, as soon as the stress of caring for a "difficult" child has been removed, will unrealistically claim that if the child is returned, the child-rearing problems of the past will no longer exist and all will be well. Here is an example:

> A 2½-year old child was thankfully given up to care by his exhausted and erratic mother. He left the Park Hospital and spent less than 2 months with foster parents. This placement was sabotaged by his interfering mother and he was transferred to a residential nursery. Then, 8 months later, the mother was granted the new home which she was convinced would solve all her problems. She demanded the return of her son. Within 3 months she was requesting his reception into care once again.

Removal of children in care under section 1 can be prevented if a section 2 resolution is passed, but defined grounds must exist before this resolution can be passed and the parents can challenge the action in court. An alternative and increasingly used way of preventing a child's removal is to make the child a ward of court. The Children Act 1975 has made the position easier for the local authorities when the child has been in care for 6 months or longer under section 1. The parent then has to give 28 days' notice before removing the child. This breathing space allows the authorities time to consider appropriate action if they feel it is not in the best interests of the child to return home to the parents. Unfortunately, with abused children, the parents not infrequently demand their children home relatively soon after their reception into care.

The grounds on which a resolution 2 can be passed were set out in section 2 of the 1948 Act and substituted by Section 57 of the Children Act 1975 (Now section 3 of Child Care Act 1980). The grounds include those circumstances where a parent is incapable or unfit to care for the child. Orphaned and abandoned children are thus included, together with those who have a parent with a permanent disability, mental disorder or unsuitable lifestyle, or a parent who has consistently failed to discharge parental obligations. The 1975 Act added two further provisions: the first relates to cases where a resolution has been passed in relation to one parent only, the other retaining parental rights. The new provision means that the child would be unable to live in a home with the parent with parental rights if the "unfit" parent was also living there. The second new provision allows a section 2 resolution to be passed on any child who has been in care for more than 3 years.

Parents can object to the passing of section 2 resolutions and the matter is then resolved in the juvenile court. Otherwise the passing of a section 2 resolution does not require appearance in court. Once in force, section 2 resolutions usually last until the child is 18, although it can be rescinded by the local authority at any time, and the parents can appeal to the juvenile court for such a rescission. The resolution will also cease if the child is adopted or a guardian of the child is appointed under section 5 of the Guardianship of Minors Act, 1971.

Despite the problems associated with the voluntary reception of abused children into care, 27.3% of the children in Creighton and Owtram's study (1977) who were given statutory protection were received into voluntary care. This was the commonest process used for both the moderately injured children and the "prodromal" group. Little detail is given in the earlier NSPCC studies of children taken into voluntary care. Of the 34 children studied in Manchester in 1973, six were taken into voluntary care, two of whom were rapidly placed on statutory Care Orders.

A. Voluntary reception into care and section 2 resolutions in the sample

One abused child was in voluntary care at the time of her admission to the Park Hospital. She was subsequently made subject of a Place of Safety Order followed by a Care Order. Two children were taken into voluntary care directly after the Park admission and one early in the follow-up interval. Section 2 resolutions were later passed on all three and they were all in care away from their parents at the time we saw them on follow-up. These three section 2 resolutions were all taken on three different grounds and none was opposed by the parents. One single mother was a firmly diagnosed schizophrenic and the section 2 resolution was made on the grounds that she was suffering from a mental disorder within the meaning of the Mental Health Act 1959, which rendered her unfit to have the care of the child. Another young single mother had clearly demonstrated her inability to care for her baby, without resorting to violence, while she was in the family unit but the section 2 resolution was made because of her "habits or mode of life". Thirdly, a young couple who had previously removed their child from voluntary care finally gave up and demanded his reception into care. For them the grounds for the section 2 resolution were that they had so consistently failed, without reasonable cause, to discharge the obligations of a parent. No other children went into voluntary care as a direct result of their Park Hospital admission. However, during the follow-up interval, as we shall see when discussing placements, a number of other children had short periods in voluntary care. These placements were not made specifically for protection of the child but because of family crises, such as the illness of a single parent. In none of these cases was the possibility of assuming parental rights ever considered by the social services department.

IV. POLICE INVOLVEMENT AND CRIMINAL PROCEEDINGS

The DHSS is clear in its recommendations that the police should be involved in the management of child abuse. When recommending the setting up of Area Review Committees (LASSL (74) 13), police officers were among the suggested members and more recently a circular issued jointly by the DHSS and the Home Office (LASSL (76) (26)) urged Area Review Committees to work towards police attendance at all case conferences concerning non-accidental injury to children. Even where this has become accepted practice, there are often cases where the police need to start investigations before the conference has taken place. This, together with the power of the police to take unilateral action at any time, continues to make other professionals reluctant to share information. The NSPCC research team (Baher et al., 1976) expresses well the ambivalence felt by the majority of social workers and doctors in relation to police involvement in child abuse cases:

> "We did not feel that trial or punishment had any value in battering situations and believed that we would more easily be able to help the parents if the police were not involved. At the same time, we realized that the police had a legal right to be informed of cases involving a possible offence and an obligation to make an investigation."

Often in practice this conflict remains unresolved and, as in the

NSPCC study (Baher *et al.*, 1976), the involvement of the police "left to chance."

It cannot be claimed that a clear policy regarding the involvement of the police existed at the Park Hospital throughout the study period. However, a good working relationship had developed between the senior staff at the hospital and the local police department. This was probably considerably easier to establish in a place like Oxfordshire than it would have been in a metropolitan area beset by inner city problems, and where the turnover of police officers is high. In a number of cases the police had already been informed of the injury before the child was transferred to the Park Hospital. Indeed, the police were responsible for some referrals. In other cases the decision to inform the police was taken after the child was admitted to the Park Hospital. As with actions over care proceedings, Park staff are honest with parents over any discussions they might have with the police. For some families the police involvement had positive effects, making the parents realize the seriousness of their predicament. For one mother in the sample the sympathetic taking of her statement acted as a catharsis leading to a full description of the despair and hopelessness that had resulted in her injuring her son. She was not prosecuted and, following her confession, it became easier for the Park staff to help her: the outcome for the whole family has been excellent.

Few abusing parents are eventually prosecuted and even fewer are imprisoned. From our knowledge of police involvement in Oxford and elsewhere, it seems to us that parents who have been in trouble with the police before are more liable to prosecution, as are the illiterate and inarticulate. While for a few selected parents a period of probation or a suspended sentence can have positive effects encouraging their participation in therapy, it is difficult to see how a custodial sentence can offer anything other than retribution, being totally contradictory to the principles of rehabilitation. The highest level of police involvement reported in the English literature is in the early NSPCC study (1969): 29% of the perpetrators were actually charged and eight went to prison (seven men and one woman). In the subsequent NSPCC studies, the rate of criminal proceedings is much lower — 5% in the 1972 study and 6.5% in the study published in 1977 (Creighton and Owtram) However, it must be remembered that the proportion of severely abused children was lower in these later studies. Of the 25 cases studied in detail by Baher *et al.* (1976), four were investigated by the police who had either been informed by another agency or had picked the case up in the juvenile court. Only one prosecution resulted and that mother was given an absolute discharge by the court.

A. Police involvement in the sample

There was some form of police involvement for ten of the 39 abused children (26%) around the time of admission to the Park Hospital. All these children had severe injuries. For several families the investigations included discussion with the Park Hospital staff but did not involve the parents in giving a statement. Where statements were taken from parents resident in the hospital, it was usually possible for a member of staff to be present. Two parents were prosecuted, resulting in probation for a mother and a jail sentence for a father. Investigations in the latter case had started before the child was referred to us. The father pleaded guilty and spent 8 months in the local prison where he was visited regularly by the staff from the Park Hospital. The irony in this case was that the family were well on the way to successful rehabilitation by the time the criminal case came to court. It is possible that his sentencing was influenced by the fact that a famous "baby-battering" scandal hit the press that very week.

CONCLUSION

While the Park Hospital clearly aims to rehabilitate the child with the family, this chapter has shown that the staff do not hesitate to use the law to protect the child: 23 of the abused children (59%) and five siblings (12%) had some form of legal or statutory protection at some time after the identifying abuse incident. The form this took is summarized in Table 10. In addition, the abuse incident led directly to the criminal prosecution of two parents, there being no further prosecutions for abuse or neglect during the follow-up interval.

Our rate of initial legal orders and statutory protection is very similar to that of the NSPCC despite the likely social differences between our sample and their clients. Sixteen (41%) of the abused children in our sample had been given statutory or voluntary protection around the time of admission to the Park Hospital. A direct comparison can be made with the large NSPCC study (Creighton and Owtram, 1977) where 35% of those actually injured were given some form of initial statutory or voluntary protection. The NSPCC found that the more serious the injury, the more likely it was for the child to be taken into some form of protective care. This was also true for our sample: 62% of the severely abused children had some form of legal or voluntary protection around the time of admission compared with only 17% of the moderately abused children. When we include action taken

Table 10   Legal and statutory action

	Abused $n = 23$	Siblings $n = 5$
Place of Safety Order only	5	—
Place of Safety Order leading to Care Order	10[a, b] (9)	4[b] (4)
Place of Safety Order leading to Supervision Order	1 (0)	—
Care Order only	3 (3)	—
Supervision Order only	1 (1)	1
Voluntary Care leading to section 2 resolution	3 (3)	—

[a]For one child this happened twice.

[b]For one abused and three siblings from the same family this had been preceded by a Supervision Order.

( ) In force at time of follow-up.

during the follow-up interval, the difference is less marked and we find that 71% of the severely abused and 44% of the moderately abused children had required some form of legal or statutory protection at some time after identification of abuse.

Excluding Place of Safety Orders, we find that 12 (31%) of our abused sample were subject to continuing legal protection (Care or Supervision Order or voluntary care leading to a section 2 resolution) as a result of action taken at the time of the Park Hospital admission. By the time of follow-up, two children were no longer subject to orders; six further children had acquired continuing legal or statutory protection giving a total of 16 (41%), of whom nine (56%) were in long-term care. These rates of "legal sanctions" are much lower than those given by Speight et al. (1979) for their sample of 59 abused children admitted to Newcastle General Hospital. Legal action for 41 (69%) abused children taken in relation to the original incident had resulted in Care Orders under Children and Young Persons Act 1969, or section 2 resolutions under Children Act 1948. In a further three cases, care proceedings were taken but orders were not granted. At the time of follow-up, 2 to 4 years later, the proportion under legal sanction had risen to 75% of whom 73% were considered to be in long-term care.

The higher rate of initial care proceedings might in part be due to the fact that Speight *et al.* were studying a sample of children who had all required admission to an acute paediatric ward for physical abuse and neglect. The authors themselves suggest two further factors which might have contributed to a high legal sanction rate and low rehabilitation rate: the lack of specialized help and resources in their area and the fundamental "untreatability" of many of the families. It is pointed out that most of the parents came from a section of the population with high rates of delinquency and psychopathy. It is a dangerous assumption that people from such backgrounds are likely to be "untreatable": a superficial knowledge of many parents in our sample could have placed them in the same category and possibly denied them the chance of learning to rear their children successfully.

There is always a need to look beyond the severity of a physical injury when considering legal proceedings. In practice it is relatively easy to obtain a legal order when there is clear-cut evidence of injury. Thus in our sample, legal protection was most often granted because of definite evidence of physical abuse to the child. Occasionally, as in the cases of the five siblings, the child, although not actually injured, was thought to be at greatly increased risk. However, later in the book it will become apparent that there were other children, often siblings, who might have benefited from legal protection and even separation because of parental rejection and emotional abuse which were producing long-term consequences far more devastating than those following physical abuse alone. Even when emotional abuse is recognized, the difficulty of proving such damage in court leads to reluctance to initiate legal proceedings. It is to be hoped that in the future a wider knowledge of the different forms of child abuse and their consequences will encourage social workers to seek, and magistrates to grant, legal protection to the victims of emotional abuse. We hope that our study will suggest ways of assessing children to pick up signs of the less overt types of continuing child abuse.

SUMMARY OF FINDINGS

(1)   Sixteen (41%) abused children ($n = 39$) and four siblings ($n = 41$) were given statutory or voluntary protection around the time of admission to the Park Hospital. For 12 abused (31%) and all the siblings this was, or became, long-term (Care Order, Supervision Order or voluntary care leading to a section 2 resolution).

(2)   At follow-up 16 (41%) of the abused children were subjects of continuing legal or statutory orders. Nine (56%) of these were considered to be in long-term care. Five siblings were subjects of continuing protection, only one of whom was in long-term care.

(3)   Sixteen (41%) of the abused and four siblings had at some time been subjects of Place of Safety Orders. Eleven of these orders were succeeded by more permanent orders.

(4)   Thirteen (33%) of the abused and four siblings were made subjects of Care Orders. Only one, on an abused child, was not still in force at the time of follow-up.

(5)   Three abused and four siblings had been subjects of Supervision Orders. One order on an abused child had been rescinded and four orders (on one abused child and three siblings) replaced by Care Orders.

(6)   Three abused children were taken into voluntary care leading to section 2 resolutions.

(7)   The police had been involved with ten (26%) of the 39 cases. Prosecutions occurred in only two.

(8)   Legal protection and police involvement were both more likely to occur if the abuse had been severe.

IV. The children's growth

I. THE LITERATURE

It is widely acknowledged in the literature that there is a close relationship between physical abuse and growth failure. Indeed, some consider failure to thrive to be diagnostic of child abuse and therefore include cases in their definitions of physical abuse, even when there is no evidence of trauma (McRae *et al.*, 1973; Creighton and Owtram, 1977). Such studies are not included in this review which aims to examine the growth data available on physically abused children from the time of birth onwards.

There is evidence that a significant proportion of abused children start life as low birth weight babies. Table 11 summarizes the findings from a number of North American and U.K. studies that all define low birth weight as under 2500 g.

Table 11   Incidence of low birth weight

Author	% below 2500 g	Expected rate
Elmer and Gregg (Pittsburg), 1967 $n = 20$	30%	
Klein and Stern (Montreal), 1971 $n = 51$	23.5%	(7⁻8%)
Castle and Kerr (U.K.), 1972 $n = 78$	14.5%	
Martin *et al.* (Denver), 1974 $n = 58$	19%	(9.2%)
Smith and Hanson (Birmingham), 1974 $n = 77$	24.7%	
NSPCC (Manchester and Leeds), 1975 $n = 81$	28.4%	(7.1%)

Other studies are less precise with their definitions but indicate that a significant number of children in their samples had been of low birth weight (Weston, 1968; Skinner and Castle, 1969). Usually, such children are merely referred to as "premature". While the majority of these low birth weight babies are likely to have been pre-term (under 37 weeks gestation), some may have been *small for dates*, that is growth retarded with a birth weight that fell under the tenth centile for gestational age (Davies *et al.*, 1972) This possibility is discussed by the NSPCC study (1975) but none of the above-mentioned series gives separate figures for growth-retarded babies. It must also be remembered that a baby can be both pre-term and *small for dates* and that a *small for dates* baby delivered at term or later may not be included in a group of low birth weight babies (i.e. be under 2500 g). To get an accurate figure for the incidence of both pre-term and *small for dates babies*, there must be reliable gestational ages available. This was possible to achieve in one of our recent studies (Lynch and Roberts, 1977) where all the babies were born in a hospital which routinely assesses gestational age. We found that 22% of the abused had been pre-term and 28% of the singletons, *small for dates*. This compared with 2% and 10% respectively in the control group.

The characteristics of abusing parents may well predispose them to produce a pre-term or *small for dates* baby and certainly make them ill-equipped to cope with the extra stress such a baby produces. The detrimental effects of separation and illness on parent–child bonding is now widely accepted (Klaus and Kennell, 1976). However, it is also worth considering the effects the behaviour and appearance of premature and *small for dates* infants can have on parent–child interaction and bonding. There is evidence that both pre-term and *small for dates* babies are often more difficult to cope with than normal full-term infants. Pre-term babies handle differently and some even have transient dystonia, feeling stiff and arching away when cuddled, with a grimace instead of a smile (Brown and Thistlewaite, 1976). *Small for dates* babies look scraggy and anxious and are more likely to have unpredictable feeding and sleeping patterns. Sometimes they continue to be more difficult to live with throughout the first year of life (Als *et al.*, 1976). It is therefore understandable that the risk of physical abuse is greater for pre-term and *small for dates* babies than for those who are well grown and full-term.

After the neonatal period, the next time at which growth data has been recorded on a large number of abused children is at the time of identification of abuse, when a significant number of children are found to be failing to thrive. Table 12 summarizes the rates of failure

to thrive found in four American studies that used similar criteria for
identification of growth retardation: below the third centile or more
than two standard deviations below the mean for height and/or weight.

Table 12   Growth failure

Author	At identification	On follow-up
Elmer and Gregg (Pittsburg), 1967 $n = 20$	55%	25%
Ebbin et al. (Los Angeles), 1969 $n = 50$	30%	
Martin (Denver), 1972 $n = 42$	33%	
Martin et al. (Denver), 1974 $n = 58$	36%	31%

Other studies also give high incidences of failure to thrive (Gregg and
Elmer, 1969; Greengard, 1964), but use less precise definitions. In the
U.K., Smith and Hanson (1974) considered 16% of their 134 children to
be failing to thrive.

There can be little doubt that for some children growth retardation
precedes severe injury. For example, 17% of Smith and Hanson's
sample had a history of previous hospital admissions for failure to
thrive. Koel (1969) saw failure to thrive and fatal injury as a continuum and described three cases who had been admitted for failure to
thrive and subsequently met a violent death or near death. Two also
had evidence of earlier injury. This idea of the "spectrum of failure to
thrive and child abuse" was further developed by Oates and Hufton
(1977). They conducted a follow-up study of children admitted to an
Australian hospital for failure to thrive in 1967–1969. By 1975, two of
the original group of 30 had been killed and at least three others had
suffered significant injuries. While most of the survivors no longer
showed traditional medical problems, they were rapidly becoming
"problem children" with "intellectual and verbal failure to thrive".
Thus there would seem to be enough evidence to consider children with
non-organic failure to thrive to be at increased risk of physical injury
and to institute steps to help prevent it.

Two of the studies referred to in Table 12 (Elmer and Gregg, 1967;
Martin et al., 1974) provide follow-up growth data and show that a
significant number of children continued to fail to thrive, some years

after identification of physical abuse. The Elmer and Gregg study (1967) has available for comparison, weights at birth, identification and follow-up. All six low birth weight babies were failing to thrive at identification and three were still doing so at follow-up. Five normal birth weight babies were failing to thrive on identification and two on follow-up. In the study reported by Martin *et al.* (1974) 11 of the 21 children failing to thrive at identification continued to do so, while seven of those not initially growth-retarded were so at the time of follow-up. It was found that those with normal growth patterns at follow-up were at an intellectual advantage.

Other authors are not so precise in their definition of growth failure. However, those who have commented on growth patterns in follow-up, report a worrying persistence of retarded growth (Johnson and Morse, 1968; Morse *et al.*, 1970). Martin *et al.* (1974) is the only study to give head circumference measurements. Eight children, 14%, had circumferences two or more standard deviations below the mean at identification. At follow-up, three of these eight children remained microcephalic with associated poor intellectual performance.

Therefore, the impression gained from the literature is that a large number of children who are identified as abused will also be failing to thrive. This would support the idea that failure to thrive is part of the complex syndrome of child abuse. In follow-up, a significant proportion of abused children are still failing to thrive, and continuing growth retardation seems to be associated with poor outcome, especially in the intellectual sphere (Martin *et al.*, 1974).

II. THE STUDY SAMPLE

A. At birth

Among the 42 abused children admitted to the Park there were eight who had been premature at birth, four *small for dates* and four others both *small for dates* and premature. This gives a rate among index abused children of 29% for prematurity, and a *small for dates* rate of 19%. Of the siblings who were living in the families at the time of admission, 7% had been premature and 11% *small for dates*. Among those born to the same mothers after identification of abuse, none was premature but 24% were *small for dates*. Thus, the overall prematurity rate among the siblings was 4.5% and the *small for dates* rate 16%, so we can see that the child identified as abused in the family was far more likely to be premature than were his siblings. However, the rate for small for dates babies was almost as high for siblings as abused (expected rate 10%). This is partly explained by three mothers in the sample producing seven of the 15 small for dates babies. Most of the mothers of the growth-retarded babies were themselves of small stature and had smoked heavily during the pregnancy. One interesting child had been both small for dates and premature. Her birth weight was 1670 g at 34 weeks or more gestation, she continued to fail to thrive, and at follow-up she showed neurological damage that was difficult to attribute to abuse (a fractured femur from an isolated attack). In retrospect, it was felt that she might well have been an example of the foetal alcohol syndrome: at follow-up interview her mother admitted to a long history of drinking. She consumed at least a bottle of wine a day and in addition was a heavy social drinker.

B. At identification

Growth data were available for all the abused children at the time they were referred to the Park. For the majority this was within days of the recognition of physical abuse. Their heights and weights were plotted on Tanner and Whitehouse charts, adjustments being made for prematurity in babies presenting under a year. Seven (18%) of the 39 children subsequently seen in follow-up had identification heights and/or weights which fell below the third centile; we considered all these children to show evidence of growth retardation. Three had been full-term babies and four premature. One of the term babies and three of the prematures had been small for dates at birth.

Figure 1 (a) shows the distribution of weights for all 39 children at identification. While our sample of abused children did not have such a high incidence of growth retardation as the American samples cited above, there was still four times the expected number of children, 16 (41%) with weights below the tenth centile. At the other end of the scale, six (15%) of the abused children had weights over the ninetieth centile. Most of them were frankly obese, having weights out of proportion to their heights. There are several possible explanations for these over-weight children. Some of the mothers had undoubtedly high, unrealistic mothercraft ideals and equated a fat baby with successful mothering. Others were trying to compensate for their feelings of rejection by overfeeding.

Head circumference measurements were available for 34 children. Only one of these had a circumference below the third centile. Three others had measurements below the tenth centile.

For the 27 siblings living in the families at the time of abuse, growth

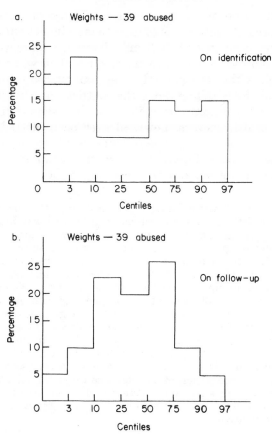

Fig. 1 Distribution of weights for 39 abused children (a) on identification (b) on follow-up.

data were less well documented, especially for those admitted at the beginning of the study period. However, it is likely that those with possible growth retardation were identified and had weights and heights recorded. Two siblings were certainly known to have heights and weights below the third centile. One of these was a physically un-harmed but emotionally rejected sister of one of the obese babies previously described. She had been a full-term, normal birth weight baby. The other was subsequently placed for adoption and does not appear in the follow-up data. He had been a full-term but small for dates baby.

If we look only at the state of children's growth at one point in time, i.e. at identification of abuse, previous evidence of failure to thrive could be ignored. A child's rate of growth is as important as his actual weight. Patterns of growth will only become apparent when serial weights are plotted on a centile chart. Only then will a child whose weight is still within the normal range, but whose rate of gain has diminished (i.e. he is falling down the centiles), be identified. We did seek out previous weights on children in our sample from hospital records and health visitors. Few had ever been plotted on a chart, though for some this would have produced evidence of growth failure prior to physical abuse. Figure 2 illustrates the fall-off in weight gain that preceded the serious injury of one boy, Simon, in our sample.

> Simon was referred to the Park Hospital at the age of 3: his leg had been broken by his father. He exhibited classical "frozen watchfulness" (see Chapter VII). In addition to the fracture there were burns, bruises and signs of recent weight loss. He had not been weighed in the accident and emergency department before his limb was encased in plaster, but in the cast he was just above the third centile (we have included him in our growth-retarded group). Simon had been a low birth weight baby and therefore had been followed up by a paediatrician. At first, clinic appointments were kept regularly and his weight increased until he reached the fiftieth centile. There then followed a series of failed appointments. At the age of 2½, he was referred back by his family doctor because of concern over his general level of development. If his weight had been charted at that out-patient visit, it would have been seen to be on the tenth centile. A recognition of the significance in the fall-off in rate of growth may well have led to the action that could have prevented the subsequent injuries. The chart also clearly shows the weight gain that followed intervention.

C. At follow-up

After admission to the Park, growth measurements are available on a number of occasions for the majority of abused children. We considered a child to show evidence of growth failure during the follow-up interval if his or her height and/or weight remained below the third centile, fell below the third centile, or if the yearly growth velocity (height or weight) was below the third centile. Six (15%) of the 39 abused children available for follow-up assessment came into this category; four of these still had height and/or weight below the third centile, actually at the time of follow-up examination. Only one child who failed to thrive in the follow-up period had not been failing to

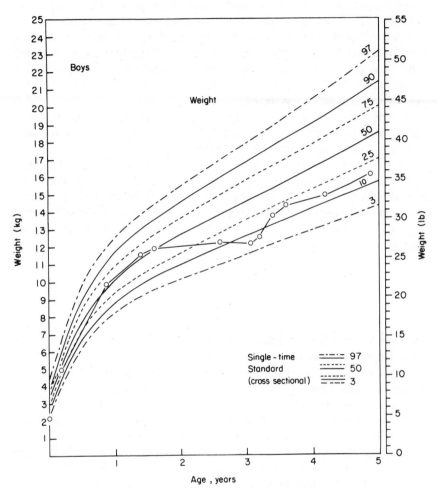

Fig. 2 Weight chart of abused child, Simon.

thrive at the time of abuse. Her fall-off in weight gain had corresponded to a difficult transition period, when she was gradually being returned from foster care to her parents. Once settled, she began to gain weight and was not failing to thrive at the time of follow-up examination. Figure 1 (b) demonstrates the distribution of weights for all the abused children seen at follow-up. When compared with distribution at the time of identification, it has now become much nearer that expected for the population. These findings on follow-up are encouraging, with a much lower rate of growth retardation than reported by Elmer and Gregg (1967) and Martin *et al.* (1974).

The sibling showing growth retardation when first seen at the Park and included in the follow-up, was still failing to thrive. Another sibling, who had been born since the abuse incident, was found to have height and weight both below the third centile. He had been neither premature nor small for dates.

At the time of follow-up, three children had skull circumferences below the third centile. All had suffered head injuries; two were severely, and one moderately, neurologically handicapped. The one child who was identified as having a small head at the time of abuse now had a head between the third and tenth centile. She was neurologically and intellectually intact. None of the siblings had a head circumference below the third centile. As in Martin's study, microcephaly in our sample was associated with poor neurological and intellectual prognosis.

III. DISCUSSION

The association between failure to thrive and child abuse is obviously very important, yet often overlooked.

From clinical experience with abusing families it is possible to suggest various reasons why there should be this association. Firstly, if parents have failed to bond to a new baby, they will not be in tune with the baby's signals and, because of their detachment, when overwhelmed with their own problems, may even ignore a baby who is screaming with hunger. Furthermore, chronically underfed babies are more likely in time to be apathetic, not to persist with crying when hungry, and therefore less likely to evoke an appropriate response in their parents.

Some abused children may fail to thrive because the chaotic environment in which many of these families live makes it very easy to forget to feed them. In contrast, we have known some families, with an obsessional need to keep everything clean and tidy, whose efforts to avoid the mess that invariably accompanies a baby's meal-time, result in restrictions on the amount and variety of food offered. Some babies respond to this by becoming inhibited in their demands for food, making meal times a miserable experience for everyone.

Some abused children live under a permanent threat of violence and in constant fear. Some will be too frightened to eat, while others —

though their actual calorific intake is adequate — suffer from intestinal hurry with diarrhoea. This has been vividly described by Erin Pizzey when she talks about the children in her Battered Wives' Refuge. The withholding of food as a form of punishment is also fairly common in abusing families, and in some cases this may be so extreme as to cause overt failure to thrive (Krieger, 1974; MacCarthy, 1979).

When assessing the reasons for the failure to thrive, organic illness must be excluded. For example, a baby with coeliac disease will fail to thrive and may be so bad-tempered as to provoke abuse by vulnerable parents. Treatment of the cause of failure to thrive could prevent further abuse. For this reason, any abused child who is failing to thrive must have the same medical examination and basic investigations as any child presenting with growth failure. Once a child has begun to fail to thrive he is more likely to succumb to intercurrent illness and therefore continue to fail to thrive, putting himself at even greater risk of abuse.

As growth failure is so often closely linked with child abuse, it is essential that proper assessment of an abused child's growth is made. Full information on the previous rate of growth is desirable as well as actual measurement of height, weight and head circumference at the time of identification. When providing therapy for a family in which abuse and failure to thrive have occurred, particular attention needs to be paid to feeding problems and practices. The parents may well require a lot of practical advice and help before feed-time can become an enjoyable experience for them and the child. When a decision is made that an abused child should be removed from the care of his parents, clearly charted rates of growth can be used as evidence in court when trying to prove that the child has been neglected, especially when separation from the parents has resulted in large weight gains.

In our study it was possible to relate fluctuations in the child's rate of growth to the general well-being of the family. This was certainly true in Simon's family. Both Simon's and his siblings' follow-up weight charts clearly reflected the ups and downs of relationships within the family. Figure 3 is the weight chart of his younger sister, Lisa. The occasions when her weight-gain slowed corresponded to periods of upheaval within the family, when we became fearful for the children's safety. Each time when circumstances changed for the better and the family settled down, Lisa resumed a normal growth pattern. The lesson to be learned is obvious: all children in families where child abuse is suspected must be weighed regularly and their weights plotted on a chart. This is a simple procedure and an invaluable way of monitoring the progress of both child and family.

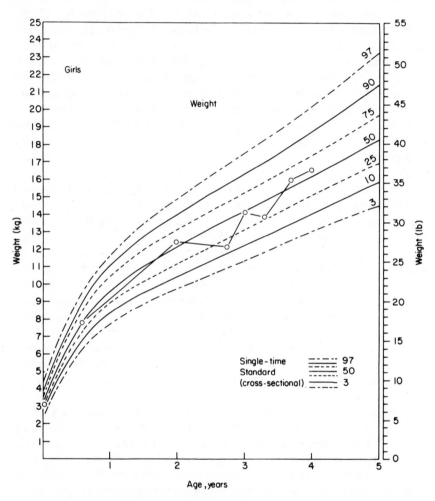

Fig. 3 Weight chart of Simon's younger sister, Lisa.

SUMMARY OF FINDINGS

(1) At birth 29% of the abused children were pre-term and 19% small for dates. Among the siblings 4.5% were premature and 16% small for dates.

(2) At identification 18% of the abused children ($n = 39$) had shown evidence of growth retardation. A total of 16 (41%) had weights below the tenth centile.

(3) During the follow-up interval 15% of the abused children showed evidence of retarded growth. Four (10%) were still retarded at the time of the follow-up examination. Only two siblings were growth-retarded at follow-up.

(4) The three abused children with skull circumferences below the third centile at follow-up were neurologically handicapped.

(5) In our sample there were clear examples of uncharted and undetected fall-off in weight gain which preceded serious injury.

V. Ill-health and physical handicap

As observed by Steele and Pollock (1968), it seems likely that parents with a high potential to abuse, because of their personalities, backgrounds and social circumstances, will find it particularly distressing to have to cope with an infant who is pre-term, ill, or who has a congenital abnormality. As we have already discussed there is certainly an increased rate of prematurity and growth retardation among abused children. Other evidence in the literature suggests that even abused children who were of normal birth weight frequently have a history of congenital abnormality or ill-health prior to injury. Klein and Stern (1971), as well as reporting a low birth weight rate of 23.5% in their sample of 51 cases of physical abuse, found that 15 of the 39 normal birth weight babies had been identified as having significant medical illness. In at least six this would have been evident in the neonatal period. Likewise, Elmer and Gregg (1967) who reported the incidence of prematurity in their sample as 30%, mention that a further 15% had serious illnesses prior to abuse, and Birrell and Birrell (1968) reported that over 25% of their sample had some kind of congenital abnormality. Smith and Hanson (1974) considered 7.45% (10) of their 134 children to have serious congenital defects compared with an expected rate of 1.75%. Eight other children were reported as having minor abnormalities. In Holman and Kanwar's series (1975) from the London Borough of Lambeth, six of the 28 abused children (21%) had previously been admitted to hospital with a serious illness, and in five cases (18%) a congenital disorder was present. The impression gained from the studies cited above is that there is indeed a high rate of congenital abnormality among abused children. However, the term "congenital abnormality" is seldom defined, and expected rates for the study population are infrequently given. Similarly, expected rates for general ill-health after the neonatal period are not given.

In this country the admission rates to special care baby units can be taken as a good indication of neonatal problems. Two of our own studies looked specifically at this factor. One study (Lynch and Roberts, 1977) compared 50 abused children with 50 controls born in the same maternity hospital. Forty-two per cent of the abused had been admitted to the special care unit compared with 10% of the control babies. While 11 of the babies admitted were pre-term, ten were full-term, six of whom were extremely ill and gave rise to much medical anxiety. The longest stay of 50 days on the unit was for a baby with viral meningitis.

In the other study (Lynch, 1975) a comparison was made between the early life histories of 25 abused children and those of their 35 unharmed siblings. It was found that 40% of the abused had required admission to the special care baby unit for more than 48 hours compared with only 6% of their siblings. In this study the incidence of ill-health among the children in the first year of life was also examined. Far more of the abused had been ill in that first year: 60% compared with 9% of their siblings. All illnesses that were reported by parents or doctors as being serious or recurrent were included. Thus, there were examples of both serious illness requiring admission to hospital and recurrent minor health problems. The abused group included some very ill children with examples of pneumonia, bronchitis, viral carditis with congestive heart failure, pyloric stenosis, severe cleft palate and hare lip and convulsions. There were also many irritating and persistent health problems: eczema, recurrent colic, with vomiting and failure to thrive. This study, comparing ill-health within families, does show that the abused child is more likely to have been a health problem than his unharmed siblings.

The serious nature of some of the congenital abnormalities described in the literature implies that a number of the children were physically and possibly mentally handicapped before abuse occurred. Sandgrund et al. (1974) imply that some children are abused because they are inherently retarded. Other babies who may be at increased risk are those who superficially appear normal but manifest subtle signs of CNS dysfunction or immaturity. As Martin (1976) points out, parents are left to cope with such babies without all the support systems that are called into play for a family whose child is obviously grossly abnormal. It has certainly been our own experience that stress was greatly increased where the presence of an abnormality had been suspected by the parents but left unrecognized and undiagnosed by their medical advisers (Ounsted *et al.*, 1974; Lynch, 1976).

For any sample of abused children the number with pre-existing handicap is small compared with those who suffer permanent damage as the result of abuse. Kempe *et al.*, in a paper published in 1962, where the term "battered child syndrome" was first used, stated that 28% of physically abused children suffered permanent brain injury. There are two main forms of permanent injury: firstly the scars and deformities that result from visible injuries, e.g. burns, cuts and fractures, and secondly, the handicap that results from inflicted brain damage, which may or may not have been accompanied by external injuries. Often, the reader is left in doubt about the author's interpretation of the term "permanent injury". For example, Smith and Hanson (1974) refer twice to permanent damage and give two different rates. They tell us that 15% of the children had serious injuries resulting in permanent damage but later state that 31% could not be intellectually assessed because of "permanent damage." Presumably the first figure refers to scars and deformities and the second to brain damage. Another form of permanent handicap is the visual impairment that can follow intra-ocular bleeding that commonly accompanies subdural and other intra-cranial haemorrhage. Often this takes the form of transient retinal haemorrhages, but can result in retinal scarring, squints and loss of visual acuity. Later, at follow-up, optic atrophy can be found (Harcourt and Hopkins, 1971; Mushin, 1971).

All follow-up studies looking at the neurology of physically abused children have found a high incidence of abnormality. However, only one author (Martin *et al.*, 1974), has fully defined the degrees of handicap experienced by the children. After a relatively detailed neurological examination the children were allocated to one of four neurological classes:

Class 3: Serious and significant neurological abnormalities.
Class 2: Less severe neurological handicaps and abnormalities.
Class 1: Mild neurological findings not severe enough for the child to show significant functional handicap.
Class 0: No neurological dysfunction, immaturity or damage.

Of the 42 children seen for Martin's 1972 study, 43% had abnormalities on follow-up neurological examination. Two-thirds of these children had obvious findings, i.e. came into classes 3 or 2. The other third had more subtle signs, i.e. class 1. Of the 18 children with neurological problems, only half had a history of head trauma and just under half had normal intelligence. In the study published in 1974, 53% of the 58 children showed some abnormalities on neurological examination; 17% had severe deficit (class 3), 14% moderate deficit (class 2) and 22% mild dysfunction (class 1). Neurological problems were related to IQ scores and history of head trauma. However, while 15 of the children with neurological impairment had a history of skull fracture and/or subdural haemorrhage, 16 had no such history. Thus, 43% of the children with no history of head trauma had neurological abnormalities. It seems likely to us that children such as these, with no documented evidence of head injury, may well have been the subjects of severe shaking (Caffey, 1972).

Despite the prevalence of long-term handicap in abused children, the descriptions that are available of the children's general health in the years following intervention, seem to indicate that illness plays a less prominent part in the child's life. The 20 children followed up by Elmer and Gregg (1967) were found to have suffered no new serious acute or chronic illness during the follow-up period, although many had a history of ill-health prior to abuse. Morse and colleagues' (1970) follow-up study reported that at least one-fifth of the children had health or somatic problems thought to be secondary to stress. Martin *et al.* (1974) found that the general health of the abused children on follow-up, as determined by history and physical examination, was generally good.

II. THE SAMPLE: EARLY HEALTH PROBLEMS

An attempt was made to look at the health of both abused and siblings prior to admission to the Park Hospital. It was possible to get some idea of the extent of neonatal problems by looking at the rate of special care baby unit admissions. Sixteen of the abused children (41%) had required admission to the special care baby unit. Three quarters of them had stayed there for more than 2 weeks. Obviously the main reason for admission was prematurity (12 of the 16 were under 37 weeks' gestation) but a number of the full-term babies also caused anxiety in the neonatal period and some were extremely ill. Among the siblings, five (12%) required admission to the special care baby unit. This included four of those who were born before admission to the Park, and one of those born subsequently.

Data on health problems experienced between the neonatal period and identification of the abuse were also examined. The following classification of illnesses was used:

Serious acute: An episode of ill-health which was life-threatening and/or required urgent medical treatment with admission to hospital, e.g. pneumonia, pyloric stenosis.

Minor acute: An episode of less severe ill-health, self-limiting or responding rapidly to medical treatment. If admission occurred, this was very brief, e.g. bronchitis, otitis media.

Serious recurrent/chronic: More than two episodes of the same life-threatening illness, e.g. severe asthma or a disease which physically handicaps for life or shortens life, such as haemophilia.

Minor recurrent/chronic: Recurrence of chronic symptoms which can interfere with life without shortening it or producing actual physical handicap, i.e. more a nuisance, e.g. eczema.

A child was considered to have been a significant health problem if he had suffered a serious acute illness, a serious recurrent/chronic illness or a minor recurrent/chronic illness. Minor acute episodes were not included because they are an expected part of every childhood. Illnesses associated with the abuse incident were excluded, as were "accidents" and routine surgical operations. Information about illnesses occurring before identification of abuse was of course retrospectively collected. However, wherever possible, it was checked out with the child's doctors and medical records. When comparing the rates of illness obtained for abused and siblings, the relative ages of the two groups must be considered. The average age of the abused children at admission to the Park Hospital was 1.2 years and for siblings 2.5 years. Thus the siblings had both longer to establish themselves as a health problem and for incidents in early infancy to be forgotten. Using the criteria outlined above, 50% of the abused children and 19% of their siblings were, or had been, a significant health problem to parents and/or doctors between the neonatal period and admission to the Park Hospital. Five abused children had one or more potentially life-threatening illnesses before abuse was identified (one had pyloric stenosis and four children had one or more severe attacks of pneumonia, in two cases with accompanying heart failure). All these illnesses occurred in the first year of life. None of the siblings were recorded as having had a serious acute illness before admission to the Park. Three probands suffered from a serious chronic disorder; two of these were neurological problems and the third child was a haemophiliac. In each case the diagnosis was only finally confirmed after the abuse. The only sibling considered to have evidence of a severe/chronic health problem — a serious visual abnormality — was also attending paediatric out-patients for failure to thrive. A large proportion of the abused children who were identified as health problems had had minor recurrent episodes of irritating ill-health such as eczema, wheezy bronchitis, vomiting and other feeding difficulties. For some, this was in addition to serious acute or other chronic disease.

The injuries which brought about the child's admission to the Park Hospital have already been described in Chapter II. It will be recalled that out of the 39 children seen at follow-up, 21 were seriously abused. This included six children with intracranial bleeds, 11 children with fractures (including four fractured skulls), one child was nearly drowned, two were poisoned, losing consciousness, and the remaining child suffered a severe burn.

III. THE SAMPLE: PHYSICAL HANDICAP ON FOLLOW-UP

A. Deformities and scars

On follow-up examination, six children had obvious scars or deformities that we considered to be, at least in part, the result of abuse. These included three severely neurologically handicapped children. Another child, who had suffered a fractured skull, had a small, flattened head. The child with a severe burn was scarred both on his hand and his thigh and another child had a deformed, troublesome nose. We excluded a variety of minor scars (similar to those one might find on any group of children) which, in a few cases, could have been the result of minor abuse. The operation scars for those children who had had burr holes were all well hidden and so were not included.

B. Neurological status

A standard neurological examination (Paine and Oppé, 1966) was part of the follow-up assessment of all the children. They were also observed for any signs of minor neurological dysfunction (see Appendix A). For the younger children under five who were having a Sheridan assessment, much of this observation was carried out while the children were being tested. More formal tests were carried out on the older children but these, too, were often incorporated into a game. They were based on Touwen and Prechtl's (1970) scheme. Following the assessment, the children were classified into four categories which were as follows:-

(1) *Severe Neurological Impairment:* Children with very definite and obvious neurological signs producing severe functional handicap.

(2) *Moderate Neurological Impairment:* Children with obvious signs (including extreme clumsiness) producing significant but not severe functional handicap. Nevertheless, their neurological problems would not necessarily be obvious to a casual observer. This group of children, we felt, warranted remedial help and follow-up.

(3) *Minor Neurological Impairment:* Children with minor signs and/or clumsiness. This includes children with minor difficulties with fine or gross motor co-ordination, poor balancing skills, evidence of poor motor planning, and mild visuo-perceptual or spatial problems. For some of the children in this category there seemed to be little, if any, functional handicap, e.g. (a) a child with an intention tremor who performed well for her age on developmental testing; (b) a boy with balance problems who was in the football team. Others, however, while their signs were no more obvious, were experiencing problems. These were often the children who were reluctant to participate in ball games, etc., thereby becoming even more ill-practised.

(4) *Neurologically Intact:* Nothing abnormal demonstrated or observed.

Children with visuo-perceptual and spatial problems were considered to show neurological impairment. Not included in the classification, however, were children with isolated squints, minor reduction in visual acuity, or minor hearing defects. Nor, unlike some American studies, did we include children with abnormal language development or "hyperactivity". Any deviations of behaviour were noted and are referred to in Chapter VII.

Among the abused children, at the time of their Park Hospital admission, it had been obvious that a number of them were at risk of long-term neurological handicap. In Table 13 we attempt to relate the type of abuse to the degree of handicap detected at the follow-up assessment. The known injuries have been classified to show any possible neurological insult. Where a child suffered more than one injury, only the one most likely to produce neurological problems is included.

Table 13   Injury and neurological handicap

	Severity of handicap — 39 children		
	Severe $n=4$	Moderate $n=6$	Minor/none $n=29$
Intracranial bleed $n=6$	3	—	3
Fractured skull $n=4$	—	2	2
Minor head injury $n=17$	1	2	14
Asphyxiation $n=3$	—	—	3
Poisoning $n=2$	—	—	2
Other injury $n=7$	—	2	5

Three of the four abused with evidence of severe neurological handicap had suffered intracranial bleeding. The most severely handicapped was spastic, microcephalic, epileptic and blind. He was living in an institution for the mentally retarded. The aetiology of his handicap is complicated because although undoubtedly damaged by his mother's assault there was evidence that he had a congenitally abnormal brain. The other two children suffering intracranial bleeds with subsequent handicap had as far as we know been previously neurologically intact. One had remained with her parents and though hemiplegic and partially sighted was able with some specialized help to cope in a normal village school. The other was making excellent progress in a foster home, despite left-sided weakness, retardation and boisterous behaviour. The only abused child without a proven history of serious head trauma to be severely neurologically handicapped was certainly considered to have been neurologically abnormal before she was physically abused (minor head injury). She had been previously investigated for delayed development and, by the time she was seen at the Park at 2 years 5 months, had obvious cerebellar ataxia. However, looking at the case retrospectively, the possibility that all her handicap was the result of early violent shaking cannot be dismissed.

Four of the six children identified as moderately neurologically handicapped did not have a history of significant head injury, or loss of consciousness. It will be remembered that Martin (1974) also had a proportion of his sample showing neurological abnormalities without a history of head trauma. There are several possible explanations for these findings. We have already discussed a couple of examples in our sample of probable pre-existing handicap. How often this happens is impossible to know. Certainly children who are abused have a high prevalence of adverse perinatal experiences that in themselves might explain subsequent handicap. Unfortunately these same children's poor attendance at clinics frequently means that we have no reliable observations made before the abuse to help date the onset of neurological signs and symptoms. Reviewing our data on one of the moderately handicapped children, a girl whose only injury had been a fractured femur, it seemed likely that she had been a victim of her mother's excessive alcohol intake during pregnancy. Her growth retardation has been discussed in the preceding chapter. On neurological examination she was found to have very definite visuoperceptual problems which very noticeably affected her performance on developmental and intelligence testing.

For a number of children the extent and duration of the abuse will never be known. While the majority of the recorded head injuries were minor bruises and scratches, such a history does indicate that blows were directed towards the head rather than, or in addition to, less dangerous parts of the body. For some children this happened repeatedly. Another vulnerable group, difficult to identify, were those children being recurrently shaken. Even when the parents admitted to having shaken a child, it was seldom clear how much force had been used. A documented example of shaking was a pair of twins presenting with minor scratches — one on the face and the other on the chest — who, on several occasions, had been shaken and thrown across the room in front of witnesses. The twin who came in for the roughest handling and who, because her injuries were on the chest, was not classified even as a minor head injury, was found to have moderate neurological impairment on follow-up while her sister escaped neurologically intact.

In contrast to those children whose neurological problems could not be explained by their presenting injuries, there was a group of children who despite suffering serious insults to their brains had escaped without neurological handicap. A number of the children with severe head trauma had done better than we had expected from their condition at the time of their emergency admission to hospital. All six babies with evidence of intracranial bleeding had been seriously ill in the acute episode and all had had convulsions. However, three of these survived with little or no neurological handicap. This raises the question of how often in the past children with a diagnosis of "subdural haematomata and intracranial bleeding — cause unknown" were sent back into homes where physical and emotional abuse were continuing unrecognized. In later years all the subsequent severe handicap could then easily be seen as the direct result of an isolated bleed. Another child who certainly was a candidate for long-term neurological deficit was the child who survived near-drowning. On admission to the intensive care unit she was unconscious and convulsing. She survived with no neurological handicap. Of the four children with fractured skulls without evidence of intracranial bleeding, none was severely handicapped on follow-up but two did have moderate neurological impairment. One of those who escaped with only mild neurological handicap, mild motor clumsiness and minimal fine motor incoordination had suffered infantile spasms. At 3 years 9 months he was seizure free and of high, normal intelligence.

Table 14 summarizes the neurological status on follow-up for the 41 siblings as well as the 39 abused children. It will be seen that in addition to six abused, three siblings were found to be moderately neurologically handicapped at follow-up. One of the siblings had a

Table 14   Results of neurological assessment

	Neurological impairment			
	Severe	Moderate	Mild	None
Abused $n = 39$	4 (10%)	6 (15%)	11 (28%)	18 (46%)
Sibling $n = 41$	— —	3 (7%)	9 (22%)	29 (71%)

severe squint, was almost blind in one eye, and had a minor tremor. She had a history of failure to thrive and we were deeply concerned over her emotional care. At the time of admission there had been no overt evidence of abuse of the other two moderately impaired siblings — both boys. One was obviously bright, but clumsy with minor unilateral signs. He had been born prematurely and had been seriously ill in the neonatal period. The other was a very clumsy 6-year old with visuo-spatial problems and minor right-sided signs. He was an intelligent child but not progressing as well as he should have at school. During the follow-up period there had been an incident which his social worker thought might have been due to physical abuse.

Almost as many siblings (22%) as abused (28%) were found to show mild neurological impairment. While we did not have a local control group of Oxfordshire children for comparison, it is likely that the incidence of mild neurological impairment in our sample is higher than one would find in a random group of children. In the Isle of Wight study (Rutter *et al.*, 1970), 13% of a random control group of 9 and 10-year olds were classified as showing possible neurological abnormality. The neurological examination and criteria employed, while not identical to ours, are comparable (Rutter *et al.*, 1970). We had the impression that for some children, the minor abnormality was due to lack of opportunity and experience that was often the direct result of restrictive parental attitudes. For younger children, adventurous and "dangerous" play was discouraged by parents fearful that an accident would result and that they would then be called upon to explain it. Older children were often forbidden to "play out" with peers and sometimes not allowed to go swimming with the school or take part in sports activities after school hours. Once a child is recognized as clumsy by his peers, he is put at a disadvantage and is unlikely to be popular; he will be incompetent at sports and therefore will not be picked by his classmates for the team — a further blow to his already fragile self-esteem. By anticipating these problems, parents and children can be helped to overcome them. For example, one little 4-year old (a study child) was shown to be clumsy and delayed in gross motor activities, although developing satisfactorily in other areas. The parents had nowhere at home for her to play outside and were in any case very apprehensive about allowing her to climb. A suggestion was made that the child should be taken regularly to an outside play area or park. The parents adapted the plan and went often to a local pub garden with play apparatus. A year later their daughter was as nimble as her peers when she entered school. The parents also benefited as their trips to the pub had helped break through their social isolation.

During the course of the follow-up assessment, it became clear that it was very important to define any neurological problems that the children had and ensure that they were receiving the appropriate help. All too often the subsequent concern over an abused child is restricted to detecting further possible "non-accidental injury". For instance, one of the four severely handicapped children, who had been abused at the age of 7 months, was subjected to frequent medical examination after teachers reported minor bruising and yet this child was not receiving the special attention and assessment she needed as a partially sighted hemiplegic pupil. The original abuse was always being recalled, whereas it was forgotten that the parents were successfully rearing a second child, were 6 years older and living in very different circumstances. As a result of our examination she did, in fact, get the extra help that she needed from a local educational psychologist. Her behaviour improved and any doubts about her remaining in a normal primary school were removed. Another child, whom we tracked down in a children's home in another part of the country, had difficult behaviour and was failing in school. It was thought that this was all the result of his deprived and disrupted background. However, on neurological examination, he was found to have moderate neurological impairment. In particular, he had poor eye/hand coordination, and severe visuo-perceptual problems. Not surprisingly, he was having great difficulty in learning to read and write.

C. Vision and hearing

As part of the follow-up medical examination, every child had his vision and hearing tested. For the younger children this was done as part of the developmental assessment and for the older children it was incorporated into the neurological examination. Visual acuity was tested in the very young with graded balls and then stycar letters, passing as soon as possible to the linear wall-chart. The "cover test" was used to detect possible squints.* Among the abused children there were two children with marked visual problems; both had been severely injured and had severe neurological handicap. One had bilateral optic atrophy and was blind, the other had a field defect, together with a squint and reduced visual acuity. In addition to this, eight children were considered to have squints. Usually the acuity in the squinting eye was reduced. One child had reduced acuity without a squint. If the children had not already seen an ophthalmologist, referral was arranged. Among the siblings, two children had squints detected and were referred. In addition we found one boy to be strikingly colour blind. Another child was already known to have visual problems: she had already had squint surgery on an eye with posterior synechia and greatly reduced acuity. The children's hearing was tested with distraction tests in the babies, passing as early as possible to vocal tests, first with toys and then with stycar pictures. Two abused children failed their hearing tests: one was already attending an ENT department and the other had already been detected by the school health service. One sibling who failed was referred to the local ENT de-

*strabismus.

partment, where the defect was confirmed.

The striking finding was the large number of abused children who on follow-up had visual problems. Eleven (28%) were known to, or required, referral to an ophthalmologist. The more severe defects were, as one might expect, in the neurologically handicapped children. Nine (23%) of all the abused children had squints. These ranged from the obvious and unsightly to those detected only on careful observation and testing. The incidence is much higher than is found in population studies. For example, Chamberlain and Simpson (1979) found 3.8% of 3½-year olds to have a definite or probable squint which is not significantly different from the rate for the siblings of 7% (three children). The association between visual defects and child abuse which is highlighted in this study needs to receive greater attention by both paediatricians and ophthalmologists. We felt that often these children were too easily allowed to default from attendance at ophthalmology clinics.

IV. THE SAMPLE: MEDICAL HISTORY AT FOLLOW-UP

A. History of subsequent abuse

Details of abuse incidents during the follow-up interval were collected from the social work and family doctor questionnaires. Further information was also obtained from entries that had been made in the Park Hospital files. While the social workers and family doctors were being asked to supply evidence retrospectively, it was evident from the precision with which dates were given that they were in fact reporting incidents which had been recorded in writing by them at the time of occurrence. Eight previously abused children were recorded as having definite evidence of abuse by their social worker, GP or by a member of the Park Hospital staff (some were, of course, recorded by a combination of these workers). Only five of the eight had actually had demonstrable injuries. The most serious was a spiral fracture of the tibia, recorded as definite abuse by the family doctor but as only possible abuse by the social worker. Two children had had bruising reported initially by their school; in one case a mother and in the other a stepmother subsequently gave accounts of inflicting the injuries. The child in the latter case was removed on a Place of Safety Order. A further case of minor bruising was reported as definite abuse by a social worker. No further details were given. The fifth injury was so minor that it could easily have gone unnoticed. The social worker reported: "Father admitted attempting to kick S. during a temper outburst (father's). Small, insignificant skin abrasion behind right ear." This very minor injury occurred at a time of mounting tension within the household, which led to this child and his siblings being temporarily removed from the home. In two of the three remaining cases the evidence of definite abuse was dependent on accounts by the mothers of their own assaults on their children. There had been no detectable injuries. In the third case the father had summoned help, alleging that the mother had kicked one of her twins. Once again there were no detectable injuries but the mother proceeded to throw the twin across the room in front of witnesses, including the reporting social worker. Both twins were subsequently taken into care.

Only one sibling was reported as showing definite evidence of abuse during the follow-up interval. He had been admitted to the paediatric ward with a large bruise on his forehead. Mother admitted to the social worker that she had inflicted this. There was no evidence of further abuse to the child, to the originally abused sister or to the other sibling in the household. Interestingly, however, before the abused child had been referred to the Park Hospital, we had known the family because of the problems the mother was having handling the behaviour of the older sibling.

B. General health

The general physical examination which was part of the follow-up assessment did not reveal any serious conditions, which were either unknown to the parents or had been disregarded by them. Apart from the occasional minor acute respiratory tract infection all the children, except the boy in a mental subnormality hospital, were judged to be in good general health at the time they were examined.

Information on the health of the children during the follow-up interval was obtained from parents, hospital records and from a short questionnaire circulated to the family doctors. The same categories of illness were used as when examining the children's health prior to admission to the Park Hospital. There had been no incidents among the abused that could be considered serious acute episodes, but one sibling at the age of 5 years had required emergency tracheotomy for acute respiratory tract obstruction. The only serious chronic illnesses were in the children with severe neurological handicap, together with the haemophiliac child. One in five of the children suffered, or had suffered, in the follow-up interval from minor recurrent or chronic symptoms. These were almost exclusively recurrent respiratory or chronic skin problems, i.e. wheezy bronchitis, tonsillitis, otitis media and eczema. The difference at follow-up between abused and siblings was much less striking with 23% of the probands and 19% of the siblings being identified as health problems.

Enquiries were made to ascertain the use the families had made of hospital services for their children. Twenty-six of the children had had at least one admission to hospital during the follow-up interval. This included 36% of the abused and 29% of their siblings. The admissions were mostly for minor complaints and included a number for routine surgical procedures. Information was also sought on out-patient attendances. Follow-up at the Park Hospital or in a local paediatric clinic which was the direct result of abuse was not included. Five (13%) of the abused were currently attending out-patient clinics for other reasons and a further seven (18%) had attended at some time during the follow-up interval. Among the siblings the numbers were smaller with three (7%) currently attending and a further four (10%) having attended previously. Overall 46% of the abused and 36% of the siblings had been known to an in-patient and/or out-patient hospital department during the follow-up interval. The parents were also asked to report on occasions that they had taken their child to casualty during the follow-up period: wherever possible, confirming document-ary evidence was sought and not infrequently the Park had been informed at the time of the visit, especially if it was for an injury. Thirty-eight percent of the probands and 22% of the siblings were known to have attended casualty. Most of the visits were for accidents and the families with easy access were most likely to have attended. Only three abused and none of the siblings had been more than once. Looking at the number of children who had some contact with the hospital during the follow-up interval we find that 51% of the children (64% of the abused and 39% of their siblings) were either admitted to hospital, seen in the out-patients, or attended casualty. Of course, some had been seen in two or all of these places.

The initial impression of the admission and hospital attendance rates found by us in this study might well appear to be high especially among the abused children. However, similar high proportions of children in the general population are found to have utilized hospital services. For example, Chamberlain and Simpson (1979) when study-ing a cohort of children ascertained as part of the British Births Child Study found that by the age of 3½ years half had been a hospital patient. This rate includes admissions and attendances at out-patient or casualty departments. Twenty per cent of all the children had actually had at least one admission. Because of Chamberlain and Simpson's exclusion of unsupported mothers and the relatively high number of children not available on follow-up, their sample is likely to be less disadvantaged than ours, making any detailed comparisons inappropriate.

When considering the rates of casualty attendances recorded for our sample, they are relatively low compared with some population studies. For example, it is estimated that approximately one in every six Sheffield children attends in a year (Illingworth, 1977) and that in Cardiff the equivalent of 20% of the child population is seen annually (Sibert et al., 1981). While the population for which our sample is drawn is less urbanized than those of Sheffield and Cardiff, our families, because of their medical and social characteristics, might well have been expected to be relatively heavy users of accident and emergency departments (Cooper and Lynch, 1979).

In their questionnaire the family doctors were asked how frequently they had seen each of the children in the last year. Eighty-two percent of the abused and 68% of the siblings had been seen at least once. These rates, too, are very similar to population figures. Nationally it was found that 69.5% of 0–14 year-olds consulted their family doctor at least once in the year 1971 — 1972 (H.M.S.O. 1979). Within our sample the average number of visits for the children who had been abused was 3.7 in the year with a top attendance of 13. For the siblings the average was three visits in the year with a top attendance of nine. Some families were noticeably heavier users than others.

When considering the use made by the parents of the acute medical services available for their children, it seemed to us from the available data and our personal knowledge of the families, that after discharge from the Park, many parents were using the services more appropriately than they had in the days before abuse was identified. Some parents, prior to admission to the Park, had recurrently demanded immediate medical attention for minor illness while others had delayed dangerously before seeking help for a seriously ill child. The children's contact with hospital and primary health care services did not appear to differ significantly from the normal population rates.

While we found the general health of the children to be good, the high incidence of minor handicap which we found among both the abused children and their siblings, confirms a need for continuing developmental and neurological assessment of these children.

SUMMARY OF FINDINGS

(1)   There was a high rate of neonatal ill-health among the abused. Forty-one per cent required admission to the S.C.B.U. compared with only 12% of the siblings.

(2)   Fifty per cent of the abused had a significant health problem before admission to the Park Hospital compared with 19% of the siblings. Five abused children had a life-threatening illness in the first year of life.

(3)   Six abused children had obvious deformities or scars.

(4)   Four abused children were severely neurologically handicapped and six moderately so. While those with severe head trauma were more likely to have major neurological handicap, this was not inevitable. On the other hand, a number of children showed significant neurological handicap without a history of any serious head injury.

(5)   None of the siblings were severely neurologically handicapped but three were moderately so.

(6)   The proportion of children showing minor neurological handicap was very similar in both the abused and the sibling groups.

(7)   Eleven (28%) of the abused were known to, or required referral to, an ophthalmologist.

(8)   Eight previously abused children were recorded by at least one professional as having evidence of further physical abuse during the follow-up period. Only five had demonstrable injuries and only one was serious (a fractured tibia). Physical abuse was reported in only one sibling.

(9)   At follow-up, one in five of all the children gave a history of minor recurrent or chronic symptoms of ill-health. The difference between abused and siblings was less striking than it had been prior to admission. The only serious acute illness was in a sibling. The serious chronic illnesses, except for a case of haemophilia, were in the children with severe neurological handicap.

(10) During the follow-up interval the children's contact with hospital and primary health-care services did not appear to differ significantly from that of the general population.

APPENDIX A — DETAILS OF THE NEUROLOGICAL ASSESSMENT

Every child had a standard neurological examination (Paine and Oppé, 1966). It included an assessment of muscle tone, passive limb movements, deep tendon and plantar reflexes. Any assymetry of face or limbs was noted. The examination of the cranial nerves included an assessment of eye movements, pupil size and reaction to light, facial movements and pharyngeal arch symmetry. The tongue was observed for mobility and any associated movements. The child was examined for the presence of a squint using the cover test and, where possible, the fundi were visualized. Sensation was not routinely tested. For the younger children, the observations for signs of minor neurological dysfunction were carried out during the Sheridan developmental assessment. Particular note was made of any associated movements, e.g. intention tremor, quality of eye–hand coordination, grasping and releasing patterns, mirroring and ability to cross the midline. The child's eye, hand and foot preferences were ascertained. The child's posture and gait when lying, sitting, walking and running were observed. The child was also seen going up and down stairs, climbing and participating in a ball game. Further observations were made during the period of free play.

The tests carried out on the older children were more formal and based on Touwen and Prechtl's (1970) scheme. The children were observed for the following:

(1) Posture standing: (a) with arms at the side, (b) with arms extended.
(2) Evidence of involuntary movements: feet together with arms out and fingers spread (eyes closed over 6).
(3) Co-ordination and associated movements: (a) mouth opening and finger spreading phenomenon, (b) diadochokinesis, (c) finger/nose test for smoothness and accuracy, (d) finger tip touching for smoothness and accuracy, (e) finger opposition for smoothness, ease of transition and mirror movements.
(4) Balance with eyes closed: standing and kneeling.
(5) Walking: (a) along a straight line, (b) on toes, (c) on heels.
(6) Standing on one leg and hopping.
(7) Lying: knee–heel test for accuracy and smoothness.
(8) Ability to sit up without help of hands.

In addition to this, the children were observed undressing and dressing, running, going up and down stairs, climbing on large apparatus, kicking, catching and throwing a ball. They were observed throughout for quality of posture and large movement. Their hand preference, eye and foot preferences were all ascertained. If necessary, further tests of eye/hand coordination and of fine motor movement were included e.g. a race against a stop watch with a pegboard or picking up small objects with alternate eyes covered.

The older children, too, had a period of free play which added further information about the quality of their movements and their ability to plan them. We were prepared to repeat portions of the test where it was felt that anxiety or silliness was inhibiting the child's performance.

VI. Developmental and intellectual assessment

There is limited evidence available on the developmental status of abused children prior to the recognized abuse incident. Few of these children would have been under regular developmental surveillance as they came from families unlikely to attend regularly baby clinics or keep follow-up hospital appointments (Cooper and Lynch, 1979). Therefore, for most children, the first time they are available for testing is the time they are admitted to hospital or medically examined for abuse. Those observations that are available indicate that for the older infant or child, developmental and behavioural problems are likely to have existed for some time prior to identification of the abuse. For example, the Denver Department of Welfare (Johnson and Morse, 1968) published a study of 101 children under their care who had had inflicted injuries. They reported that child welfare workers had observed that nearly 70% of the children exhibited some physical or developmental deviation prior to the reported injury. When one looks at the development of children of parents referred because of threatened abuse, one does find a high incidence of developmental delay. For example, when we assessed the children of mothers in a community therapeutic group we were surprised at the developmental deviations we found. One of these children had had a minor injury but none had been admitted to hospital because of physical abuse (Roberts *et al.*, 1977).

Most accounts of the development of abused children do not even give results of developmental testing carried out at the time of the hospital admission for abuse. As Elmer and Gregg (1967) observed when retrospectively examining the admission data available on their follow-up sample, "little attempt had been made to estimate the

79

children's precise developmental levels." This may result from pre-occupation with the injuries. But as Martin (1972) explains:

> "objective data on children at the time of abuse are difficult to obtain. Most of these children are initially untestable, being quite withdrawn, oppositional or fearful. Many are very weak and apathetic and are engaged in recovery from serious trauma and often associated under-nutrition."

Nevertheless, both these studies indicate that a high proportion of these children are developmentally delayed, some severely.

One British study (Smith and Hanson, 1974) does give the details of the developmental test results for 83 children from a larger sample of 134 battered children admitted to Birmingham hospitals. The remainder were either untestable (41), unavailable (6) or excluded because of major congenital abnormalities (4). Those tested were all under the age of 5 years and 39% had suffered a head injury. The children were tested after adaptation to hospital and were compared with a control group of 55 children in-patients. The Griffiths Mental Development Scale was the assessment used. The mean general quotient on the Griffiths Scale was 89 for the battered and 97 for the control children ($p < 0.01$). Excluding those who were recovering from their head injuries, the contrast between battered children and controls was of smaller significance ($p < 0.05$). Battered children tested after the head injuries scored significantly lower than controls on personal and social behaviour, hearing and speech and hand/eye coordination. Only hearing and speech quotients were significantly lower for those children who had suffered no head injury. Judging from the average length of stay, the majority must have been tested within a week of admission but, even so, it is stated that only one child behaved mis-trustfully throughout the testing. No other details of the children's behaviour on the ward or during testing are given. We find surprising the apparent ease with which the assessments were completed, in the light of other people's difficulties and our own experience in the assessment of the recently injured child.

Two American studies, both indicating a high level of intellectual deficit among abused children, are summarized in Table 15. Gregg and Elmer (1969) compared the development of 30 physically abused children with 83 children presenting with accidental or questionable injuries. Almost all the children were under the age of 13 months. They found that, excluding four who were too ill for evaluation, 42% of the abused and 18% of the accident children were "retarded in development." ($p < 0.001$). Sandgrund et al. (1974) studied 120 children to assess the possible impact of abuse and neglect on cognitive development. The criteria used for abuse was that it was of "an ongoing or recurrent nature." All the children were between the ages of 5 and 12.9 years. Of the abused children, 25% had IQ's below 70 ($n = 60$). This compared with 20% of a matched group of neglected children who were known not to have been physically abused ($n = 30$). Of another matched group of children who had been neither abused nor neglected ($n = 30$), only 3% were retarded. The abused sample did not include those children who had had "massive central nervous system impairment." The psychologist who did the testing did not know to which group each child belonged. All the children came from families receiving public assistance so the low IQ's could have been the result either of abuse or neglect. The other possibility suggested by Sandgrund is that some of the children could have been abused because they were retarded.

Table 15 Incidence of mental retardation at identification

Author	% Retarded (with definition)	"Control" rate
Gregg and Elmer (Pittsburg), 1969 $n = 30$	42% (none given)	18% (accident cases)
Sandgrund et al. (New York),1974 $n = 60$	25% (IQ < 70)	3% (matched controls)

Follow-up studies should provide information on the later development and intellectual status of abused children. However, it is difficult to compare the different studies. The severity and definition of abuse varies. The children have been abused at different ages and are assessed after varying intervals using different tests (sometimes not even named). Some children are still subject to abuse while others have received successful intervention. Nevertheless, one is forced to conclude that many children have not done well. Table 16 summarizes the incidence of retardation reported in the literature.

Elmer and Gregg (1967) reported that on follow-up 50% of 20 children who had suffered multiple bony injuries had IQ's below 80. As Martin and Rodeheffer (1976) comment, in a normal American population only 11% would have been expected to have IQ's below 80. Morse et al. (1970) saw 21 abused and/or neglected children 3 years

Table 16   Incidence of mental retardation on follow-up

Author	% Retarded (with definition)	"Control" Rate
Elmer and Gregg (Pittsburg), 1967 $n = 20$	50% (IQ < 80)	11% (American pop.)
Morse et al. (Rochester N.Y.), 1970 $n = 21$	43% (none given)	— —
Martin (Denver), 1972 $n = 42$	33% (IQ < 80)	11% (American pop.)
Martin et al. (Denver), 1974 $n = 58$	33% (IQ < 85)	15% (American pop.)

after injuries or illness: 43% of these were mentally retarded. In Martin's study (1972) of 42 physically abused children evaluated 3 years after the injuries, 33% were said to have IQ's below 80. Of the children who had had skull fractures or subdurals, 69% were retarded. Even among the children who were not retarded, 43% had "language disabilities" on formal testing. Martin and colleagues' later follow-up study (1974) of 58 abused children included some who were less severely abused, 31 having only soft tissue damage. Despite a high incidence of disturbed behaviour, this group of 58 children obtained a mean IQ of 92.3. However, 33% had IQ's below 85 compared with an expected rate of 15% in the normal population. Once again it was the sub-group of children with a history of head trauma who had the lowest scores. Brain damage, neurological handicap and the quality of the home were all found to have an independent effect on the scores. Nine of the 24 school-age children with no neurological handicap and normal intelligence were identified by school personnel as having learning problems (Martin and Rodeheffer, 1976). Gil (1970) conducted a nationwide survey of nearly 13 000 legally reported incidents of child abuse with more detailed data collection on 1380 of the cases. Thirteen per cent of school-age children included were attending special classes for the retarded or were in grades below their age level and 3% had never attended school.

The NSPCC research team (Baher et al., 1976) when reporting at the end of their 3-year therapeutic project, stated that "in our estimation only 8 out of a possible 23 children seemed to be making reasonably satisfactory and sustained developmental progress."

When reporting on a 2-year follow-up study of the children's IQ scores, they gave a slightly better picture. Fourteen out of the original 25 children were available for retesting and they had a mean IQ score of 100.4. The scores ranged from 81–121 and they therefore resembled a normal population of children. These 14 children came from families who were all still receiving specialist social work help.

One aspect of the abused child's development which is worthy of further consideration and investigation is language. Ruth Kempe (1976) observed that a consistent feature in abused children was their "considerable delay in speech." The findings of several of the authors already cited, support this observation (Smith and Hanson, 1974; Martin et al., 1974). Blager and Martin (1976) studied in detail two small groups of abused children. One group consisted of ten 2½–4-year olds assessed within six months of abuse. Almost all these children showed delay in comprehension and expressive language with poor articulation. Some improvement after speech therapy was demonstrated. The other group contained 13 older children who had been abused some years previously and who were receiving psychotherapy. The authors comment that "these older children had caught up in many of the rudiments of language .... and yet, when using language outside a testing situation, the form and complexity of their language was of a younger age."

The NSPCC battered child research team (Baher et al., 1976) found that language retardation was a striking feature among the 25 abused children referred to them. "Of the 12 children aged 12 months or over, 2 were showing no evidence of speech and the speech of 9 children was retarded."

This review of the literature paints a grim picture of the developmental and intellectual prospects for an abused child, even when the abuse has been recognized and "treated". It is important to bear this in mind when considering the data collected on our sample, both on admission and on follow-up.

II. THE STUDY SAMPLE DURING ADMISSION

Our data on the intellectual development of the abused children at the time of admission to the Park Hospital were available from several sources. For the younger children, developmental assessments based on Mary Sheridan's method (1975) had been carried out. Some of these children were also assessed by a clinical psychologist who routinely saw the older children. In addition to this there were the more general statements and records of the direct observations made by the medical and nursing staff concerning each child's development.

The object of developmental and intellectual assessments at the Park Hospital is to produce a profile of each child emphasizing both weaknesses and strengths, upon which the therapy can be based. Therefore, traditionally, these assessments lead to descriptive reports rather than numerical scoring. Often the way in which a child tackles a task tells us more about him than his eventual score. More detailed descriptions of the children's behaviour which inevitably affected their scores, are given in Chapter VII.

Of the 39 abused children seen in follow-up 26 were over 6 months at the time of admission and 15 of these (58%) were recorded as having definite evidence of developmental delay. All these children had had developmental assessments and/or psychological tests. Examples ranged from global retardation, due to obvious neurological handicap, to delay in a specific area of development. Every single one of these 15 children was behind in their language development. We observed that there were two main groups of abused children who showed speech delay. Firstly, there were those who were silent and under-achieving in all areas, the extreme example being the child with "frozen watchfulness" (Ounsted, 1972). Then there were the children who were agile and socially competent but still silent. We noticed especially some unharmed siblings, who were also admitted, who were remarkably advanced in their social behaviour and physical skills while still relatively behind in language development. For some children this was undoubtedly in response to their parents' demands for early mobility and physical independence without being a "noisy nuisance." Even when we looked at the 13 babies under 6 months at the time of admission, four were unequivocally retarded, one of whom was obviously brain-damaged from head injuries. Developmental and intellectual assessments had not been recorded systematically for the siblings in this sample (of course, 15 had not been born at the time of admission). The results of our follow-up study will show that this was an important omission.

III. THE STUDY SAMPLE ON FOLLOW-UP

Two main procedures were planned to assess the children's developmental and intellectual status at the time of follow-up. Firstly, all the under 5's ($n = 40$) were to receive a Mary Sheridan developmental assessment. Secondly, all the children over 3 years ($n = 61$) were to be assessed by a psychologist. (Thus 21 children would receive both assessments.)

A. Developmental assessment

When planning this follow-up study, the decision was made to reassess the children still under five, using the method with which we were familiar: a Mary Sheridan assessment. Unlike many other procedures, this assessment does not give a developmental quotient for each child. It was necessary, therefore, for us to adopt the following scoring system:

> All four sections of the assessment (vision and fine movement, speech and hearing, social behaviour and play, posture and large movement) were considered separately, as an overall score could have covered up uneven development. The children's attainments in each section were divided into three broad categories: A (above average), B (average), C (below average, i.e. children with evidence of developmental delay).*

As a check on our scoring system we arranged to test a group of 25 local children whose developmental progress was considered to be normal by both parents and professionals. These children were from a variety of socio-economic backgrounds and were recruited from child health clinics and playgroups where developmental delay would have been identified. This group was made up of 15 boys and 10 girls with an age range of 10 months to 5 years — very similar to that of the sample. All but two of the 25 children gave a performance which was unquestionably normal on all sections of the assessment; 78% of the scores were "B" and 20% "A". The only two below-average scores were in the speech and hearing section. One was from a girl with language delay who was being raised in a bilingual home and the other was from a boy who refused to speak to the tester. Both these children performed competently the other tasks asked of them. Two children were found to have possible minor visual problems that did not affect their performance.

The 40 children in our follow-up study who were given a Mary Sheridan assessment came from 30 families. Twenty-two were abused and 18 were siblings (13 of whom had been born after the abuse incident). Where the abused child was now over 5 years, the family was represented only by a sibling. At the time of assessment the youngest child was 9 months and the oldest was 5 years. Most of the children were assessed during an hour's session in the hospital's occupational therapy department.

* Further details of this scoring system can be found in Appendix B.

All the children had met one of the researchers before the visit to the hospital. Each child was given an honest description of what he was going to do and every effort was made to make the whole thing fun. Separation from parents was encouraged but not enforced. The parents were given the option of watching the assessment through a one-way mirror. There was some difference in reaction to the suggestion of separation between the study group and parents of normal children. The latter (all mothers) seldom elected to leave their child and the majority stayed close beside him without interfering with testing. Study group parents who stayed often came near to sabotaging the assessment by trying to gain attention for themselves. If this was anticipated, the social worker engaged them in conversation out of earshot of the child.

For all the assesments we followed the same basic schedule, the paediatrician and an occupational therapist working together. The use of two therapists meant a careful watch could be kept on the child's reactions and mood during the testing and also increased the accuracy of recording. Descriptions of the behaviour encountered by us during the assessments are given in the next chapter. Where children needed encouragement or pushing to finish the tasks, we tried to do this in a way that would not interfere with the standard requirements of the test. We were able to complete and score assessments on all 40 children.

Forty-one per cent of the abused and 67% of the siblings showed normal development, i.e. they scored "A"s or "B"s on all sections of the assessment (Table 17). The difference between the abused and the sibling groups for the occurrence of development delay did not reach statistical significance.

The 11 severely abused children were most likely to show some developmental delay. Only two children in this sub-group of 11 gave no cause for concern over their development. One, a 3½-year old boy, had suffered multiple skull fractures at 2 months and infantile spasms at 7 months and the other, a 5-year old girl, had required resuscitation and intensive care after nearly drowning at 1 year of age. The prognosis for both at the time of identification was doubtful and the boy had shown delayed development for some months after remission of his seizures. These two cases show that life-threatening injuries do not inevitably produce developmental delay. Four abused children were globally retarded; three had been severely abused and one was thought to have been handicapped before she was injured. No siblings were globally retarded and only two (11%) were delayed in more than one specific area. All the children with moderate or severe neurological handicap

Table 17   Results of Sheridan Assessment

	No developmental delay	Some developmental delay	Total
Abused	9	13	22
	(41%)	(59%)	(100%)
Siblings	12	6	18
	(67%)	(33%)	(100%)
Total:	21	19	40

showed some developmental delay. On the other hand, there were 12 other children whose developmental delay was not associated with a similar neurological deficit. Thus, all the developmental delay identified could not be attributed to injury or neurological handicap.

The area of lowest achievement for the whole sample was language. Thirteen children (33%) showed delay in this section. For only one child was this related to a minor hearing deficit. Only a slightly higher proportion of abused (36%) than siblings (28%) were delayed in their language development. Where the sample as a whole achieved the best results was on the social items of the social behaviour and play section. Thirty-three per cent were assessed as advanced on this section, despite evidence of impoverished imaginative play. This included 36% of the abused and 28% of the siblings. Only five out of the 40 children showed delay in social skills. The group with the least developmental delay were the siblings born after the abuse incident: 77% were developmentally normal.

B. IQ scores

This was the one part of the follow-up assessment in which we were not directly involved and so for this section we are reporting the observations made and IQ scores obtained by qualified psychologists on our behalf. There were 63 children over the age of 3 years and only two of these, living in the U.S.A at the time of follow-up, were unavailable for a psychological test. The aim was to obtain formal IQ scores for each child. The majority of the children were assessed on our behalf by the two clinical psychologists at the Park Hospital; the remainder were assessed by educational psychologists.

Because of the age range of the children, several different tests were used. In general, the Peabody Picture Vocabulary test (Dunn, 1965) and the Leiter Non-Verbal Test (Arthur, 1952) were used for the 3—4 year-olds; the Wechsler Pre-school and Primary Scale of Intelligence (W.P.P.S.I.) (Wechsler, 1963) for 4–6 year-olds and the Wechsler Intelligence Scale for Children (WISC-R) (Wechsler, 1976) for the remainder. The psychologists found that to obtain a score for some children, it was necessary to be flexible about the type of test used. Therefore, occasionally the Merrill/Palmer Test (Stutsman, 1931) was used instead of the Leiter and seven children aged between 4 and 6½ years were given the Peabody and Leiter Tests instead of the usual W.P.P.S.I. These changes in design had to be made because some of the children were either so shy or difficult at the beginning of the session that they could only be engaged with the more immediately interesting puzzle type material. One severely mentally handicapped child could only be assessed on the Vineland Social Scale (Doll, 1965); another child living in an institution for the blind and mentally handicapped, was so retarded that an assessment would have been meaningless and one sibling was so difficult during testing that no formal score could be obtained. Thus, formal IQ scores were obtained for 58 children. There are obvious limitations in comparing numerical IQ scores from different tests but, to give an overall picture of the children's IQ levels, we have divided their scores into the following categories:

	IQ score
Superior	125 and above
Bright average	110-124
Average	90-109
Low average	75-89
Borderline	55-74
Mentally handicapped	below 55

The distribution of the children's scores in these categories is shown in Table 18. As can be seen, apart from the occurrence of global mental handicap, the distribution in the two groups differs very little. As 60% of both groups score average or above on IQ tests, they differ little from the expected. The rate of mental retardation (even if the "borderline" group is included) is considerably lower than those rates reported in the literature (see Table 16). Neither of the abused children in the "superior" category had suffered serious head injuries whereas four out of the six abused children in the "borderline" and "mentally handicapped" categories had suffered from intracranial bleeding. The two siblings in the "borderline" category were from deprived homes, but both of them had abused and non-abused siblings who were more

Table 18   IQ scores

	Abused	Siblings
Superior	2	1
Bright average	4	5
Average	13	15
Low average	7	5
Borderline	3	2
Mentally handicapped	1	—
Untestable	2[a]	1[b]
Total	32	29

[a]No formal IQ score was obtained for these children because of the extent of their handicap.

[b]Too difficult to assess.

intelligent.

When we look at the verbal and non-verbal IQ scores separately an interesting pattern emerges which, in spite of the limitations in the data, requires further investigation. On the one hand the mean average non-verbal IQ scores for both the abused (100.5) and the sibling groups (100.8) compare favourably with the expected mean (100). Figures 4 and 5 show the similarity of the IQ score distribution between our groups and the general population. On the other hand, the mean verbal score for the abused group (90.3) is significantly different from the expected ($p < 0.001$) but the mean verbal score of the sibling group (95.4) is not significantly different (see Figs 6 and 7). Only 50% of the abused group had verbal IQ scores in the average or above average range compared with 75% of the siblings.

The discrepancies in these children's verbal/performance IQ scores show even more clearly the pattern of lower verbal intelligence, especially in the abused children. Whilst one should expect a wide range of verbal/performance discrepancies (Seashore, 1951), the discrepancies in our group were, with one exception, weighted in the one direction. A total of 21 children (36%) in our sample had significant age-related verbal/performance discrepancies (all over 11 points difference) and only one of these children had a greater verbal than non-verbal score. According to Seashore (1951), one would have expected a much more even distribution between V >P and P >V scores. Not so many siblings (25%) as abused (42%) demonstrated these significantly higher performance scores. It is depressing that the language problems noted in the younger children in our sample seem to be

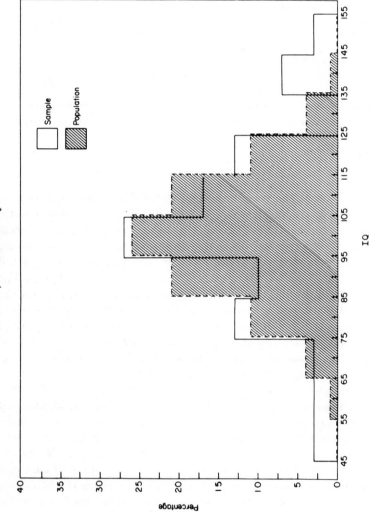

Fig. 4 Mean 100.5, sd 21.4, $n = 30$. Mean not signif. diff. from pop. mean ($p > 0.1$). Distribution not signif. diff. from pop. distribution ($p > 0.1$, Kolmogorov Smirnov).

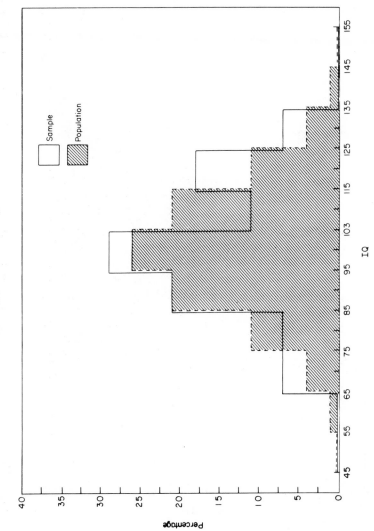

Siblings, non-verbal IQ's

Fig. 5 Mean 100.8, sd 15.52, *n* = 28. Mean not signif. diff. from pop. mean (p > 0.1). Distribution not signif. diff. from pop. distribution (p > 0.1, Kolmogorov Smirnov).

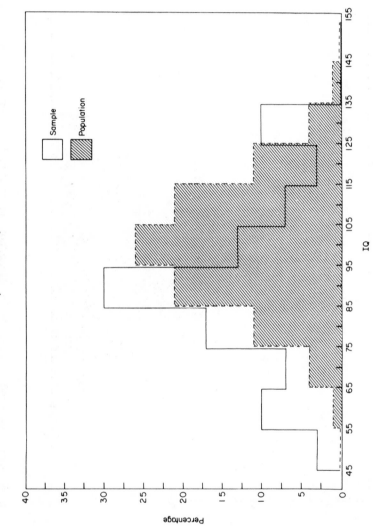

Fig. 6 Mean 90.3, sd 20.4, $n = 30$. Mean signif. diff. from pop. mean ($p < 0.001$). Distribution signif. diff. from pop. distribution ($p < 0.01$, Kolmogorov Smirnov).

Siblings, verbal IQ's

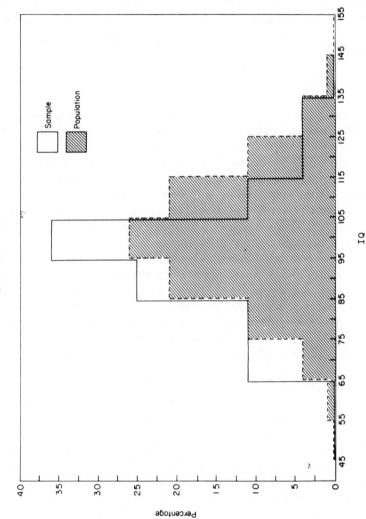

Fig. 7   Mean 95.4, sd 13.8, $n = 28$. Mean *not* significantly diff. from pop. mean ($p > 0.1$). Distribution *not* signif. diff from pop. distribution ($p > 0.1$, Kolmogorov Smirnov).

continuing in the older children. The psychologists especially noted the lack of spontaneous speech and surprising inadequacy of language compared to the children's IQ potential. We wondered whether it was the language deficiency which had affected the children's scholastic attainment: 41% were recorded by their teachers as "below average" in arithmetic and 44% in reading, which are higher percentages than we would have expected from their overall IQ scores.

IV. DISCUSSION

As has been noted in other studies and as had been observed during the children's admission, the language delay in this group of children, especially the abused, is particularly striking. It is disappointing that this specific deficit seems to have continued well after discharge from the hospital. Among the younger children, when compared to our "control" group, most of our sample were remarkably silent. Even when they were relaxed or absorbed in a game, there was little spontaneous chatter. There was a lack of questioning and rarely did they engage in verbal argument with parents or testers. Instead one received a silent, stubborn refusal or a monosyllabic "No". Some of the children's language delay was disguised by the development of limited speech designed specifically to please adults. It had the quality of "cocktail party" conversation, full of acceptable "situational phrases." We often found that the parents, too, were relatively inarticulate and there was a marked lack of verbal communication in the homes. Thus the inability to use language seems to be a characteristic that is passed from one generation to the next. Such parents often need a lot of help before they are able to talk to their children. They feel "stupid" when they try to speak to a child who, they think, is not capable of understanding or replying, preferring to go about household tasks against the comforting noise of the radio or television.

In Chapter XI we will note that the children who did well did not have a language deficit: they were full of spontaneous chatter and volunteered information. Thus it seems important to concentrate on this aspect of an abused child's development. If we find a way to improve this area, then we may find how to improve their general quality of life.

Our follow-up study high-lighted for us two omissions in our therapy at the time of abuse. Firstly, not all the siblings systematically had developmental assessments and yet, in spite of having avoided abuse, some had developed problems later on. Although at the Park Hospital it is possible not to be preoccupied with injuries, there are times when dealing with troubled, demanding and difficult parents when systematic assessments can be overlooked for the sake of keeping the family in treatment, an experience well known to all who work with abusive families. The other omission was that proper developmental or intellectual assessments were not always made at the time of discharge from the hospital. It would have been extremely helpful for us to know whether the progress that had been made during the family's stay had been maintained throughout the follow-up interval or whether even further progress had been made since the family's discharge.

Our discussion has naturally tended to high-light the children's difficulties. However, over half of the under-fives would have shown no developmental delay on the type of routine screening carried out in child health clinics, and only 19% of the abused children over 3 years had evidence of intellectual retardation, which is a much lower rate than those reported in Table 16. When comparing our results with those of other studies, it must be remembered that we, unlike others, have not excluded those in institutions or the severely brain-damaged from our final analysis. In general, considering the incidence of severe head injuries, these results are quite encouraging.

One particularly pleasing finding was the very good progress of the siblings born after the abuse incident: 12 out of the 15 (80%) were developmentally and intellectually completely normal. This indicates that the abuse of one child in a family does not inevitably lead to the abuse or disturbed development of siblings. In most of these cases the parents were receiving, or had received, intensive help from professionals who knew about the earlier abuse incident and were conscious of the need for special effort in helping the parents bond to their new baby. We gained the impression from these delightful children that once a good relationship had been established, they acted almost as their own therapists by being most rewarding and responsive children.

SUMMARY OF FINDINGS

(1)   At least 19 (49%) of the 39 abused children had shown definite evidence of developmental delay at the time of their admission to the Park Hospital.

(2)   On follow-up 40 under 5's (abused 22, siblings 18) received a Mary

Sheridan developmental assessment. Fifty-nine per cent of the abused and 33% of the siblings showed some developmental delay. Four abused children were globally retarded.

(3)   The area of lowest achievement for all the pre-school children was language, with a third showing delay. This included only a slightly higher proportion of abused (36%) than siblings (28%).

(4)   Psychological assessment of the children over the age of 3 years showed that 60% of both abused ($n=32$) and siblings ($n=29$) had IQs over 90. Six (19%) abused and two siblings were mentally retarded (IQs below 75).

(5)   Discrepancies between the children's verbal and performance IQ scores (more marked among the abused) give evidence of continuing relative language handicap.

(6)   The children's school performance was not as good as would have been expected from their IQ scores.

(7)   Overall, those with the best outcome were the siblings born after the abuse incident: 80% were developmentally and intellectually normal.

APPENDIX B — MARY SHERIDAN SCORING SYSTEM

The allocation to categories A, B and C was based on Mary Sheridan's working rule that a child should be expected to respond to three-quarters of the items prescribed for his age level (Sheridan, 1975). Such a child was graded B. If the child was also able to respond to a quarter or more of the items prescribed for the next age group, he was considered to be advanced and awarded an A. Category C was allocated to those children unable to respond to three-quarters of the items expected for their age level. We considered these children to show some evidence of developmental delay.

When testing vision and hearing, it was noted whether or not the child was able to understand how to do the age-appropriate test as it is necessary to distinguish between those children who do not respond because of generalized retardation from those who have a specific visual, hearing or neurological problem.

It was impossible to assess all the children at Mary Sheridan's "key" ages (that is the age at which precise details of the expected performance are given). Thus some adjustments had to be made to allow for the child's actual age when it did not correspond to a "key" age. In practice, the items for the two nearest "key" ages were presented to most of the children: the exception being where a child was obviously very retarded. The final assessment was made on the child's response to the nearest "key" age items. If the child was older than the "key" age, he was expected to respond to more than three-quarters of the items before getting a B, but if he was younger, a B would be awarded if he responded to between a half and three-quarters of the items.

VII. Children's behaviour outside the home

Descriptions of the behaviour of the abused child at time of identification and admission to hospital are remarkably few, most papers showing preoccupation with the injury and physical condition of the children. Morris *et al.* (1964) made one of the few early descriptions of the behaviour of abused children in hospital. He emphasized the way in which these children, in contrast to normal children, did not turn to their parents for help and reassurance. Galdston (1965) described the marked fearfulness or apathy of abused children. One of the best accounts of the abused child at the time of injury is given by Gray and Kempe (1976). They describe how, when these children are first seen, the majority have the same initial behavioural characteristics. In general they are frightened, withdrawn and extremely passive, quietly watching every move of the medical staff with wide eyes. If an older child speaks, it will be just one or two words in response to a question, more likely a mere shake of the head. Such behaviour was termed "frozen watchfulness" by Ounsted (1972). He wrote: "They make no sounds. They keep quite still. They gaze fixate the approaching adult, but they give out no facial signals. They have learned not to ask, by word or cry; not to demand, by approach or flight; not to influence, by smile or frown." Probably the very first description of this characteristic behaviour is to be found in a rarely quoted paper by Tardieu, a nineteenth century French Professor of Legal Medicine (Tardieu, 1860): "Les traits de leur visage respirent la tristesse; ils sont timides et craintifs, souvent hébétés et l'oeil éteint; plus souvent au contraire d'un intelligence hâtive qui ne s'exprime que par le feu sombre du regard."

Gray and Kempe, in their account, go on to describe two typical ways in which abused children behave during the early days of the hospital admission. The first, which they reckon applies to about 75% of children, is designed to try to meet adult demands. In their words, the child has "bought into the system." Throughout they remain compliant and "hypervigilant", looking for clues from adults as to how they should behave. When undergoing painful investigation they do not protest; they do not squirm when being dressed or changed. They also display abnormal "positioning". For example, if such a child is placed with his arm in the air, he will leave it there as if in a catatonic state. Then, as the children gain a little confidence, they begin to show evidence of role reversal — trying to look after the parents' needs and doing things such as tidying up the room. The attachments of these children appear to be indiscriminate, seeking the approval of any adult who happens to be around. Gray and Kempe have found that the 25% of children not showing this compliant behaviour tend to be provocative, aggressive and hyperactive. These are the ones of whom the nursing staff say they can understand why they were battered and who later fail foster placements. These authors also describe aspects of the child's behaviour that become apparent during a longer hospital stay. They observe that the abused child is often ambivalent towards separation from his parents and that his attachments to adults continue to be indiscriminately friendly. They also make the point that often the child's apparent passive co-operation masks its underlying fear. With the older child too they describe a reluctance to accuse a parent of inflicting the injury and the child's assumption that somehow they were to blame and deserved what happened to them. Given this severely disturbed behaviour, it is not surprising that researchers have found abused children very difficult to assess formally.

Rodeheffer and Martin (1976) describe in some detail behaviour they have found to be characteristic of abused children during developmental assessment. Their observations are drawn from their experience with the testing of a large number of abused children at varying intervals after identification. They define six types of behaviour which interfered with their testing procedures, making the child's developmental assessment difficult to interpret. The first was "Hypervigilance", where the children were so watchful of the therapist's every movement that they could not concentrate on the test procedures. Secondly, the abused children often demonstrated "fear of failure". The third problem was that they had "difficulty attending to instructions", often repeating the instructions in a meaningless fashion. Fourthly, the children demonstrated "verbal *inhibition"*; they had great difficulty finding the right word. Then, Martin found that they often showed *"failure to scan"*, tending to take the first possible solution to a problem. Lastly, the authors encountered *"passive aggressiveness and resistance"* from the children. While giving the impression of co-operating, they became half-hearted and negative, trying to do what they wanted to do rather than the activities presented.

It is obvious that an abused child is likely to show emotional problems at around the time of the abuse but what about years later? Martin and Beezley (1977) described nine characteristics commonly found in 50 abused children assessed at a mean of 4½ years after physical abuse was identified. The types of behaviour most frequently reported were:

(a) *"impaired ability for enjoyment"* — 33 of the 50 children displayed this characteristic. They could not play freely, nor laugh, nor enjoy themselves in an uninhibited fashion;

(b) *"behavioural symptoms"* — 31 of the 50 children had symptoms such as enuresis, temper tantrums and sleep disturbance, which are commonly recognized signs of emotional disturbance;

(c) *"low self-esteem"* — 26 of the 50 children showed very low self-esteem. The factors found to be related to the severity and frequency of symptoms in the child were: the number of home changes; parental emotional disturbance; a punitive home; instability of home.

Elmer (1977), in her follow-up study, found abused children had some increases in aggression and impulsivity in contrast to their comparison groups. However, 58% of all abused, accident and comparison groups showed some degree of disturbance. Nervous mannerisms were least common in the abused group. Overall, children from all three groups had an air of depression, sadness and anxiety. The author postulates that the most powerful influence on development is the social class membership of the child's family and she awaits similar controlled investigations to prove otherwise.

In England we find a similar gloomy picture for the emotional development of abused children in the NSPCC study (1976). They found that the battered children, although achieving normal levels of development, did not view their family relationships as one would expect children of their age group to do. The 13 battered children in comparison to controls from similar "deprived family situations" had very little involvement with their mothers, at the same time refusing to admit negative feelings towards or from her.

How far emotional problems are the result of physical abuse must be questioned, especially when considering follow-up studies of children who have failed to thrive. For instance, Hufton and Oates (1977) found that teachers using the Rutter questionnaire considered over half of his sample to be "deviant" and 90% of the children's mothers gave their child an "abnormal" personality score. The mothers also complained of a high incidence of behaviour disturbances in the children, such as lying, temper tantrums, enuresis, insecurity and nervousness.

Just as the literature points to a poor physical and intellectual prognosis for abused children, there seems to be a dismal forecast for their psychological and emotional well-being. It is now essential that we work out how this can be changed and, as Martin suggested in a recent publication (1979), there is need to study in detail those children who do survive abuse intellectually, physically and emotionally in order to find out why the outcome for them is good. We will do this for our sample in Chapter XI.

II. THE STUDY SAMPLE DURING ADMISSION

A. Behaviour on identification

It was possible for us to look back into the Park Hospital records and discover what behaviour problems, if any, were noted for all the 69 study children who were living in the families at the time of the abuse incident. Twenty-nine out of these 69 (42%) had behaviour problems described and recorded by the hospital staff. Twenty-two of these were the proband abused children. In seven families a disturbed sibling was identified as well as a disturbed abused child.

There were three main types of problems described in the abused children. Firstly, there were the children with "frozen watchfulness" and those who were described as looking so frightened and anxious that they did not respond appropriately to any stimulus. For example, one 3-year old boy who had one leg badly burnt and the other fractured, did not even whimper when the admitting doctor accidentally knocked his legs when carrying him upstairs. Then there were the fussy, colicky babies with difficult and discontented cries.

One such 5-month old girl was described by the nurses as unsettled and constantly crying. She had great difficulty feeding, she cried in between sucking and swallowed air, then objected violently to the teat being taken out of her mouth to wind her. During each feed, all her limbs were continually flailing about. It was during a feed that she was seriously abused by her mother. This baby seemed terrified whenever she was picked up. The third main group of children were those who were generally displaying aggressive, difficult and attention-seeking behaviour, such as the little 2-year old boy who had already been admitted to a psychiatric hospital for temper tantrums and head banging. Whenever frustrated or annoyed, this child would throw himself on the ground and bang his head. On one occasion during the admission, he bit his hand seriously. This child was being repeatedly abused and rejected by his mother as she thought he was going to grow up to be a homosexual.

Three children were noted for what we have come to term "social promiscuity". This is an inability to distinguish appropriately between strangers and familiars. In spite of their very young age, they showed no obvious attachment to their mothers and did not seem to recognize when they were passed from mother to a stranger. Two older children were described as having restless, inconsequential and clumsy behaviour. Some of the disturbed siblings were frightened and anxious and one even displayed "frozen watchfulness". She was a 2-year old girl who was admitted with her younger abused sister. This sibling was in almost a catatonic state. If any of her limbs were placed in an abnormal position during the medical examination, she stayed absolutely motionless unless told to move. In contrast, the other disturbed siblings were aggressive, moody and attention-seeking.

III. THE STUDY SAMPLE ON FOLLOW-UP

A. Behaviour during follow-up assessment

Observations on mood and behaviour were recorded for most of the children during the Mary Sheridan assessment ($n = 40$). The majority were described as "happy" during the testing; that is, both therapists and children enjoyed themselves. This included all the children who were talking or vocalizing well. Nevertheless, these children did have some initial problems in adjusting to the novel surroundings and some behaved in a way which interfered with the testing. What distinguished them from the rest of the sample was that they were able to have fun.

We thought it would be valuable to try to define more precisely the types of behaviour which we found interfered with the testing procedure. Such behaviour may not have affected the child's final attainment in the assessment but it certainly influenced his approach to the tasks, his interactions with the therapist and often his enjoyment of the assessment. The types of behaviour which we found seriously interfered with some part of testing are given in order of frequency and are in many ways similar to those described by Rodeheffer and Martin (1976). When the children displayed any of these types of behaviour, the testing required extra patience and time, sometimes resulting in serious frustration in the therapists.

(1) *Distractibility.* Some children were too easily distracted by background noises and were unable to relax and concentrate. For example, one 4-year old girl repeatedly left her chair during the assessment and seldom completed any task because of her interest in what was happening in an adjoining room.

(2) *Extreme manipulation.* At times the therapists were not allowed to control the testing. For example, one very self-willed 2½-year old dictated the terms of the assessment by refusing to complete any task unless allowed to do it all in a whisper while sitting on the therapist's lap.

(3) *Resistance and rebelliousness.* It was quite clear in some cases that the children did not want to co-operate and would not be won round, as most children are, by the interesting play material that is put before them. These children were extremely negative. For example, one 3-year old girl screamed loudly whenever she did not want to perform a task and several times threw the test material across the room.

(4) *Elective withholding of speech.* These children simply refused to talk, almost as though they were frightened of opening their mouths. One 3-year old sibling did not utter a word until right at the end of the session when she was obviously feeling less under threat.

(5) *Passive denial.* This is a very difficult characteristic which Rodeheffer and Martin also encountered. As they also noted, the assessors became confused and frustrated as they gradually realized that they were becoming involved in a very subtle battle for power. The child disguises his wilfulness in order to avoid overt anger. For example, a rather nonchalant 3-year old boy gave us the impression of co-operating by smiling sweetly but, by being very distant, he successfully avoided doing several parts of the test.

We had less trouble with the children who displayed a fear of failure or who were watchful: they were more easily persuaded to perform the tasks required of them. Most of them needed constant, firm, verbal assurance and some also needed and sought out body contact with the therapist.

There was a worrying group of 13 children who showed compliant and conforming behaviour. Such characteristics did not interfere directly with the testing but they did inhibit spontaneity and mar the child's enjoyment. We felt that a number of these children did what was asked of them rather mechanically, deriving no pleasure or interest from the tasks. They always did what they were told. Only six children from the whole sample failed to get any apparent enjoyment at all from the assessment; three resisted and rebelled angrily against the assessors throughout and three appeared extremely anxious although two of them showed a resigned compliance. Finally it was very plain and rather distressing that a number of the children were delighted with the individual attention they received and it was obviously a novel experience for them to be the centre of adult interest for so long.

When considering differences between the mood and behaviour of study and "control" children, the researchers soon realized that as a group the study children had been much harder work and that it was usual for them to feel emotionally drained at the end of the session. The assessments of the "control" children tended to run more quickly and smoothly. The younger children, under about 3½ years, were initially shy and needed winning over but the older ones were far more confident and often charmed the researchers. All but one child obviously enjoyed the assessment and three qualities were recurrently mentioned that were sadly lacking from descriptions of the majority of the study sample: enthusiasm, imagination and a sense of humour. The control children set their own limits but were prepared to negotiate and they would initiate interaction, the older ones asking questions of the examiner.

One thing we would recommend as a result of these experiences is that therapists working with abused children, if they are to keep a realistic view of childhood behaviour, must regularly spend some time with normal, happy children and families.

During the hospital follow-up visit, time was set aside for the children under 12 years to have a session of "free play". Each child was given 5 minutes on his own in a room full of toys, games, climbing apparatus, books and puzzles. Two researchers made recorded, on-the-spot observations of the child's play. It was in these sessions, when there were no formal guidelines, that the child's emotional problems came to the fore. Several children completely broke down when they did not know what was expected of them. For example, one 9½-year old girl felt so insecure that she tried to attack one of the observers. She moved round the room with a stiff, aggressive, "Dalek"-like gait and the only way she knew to obtain the observer's attention was to use physical violence. In contrast, the very compliant children also had a miserable play session. For instance, a 3½-year old boy, when left to play, simply burst into tears. He was told, rather unsympathetically by a tired observer, to stop crying. This he did, then stood silently still. The suggestion was then made that he might like to attempt a puzzle. He spent the rest of the available time sorrowfully and silently doing and redoing the same puzzle! Some of the children played very nicely, but there was often a lack of imagination. Objects remained very much themselves and there was very little make-believe or invention. The younger children rarely showed a well-developed exploratory drive and some older children asked permission before touching play material. On the whole we found the play boring. The lack of imagination was not related to intelligence. The child with the best developed imaginative play was certainly no more than low average on psychological testing, while a child in the superior range produced a very mundane performance. Again, there was a lack of spontaneous and playful chatter. Often the play was done in a deathly hush.

The psychologists all recorded their subjective opinions on the children's mood and behaviour during their assessments. Some of the children were so difficult that the psychologists had to spend a lot of time and effort in persuading them to co-operate. For instance, one 5-year old boy, a sibling, shielded his head for a full 15 minutes before attempting any of the test material. One 4-year old abused girl stubbornly refused to co-operate for about half an hour. Despite her mother's encouragement, she turned round and said. "You can't make me!" As recorded in Chapter VII, one little 3-year old sibling was so angry and resistant that no assessment was made at all. The most common problems described were signs of anxiety, extreme shyness or fear of failure. This was not restricted to the abused children. A classic example was a 6½-year old boy who was described as inhibited. He was most concerned and anxious about failure. He was frightened of exploring new material, although very willing to copy when shown how. When he came to a problem he thought might be beyond him, he was totally unable to make an attempt to use his intelligence in a constructive way.

The next common problem was one of resistance or lack of co-operation. Some children, both abused and siblings, showed no interest at all in what they were doing and were seriously lacking in motivation. One child even gave the impression of being rather cagey and withdrawn. It depended on the children's age as to whether the parents were present or not but only one father (a foster father) was noted for his ability to give encouragement without dominating or interfering with the test. Most parents seemed quite anxious about the tests and one mother was insistent on being present although her children were aged 8 and 6 years. Her own desire to help the children and embarrassment if they got the "wrong" answers, seriously affected the children's performance.

We found six children (four abused and two siblings) (8%) who were described by two independent assessors as having behaviour problems which we would categorize as severe. Their behaviour was either disruptive, uncontrollable and negative or extremely inhibited, sad and fearful so that the therapists found that their performance was seriously affected and their behaviour could not be modified. It was generally felt that these children would be at considerable risk of developing serious emotional problems in the future. There were also 15 children (19%) (seven abused and eight siblings) who did demonstrate the sort of behaviour already described which was not considered age-appropriate. However, in these children the problems created by disturbed behaviour were eventually overcome by the therapists, but not without considerable effort. It was quite clear when looking at our experiences in assessing these children that anyone working with children from abusing families must be prepared for considerable emotional strain, frustration and little reward in comparison with normal children. These children were hard work and required specialized help if they were to achieve their potential on the assessments.

B. Behaviour in school

One place where a child's behaviour and emotional adjustment can have a crucial effect on his development is in school. It could be argued that teachers make very subjective assessments of their children's personalities and behaviour but, nonetheless, the teacher's opinion has an objective reality in that it is bound to have an effect on the pupil and his achievement. For our enquiry we felt that it was just as important to know how the teachers perceived abused children as how they were achieving. We needed to know whether it was in school that an abused child's difficulties were more likely to appear, and yet again, would we find that the siblings were having fewer problems than the abused?

We were able to make à detailed enquiry about 45 (94%) of 48 school-age children. (The mother of two children refused to allow us to visit the school because she claimed she was having difficulties with the staff and the third child was in an institution for the mentally handicapped.) Twenty of the school children were abused and 25 were siblings. They ranged in age from 4½ years to just over 12 years. Over half the sample were under 7 years old (24 children) and so this was mainly a group of young school-children. Three of the children from two families in the top socio-economic group were at independent schools, four were at British Forces' schools and one child was attending a school for the maladjusted. All the children had been at the school concerned for at least a term, although six had changed schools within the last year and 12 had only started school that year. Each school was different, but the most striking similarity between them was the concern and interest shown by the head and class teachers for the children we were studying. We did not meet one teacher who did not know the child concerned extremely well. Similar concern and knowledge was shown by many, although not all, of the teachers for the parents too.

In order to ascertain the teachers' views of these children we used two standardized questionnaires, namely the Bristol Social Adjustment Guide (Stott, 1974) and the Teachers' Questionnaire Scale B(2) devised by Rutter and Yule (Rutter, 1967). Two different questionnaires were used to see whether they might pick out different aspects of the child's behaviour.

The Oxfordshire School Psychological Service distributed the questionnaires to all the teachers, giving them an explanation of the study. This was followed up by a telephone call from one of the researchers to discuss the study further, to arrange to interview the class and/or the head teacher and to collect the completed question-naires. Only the British Military schools overseas were not actually visited. During the interviews much subsidiary information was obtained and often lengthy discussions were held about the welfare of the child concerned.

When considering the results of the Bristol Social Adjustment Guide, we used the base-line score (recommended by Stott, 1974) for discovering the proportion of pupils who were considered "mal-adjusted". Using this base-line and including the child already at a school for the maladjusted, a total of 12 children (27%) were deemed maladjusted. As can be seen in Table 19, this number included seven boys and five girls.

Consequences of Child Abuse

Table 19   Maladjusted children according to B.S.A.G.

	Our sample	Population norms
Boys $n = 26$	7 (28%)	15.2%
Girls $n = 19$	5 (26%)	7.5%

The rate of maladjustment in our sample is well above the expected population rate for boys and over three times the expected rate for girls, which is a very striking finding.

If we consider the abused children and the siblings as two separate groups, then there is no significant difference between the two groups for the occurrence of maladjustment (Table 20).

Table 20   Maladjustment on B.S.A.G.: Abused v. siblings

	Maladjusted	Stable	Total
Abused	8	12	20
Siblings	4	21	25

$$x^2 = 2.2$$
n.s.

As Stott himself has suggested (Stott, 1974), it is probably more meaningful to look at the sub-divisions of the B.S.A.G rather than the total scale. The guide is divided into two main categories of behaviour disturbance: firstly, "under-reaction" which includes behaviour such as being withdrawn, depressed and unforthcoming and secondly, "over-reaction" including hostility, inconsequential behaviour and inability to get on with class-mates. When we compared our study children's scores with the expected population rates, we found practically no divergence from the expected in the "under-reaction" category but striking differences in the "over-reaction" grouping. Table 21 shows that the Park sample of boys had a maladjustment rate in aggressive and inconsequential behaviour which was 10% higher than the rate for a normal population of boys. The Park girls had the same rate as the Park boys and three times that expected for a normal population of girls (Table 22). Within this sub-division it was the "hostility" category which mainly accounted for the high scores.

Table 21   "Over-reaction" maladjustment in boys

Park group $n = 9$	36%
Population	26%

Table 22   "Over-reaction" maladjustment in girls

Park group $n = 7$	37%
Population	12%

Admittedly, the numbers in our study are small but the scores accurately reflect the high level of disturbance seen by the teachers in some of these children. For example, one girl (a sibling) of only 9 years was already being aggressive towards her class-mates. She had stolen several times and often lied. She regularly defaced school books and walls with "smutty" language. She associated with only the naughtiest in the class and yet seemed to have no friends as she was always having fights.

The youngest maladjusted child was 5½ years; the oldest just over 11 years. The 12 maladjusted children came from nine families. There were two families where, although the siblings had escaped major physical abuse, the disturbance in the family was so great that abused and siblings alike were revealing severe behavioural problems outside the family.

The Rutter questionnaire was designed to screen for "deviant" children and was based on the type of behaviour found in children who are referred to child psychiatric and child guidance clinics (Rutter, 1967). A much higher proportion of our sample were identified as "deviant" by this questionnaire: 22 children (49%). Again, we included the boy at a maladjusted school. This is a very similar proportion to that found by Hufton and Oates (1977) using the same questionnaire. The proportion of deviant boys was higher than expected for the population and the rate for the Park Hospital girls was much higher than the population rate (Table 23).

When we compared the abused and the siblings as two groups, there was no significant difference in the rates of "deviance" (Table 24).

Consequences of Child Abuse

Table 23   "Deviance" on Rutter B(2) Scale

	Our sample	Population norms
Boys $n = 29$	13 (48%)	11%
Girls $n = 19$	9 (47%)	3.5%

Table 24   "Deviance": abused v. siblings

	Deviant	Stable	Total
Abused	12	8	20
Siblings	10	15	25

$$x^2 = 1.1 \text{ n.s.}$$

Ten children not identified by the B.S.A.G. as "maladjusted" were identified as "deviant" by the Rutter B(2) Scale. Of these, seven were still under 7 years, which could explain this finding, and two of three others were children who would be more likely to be withdrawn than an actual disturbance in the class-room. In fact, eight of the ten children would have been identified as "unsettled" in an earlier method of classification on the B.S.A.G.* and were therefore borderline cases of maladjustment. The conclusion is, therefore, that both questionnaires did identify the same group of children as having problems, and anti-social, hostile behaviour was high-lighted by both scales.

As we saw in Chapter VI, children from abusing families continue to have greater problems when it comes to speech and verbal tasks. This could partly explain why these children tend to be hostile and aggressive as they find it difficult to put their feelings into words and would tend to bottle up their emotions, resulting in violence and aggression. In several cases it was obviously the children's social and emotional problems that were restricting their academic potential. For example, of the youngest of three children in a highly disturbed family, his teacher writes: "He always wants his own way and expects to get it. He is always loud. He doesn't mind spoiling things for other children. He thinks only of himself." He associated only with the naughty children and was obviously the most difficult member of the class. Although of good, average intelligence, both his reading and

---

* Please see Stott (1974) Bristol Social Adjustment Guides Manual. The Social Adjustment of Children, 5th Edition. Hodder and Stoughton, London.

arithmetic were below average. His mother sent him to school thin, undernourished and even when he was ill.

We enquired about the children's school attendance rate as we know that problems in the family could well influence whether they actually appeared at school or not and this could affect the teachers' perceptions of them. Seventeen per cent of our sample were recorded by the teachers as "frequently absent for a day or half a day", but only one child was thought to be truanting. Other examples were a 9-year old girl who, it was thought, was really encouraged to stay at home with minor illnesses because her mother, who was chronically ill, needed her there. For a couple of other families the parents obviously had difficulty in organizing things to get their child to school in time and therefore the child was kept at home rather than sent late. Two other children from a one-parent family were often kept away from school to help their mother at home or to go shopping; they were only 7 and 8 years old. This attendance rate is not strikingly different from the general school population and it is worth noting that the majority of these children had an attendance rate of 100%. Thus it seems that school is one place to reach children from abusing families and to make sure they are getting the help they need.

Although nearly half of the children were considered maladjusted or deviant by their teachers, only six of them (13%) had been referred to an educational psychologist. Three of these children were from the same highly disturbed family and during our study were in the process of being removed from home for all but the school holidays. One other child was neurologically handicapped and a problem for teachers in a normal school. Another child was a severely deprived and disturbed 8-year old who had suffered repeated rejections from his natural parents, foster-parents and children's homes. The sixth child was a lad with highly inconsequential, silly, acting-out behaviour and a real class-room management problem. We felt that there were other children who were just as much a problem for the teachers. It is only to the teachers' credit that for the most part they had identified the children's problems and were trying very hard to help them, and often the parents as well.

As a group, the siblings were as likely as the abused children to be perceived by their teachers as "maladjusted" or "deviant". However, in the 12 families where more than one child was tested, only one sibling was maladjusted when the abused child was not. The disturbance did seem to cluster in families, as four families in the sample managed to produce ten of the 22 disturbed children. Obviously, the teachers were being asked to describe a labelled problem group and that is bound to have some effect on their perceptions. It is a pity that it was not possible to assess this effect as it could perhaps teach us how we can avoid negative labelling and therefore benefit future abused children. For the most part, however, we did feel that teachers were making their own independent assessment of the family and its effect on the child. Once or twice, other professional opinions were strongly challenged and sometimes we felt that the school staff understood the child and the family better than anyone else.

IV. DISCUSSION

Despite the limitations of our small numbers, the implications of this chapter are clear: children from abusing families can very quickly grow into difficult and disturbed individuals, disliked by their peers and frustrating and antagonizing adults who try to care for them. In the families we studied, a quarter of all the children and nearly half of the school-age children had noticeable emotional and behavioural problems outside the home some time after the abuse. Unlike other studies (Rutter *et al.*, 1970) there was in our school sample no sex difference; as many girls as boys were maladjusted and an even higher proportion of girls than boys were hostile. It is perturbing that already 14 out of the 45 school-age children were showing the type of aggressive behaviour that often leads to becoming a violent and abusive parent. Certainly the girls in this group were not the individuals one would choose to be the mothers of tomorrow.

This chapter and the previous one have also shown that this sort of behaviour can adversely affect an assessment of the child's development and intellect, making it extremely difficult to get a true picture of a child's ability. Therefore, these children need individual therapy not only for them to become less emotionally disturbed but also for them to achieve their full intellectual potential.

Parental attitudes to school have been noted to have great influence on their children's scholastic performance and adjustment (Douglas *et al.*, 1968) and although we did not enquire into these parents' attitudes systematically, we did note types of parental behaviour which the school found difficult and which seemed to affect the teachers' perception of the children. Some parents were rather isolated, they neither participated themselves nor encouraged their children to participate in extra-curricular activities. This gave the teachers the feeling that they were mistrusted. Another small group of parents were very hostile to the school, to an extent that made the children feel that they had to react against the teachers too. One or two families had no interest in the school at all, never set foot inside and greatly disappointed the teachers with their apparent indifference to their children's achievements.

It is often debatable how much staff in a school should know about an abused child's background. Before a teacher can understand a child, especially a child with problems, she needs to be fully acquainted with his biography. However, there is also the possibility that the knowledge that a child has been abused could prejudice a teacher's perception of him and his family, precipitating problems that might not have occurred otherwise. This certainly was the fear of one family known to us who successfully campaigned for the removal of their daughter's name from the "At Risk" register prior to her entry into primary school. They did not want her to start school with a label or "black mark", nor did they want her to be singled out and suffer for something they had done over 4 years previously. They said that they were determined that she should start school with a "clean slate", just the same as the other children.

All the observations on the children's behaviour made during our follow-up are similar to those reported by others. It is often an abused child's hostility to adults and peers that singles him out; yet at the same time they lack confidence and are the under-achievers. Some of them are noticeably withdrawn and depressed. We felt that a number of these children desperately needed a good, consistent, trustworthy adult friend outside the home. Considering the interest we found among the children's teachers, we felt that these professionals could be included more often in the long-term therapeutic plan as they could well fill this gap. Judging from the problems we found, it is a great mistake to heave a sigh of relief once an abused child has gone to school. They may be at less risk physically but their overall development will need careful watching. With many abused children there is obviously a need for individual play therapy to continue well after the abuse has been stopped. As with developmental problems, it would have been very useful to have had more systematic behavioural assessments on the children at the time of discharge against which to monitor change.

If this chapter seems to present a gloomy picture, it must be remembered that we set out to look hard for any emotional problems these children might have. We would have found a proportion of maladjusted in a random sample of children from the population. It is perhaps more important to end with the recollection that 74% of the children showed little or no disturbance during the follow-up assessment and 51% of the school-age children were free from significant behavioural and emotional problems in the class-room. We believe that by providing more long-term child-orientated therapy, this proportion could be made higher and that children from abusing families could make a better emotional adjustment.

SUMMARY OF FINDINGS

(1) At the time of admission 29 (42%) of the 69 children living in the families were described as having significant behaviour problems. Twenty-two of these were the proband abused.

(2) During the developmental assessments the types of behaviour that interfered with the testing were distractibility, extreme manipulation, resistance and rebelliousness, elective withholding of speech and passive denial.

(3) The most common problems reported by the psychologists during their testing were signs of anxiety, extreme shyness and fear of failure.

(4) Overall during the hospital visit six (8%) children (four abused and two siblings) were identified as showing evidence of severe behaviour disturbance. The behaviour of a further 15 (19%) caused difficulties during the assessments.

(5) Using the B.S.A.G., 12 (27%) of the 45 children for whom results were available were deemed maladjusted. This includes 40% of the abused and 16% of the siblings (x^2 n.s.). There was no expected sex difference, with as many girls as boys with a maladjusted score. The high hostility rating of both sexes was a striking feature.

(6) Using the Rutter B(2) Scale, 22 (49%) of the children were identified as deviant, including 60% of the abused and 40% of the siblings (x^2 n.s.). Once again there was no sex difference.

(7) The attendance rate of the children at school was good.

(8) Seventy-four per cent of the children showed no significant disturbance during the hospital visit and 51% of the school-age children were free from significant behaviour problems in the class-room.

VIII. Placements

The follow-up samples of abused children described in the literature include children in the care of their parents and those placed elsewhere by social agencies. Studies where not all the original sample are assessed are likely to contain a disproportionate number of children placed away from home. Such children should be easier to find, and foster parents and social agencies may be more likely to co-operate with a researcher than parents who have had their children returned. This was certainly the experience of McRae *et al.* (1973) in Winnipeg where 76% of the children assessed were in foster homes. Such possible biasing of the samples should be kept in mind when considering reported outcome, especially where no comparison is made between those living at home and those in some other form of care.

Morse *et al.* (1970) describe the placements of their sample and try to relate outcome to placement. Of the 25 children in the study, 20 went home to their parents following the initial admission to hospital. By the time of follow-up 3 years later, there were 14 children who had remained at home throughout the follow-up interval; six were permanently outside the parental home and five temporarily. Full follow-up assessments were carried out on 21 of the 25 children: the six judged to be within normal limits intellectually and emotionally at the time of follow-up had all lived continuously with their parents since the original diagnosis. On the other hand, mentally retarded children were much more likely to show improvement following removal from the parental home.

In the sample of children described in "Children in Jeopardy", Elmer (1967) found that children who had experienced a change of home following abuse did better intellectually, emotionally and physically than those who remained in the same environment. However, those in foster homes were not without problems and several

115

families who kept in touch with the researchers reported behavioural difficulties later. In Elmer's (1977) later follow-up study of traumatized children, eight of the 17 abused were living with foster or adoptive families. The only difference in the development of those in substitute homes compared to those who had remained in their natural home was in their language abilities: those in substitute homes had significantly more communication and articulation problems and also tended to have poorer expressive language than those living with their parents. Elmer puts forward two possible explanations for this. She cites Goldfarb's (1945) observations that deprived children's language deficiency continues even after placement in a more favourable environment. Secondly she points out that there were ethnic and social status differences: six of the children in substitute care were lower class black children while six of the nine children in natural homes were white, four also being middle class.

Thirty-seven of the 58 children followed up by Martin *et al.* (1974) were living with their biological parents at the time of follow-up. The number of placement changes experienced by the children during the follow-up interval (mean 4½ years) were also documented and ranged from 0–8. Twenty children had experienced no change of domicile, seven had one change of home, and were living with foster parents at the time of evaluation. Eleven children had had two changes: most of these had been returned to their biological home after a foster home placement. Twenty children had had three or more changes. Those with more than three changes had lived in numerous foster homes for a variety of reasons. Frequently the child's provocative behaviour had made the foster parents ask for his removal. Of the 38 children who had been in foster home placements most were placed there immediately following hospitalization for an injury. Martin and colleagues did not find removal of a child from his biologial home to be related to the severity of the injury: 35% of the children with soft tissue injuries and 33% of the children with skull fractures and/or subdurals had never left their biological parents. When relating placement to outcome the authors came to the conclusion that the quality of a home environment had more influence on a child's cognitive performance than did the number of moves a child had to make to obtain a good environment. However, when the behaviour of the children was looked at in detail (Martin and Beezley, 1977), a relationship to the number of changes was found. The study, based on 50 children from Martin's 1974 sample, of whom 17 (34%) had had three to eight home changes, shows an increase in the severity and frequency of behaviour symptoms among children who had experienced changes of placement. The more symptoms a child had, the more likely he was to have had three or more placements. A child was also more likely to be disturbed if the permanence of his present home was questionable. Many of the children with the most symptoms were in the care of foster parents.

Unfortunately, it is difficult to follow the placement changes experienced by the 59 children followed up by Speight et al. (1979). However, by the time their study was done, a high proportion of the children (54%) were separated from their parents and considered to be in long-term care. The authors emphasize their concern that only 14 (44%) of these 32 children had found a family placement. The older children were most likely to be in an institution but even in the youngest age group of 15 children who had been under the age of 3 years when abused, there had been four foster breakdowns. Only two children had been adopted.

When evaluating the outcome for abused children in long-term care away from their parents, one must be aware of the shortcomings of the alternative placements available. After a decision has been made that an abused child is unlikely ever to return home, the commonest placement sought is a long-term foster home. Even after such a home has been found, the outcome has a soberingly high chance of being unsatisfactory. Most published studies evaluating the success of foster placements are general ones using samples of children in long-term foster care for a variety of reasons and very broadly define success as a "placement that lasts." A number of studies using 2-5 years in one foster home as their criteria of success give overall breakdown rates of 40 - 60% (George, 1970; Kraus, 1971; Napier, 1972). In these studies, breakdown rates were at their highest in the first year after placement, fairly high in the second year and falling thereafter until adolescence was reached when an increase in breakdown was seen (George, 1970). Success has been related to age of the child when placed, time the child had already spent in care, age of the foster mother and presence of other children in the household (Prosser, 1978). A child placed over the age of 4-5 years or with a record of behaviour problems before placement has an increased risk of his placement breaking down (Parker, 1966; George, 1970). This does not bode well for the older abused child who inevitably has behaviour problems. Napier (1972) found that assessments of young children carried out in a residential nursery were more likely to lead to a successful long-term placement than were assessments carried out in a short-term foster home. It will be seen that our experience supports this. The same study found that if the placement was the child's first experience of foster care, there was a 72% chance of success. If the child had had a previous foster placement, the success fell to 55% and if there had been a previous breakdown, the placement had only a 36% chance of lasting.

Absence of an overt breakdown in a fostering arrangement should not be the only criterion of success as some foster parents will tolerate many problems without requesting removal of the child. There is evidence of a high level of maladjustment amongst foster children. For example, Jenkins (1969) found that half of a sample of children who had been in foster care for 2–5 years "were behaving or had behaved over a long period in a way that suggested a considerable degree of emotional disturbance." In a small American survey, Canning (1974) studied in detail 25 school-age children. About half were seen by teachers as withdrawn, and about a third were described as aggressive, while others were found to be too compliant. Many of the children seemed to feel different and to be apprehensive about security and their own identity.

Thus it would seem from both the child abuse literature and more general literature on long-term foster care that removal from the parental home and placement with long-term foster parents does not necessarily protect against future behavioural and developmental problems.

The difficulties associated with long-term foster care have led to the support of adoption as a better method of securing a permanent substitute home for an abused child (Speight et al., 1979). The outcome for healthy babies placed in infancy and early childhood is undoubtedly good. Epidemiological studies (Bohman, 1970; Seglow et al., 1972) have shown slightly increased rates of behavioural disturbance in boys in adoptive homes compared to controls. Adopted girls were not found to be significantly more likely to be disturbed; in fact one study (Seglow et al., 1972) found them as a group less maladjusted than girls growing up in their natural families. There is less information available for the outcome of abused and neglected children placed for adoption. What there is indicates that for some the outcome is undoubtedly very successful. However, the adoption of an abused or neglected child is likely to be a very different experience from more conventional adoption and could lead to considerable problems.

Kadushin (1970) describes a follow-up study of children placed in Wisconsin at a mean age of just over 7 years. Most of them had experienced neglect or ill-treatment. One hundred and fifty placements had been made between 1952 and 1962, of which 12 had failed in the first year. Ninety-one families were available for assessment at an average follow-up interval of 6 years. In only two of the families had the adoption ended in the child's subsequent removal from the home. This study concentrated on parental interviews and used parental satisfaction in the adoption experience as the basis of criteria for success. The outcome was judged to be satisfactory for at least 82% of the placements. Among the factors related to poor outcome were behaviour disturbances in the child and the number of placements experienced before adoption. One would be happier about the optimistic findings of this study if there were an independent measure of the outcome from the child's point of view. Also in North America Loadman and McRae (1977) studied 33 adoption breakdowns and found that previous deprivation of the child seemed to be precipitating many of the problems experienced by the adoptive parents.

Pierson and Deschamps (1976, 1979) who have experience of the adoption of abused children in France, warn against seeing this as the "ideal solution of the future for abused children." Most of the children followed up by them had been over the age of 4 when placed and had had disrupted lives and most were emotionally disturbed, although in the short-term they were doing better than children placed in children's homes or with foster parents. Deschamps (1979) feels it unfortunate that it had not been suggested to the adoptive parents that they might well need psychological help with the child and is cautious about the long-term outcome. She also expresses concern about the biological parents and siblings who may no longer receive help once their contact with the abused child is severed.

Tizard (1977) studied a sample of children who had spent their first 2 – 7 years in an institution. Among those placed with adoptive parents between the ages of 2 and 4 years, five out of 20 (25%) had significant behaviour problems at age 8 years and 15% had been referred for specialist advice. Among the small group placed over the age of 4½ years, three out of the five had behaviour problems at home and at school. None of the placements had broken down but four out of 25 (16%) of the adopted couples and their child were judged not to have developed "mutual attachment". However, when the adopted children were compared with children restored to their natural parents after similar periods in institutions, they had faired undeniably better: two-thirds of those restored after 2–4 years had been referred because of behaviour disorders by the age of 8 years and more than half of the natural mothers said that they did not feel a close attachment to the child. Neither did the majority of children in this group experience a close relationship with a "father", unlike those in adoptive families where usually both parents were deeply committed. Thus Tizard's study, as well as giving information on the outcome of late adoption, illustrates the often dismal consequences for a child restored to natural parents after a prolonged stay in an institution.

Not all abused children removed from home will find substitute parents. A number, especially those removed in later childhood, will grow up in institutions. In the present atmosphere created by the drive to transfer children from residential establishments to substitute homes, such placements are likely to be seen as failures (Speight *et al.*, 1979). While it must be acknowledged that there are well documented detrimental consequences of long-term residential care (Prosser, 1976), it must be remembered that a substitute home in no way guarantees a better outcome. Indeed, as observed by Shaw and Lebens (1978) in their study of substitute family care: "It is worth remembering that there are some children for whom foster care has failed and who flourish in residential care."

The short-comings of long-term care are not necessarily restricted to childhood or to the child. In a longitudinal study of mothers and first-born children, Wolkind (1977) and colleagues (1982) identified a sub-group of women who spent time in local authority care when children. Not only have these women been shown to have more psycho-social problems, but their children are disadvantaged in many ways. When compared to controls, they have a lower birth weight, lower intelligence, poorer language development and more behaviour problems. Therefore, even if children are removed from their abusive parents for their protection, they are still exposed to a number of developmental risks and the quality of life of their own children could be jeopardized. We have found that a child removed from natural parents is often in greater need of long-term follow-up therapy than the child who had been quickly and successfully returned home. This all has implications for decision-making and service planning at the time of abuse, which will be discussed in the final chapter.

II. THE SAMPLE: PLACEMENT CHANGES

We were able to trace the placement changes experienced by all the children in our sample after their discharge from the Park Hospital. The possible effects of these changes will be discussed and the problems encountered in the different placements examined. Figure 8 compares the placements of the 39 abused children at the time of discharge with their placements at the time of the follow-up study. Also shown is a summary of the placement changes that took place within the follow-up interval. By the time of our study, nine abused children were in long-term care and 30 with one or both natural parents. Of the siblings seen at follow-up, none had been discharged to care and only one was in long-term care. The siblings' changes of placements were less frequent and will be dealt with separately.

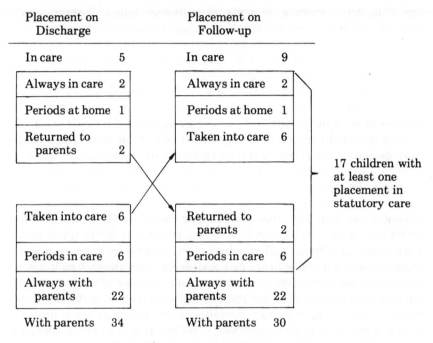

Fig. 8 Placements of the 39 abused children.

As can be seen from Fig. 8, 17 (44%) abused children had had at least one placement in statutory care since discharge, including two who had spent all the follow-up interval in care. Eight of these 17 children had returned to their parents by the time of follow-up. This included four children whose placements outside the home could not be considered major changes as they were temporary, short-term voluntary arrangements. Six of the 17 children were taken into care away from their parents at some time during the follow-up interval. Only one child in care on follow-up who had been discharged to care had had periods of "trial at home."

Five abused children (13%) had experienced three or more major changes of placement by the time of follow-up, and none of these emerged as emotionally and developmentally normal. The highest number of placement changes was seven and the average number amongst the 13 abused children who had had major changes was three.

The sequences of events that led up to the various changes of placement are worthy of detailed consideration, as are the efforts that were sometimes needed to maintain placements and prevent more of the children becoming victims of multiple home changes. Some outlines of the abused children's biographies will be presented.

III. THE ABUSED CHILDREN IN CARE ON FOLLOW-UP

All the nine children who were living away from their parents at the time of follow-up could be considered to be in long-term care as there were definitely no plans to return them to their parents.

A. Always in care

It is quite striking that out of 39 abused children only two were found on follow-up to have been in care all the time since discharge from the Park Hospital. These children had been in care for 8 years and 4½ years respectively. The first child was severely mentally handicapped, probably even before the abuse. He spent one week in a foster home following discharge from the Park Hospital and then spent the next 8 years in hospital, moving from one institution for the mentally handicapped to another after 3 years. By the time we visited this child he had been abandoned by his family who had found the strain of visiting him too much and who felt that he would be better dead. Indeed, he was a blind, pathetic, miserable child who was spastic and mentally handicapped. We admired the staff for their dedication to his well-being.

The only other child who had never been discharged from care was a child in a foster home. He still had occasional contact with his natural mother and step-father but he regarded his maternal aunt (the foster mother) as his own mother.

B. Periods at home

Only one child who was discharged from the hospital to statutory care and who was found to be in long-term care on follow-up had spent periods at home "on trial." He was first discharged to foster parents at the age of 2 years 5 months. He stayed there 2 months and was admitted to a residential nursery because of behaviour problems. Then, 9 months later, his parents were rehoused in a new town some 100 miles from the nursery and it was felt fit to return the child to his parents. This so-called rehabilitation and "trial" lasted only 2 months and the child was taken into care when his mother threatened to kill him for his misdeeds. He was admitted again to a residential nursery for 11 months and then placed with foster parents. These foster parents were older people, more set in their ways than some, and found the child's testing-out behaviour, especially soiling, smearing and bad language, far too much to tolerate. He was unable to live up to their unrealistic expectations of their "substitute son" and the placement lasted 4 months. He then spent 1 year 8 months in the residential nursery before being moved to the children's home where we visited him at follow-up. We have since heard that his violent, acting-out behaviour is becoming increasingly difficult to handle and a further change of placement — his eighth — is being contemplated. He summed up his own predicament precisely when he said: "Nobody bloody wants me!"

C. Taken into care

Six abused children had initially gone home but were taken into care during the follow-up interval. Only one of these children experienced further attempts at rehabilitation with her natural parents after removal from their care. For the other five children, once a decision had been made to remove the child, he had remained away from the parental home. The period spent with the parents after discharge from the Park Hospital ranged from only 19 days to 4 months. In all the cases there had been considerable concern over letting the child home in the first place and supervision had been close.

Two examples will illustrate how rapidly action was taken when follow-up care arrangements broke down and the child appeared to be at increased risk.

A pair of twins were discharged at the age of 6 months into the care of their mother who was living with a reliable aunt in another part of the country. When the mother suddenly left the aunt, a short further admission to the Park Hospital was arranged, after which the twins went home to both parents with intensive supervision including a daily family aide. A month later, following a violent episode between the parents during which one twin was thrown across the room in front of witnesses, both children were removed and Place of Safety Orders obtained.

The second example is another young baby who was discharged from the Park Hospital at the age of 6 months, going home on a Care Order to her mother and maternal grandmother. This placement lasted only 19 days. When the grandmother fell ill, the baby was removed because it was known from observations made at the Park Hospital that this mother would be incapable of caring for her baby safely alone.

IV. ABUSED CHILDREN WITH PARENTS ON FOLLOW-UP

This second section is concerned with the group of children found to be with their natural parent(s) on follow-up. As seen in Fig. 8, these children could have been returned to parents from care during follow-up or could have spent periods in statutory care or been with their parents throughout.

A. Returned to parents from care

Two children who had been placed away from their natural parents at the time of discharge from the Park Hospital were back living with them at the time of follow-up. Both children had suffered serious abuse. The management of the younger of the two, a baby of 5 months, illustrates well the use of foster parents in a planned rehabilitation of an abused child with her family. The baby was discharged, after the granting of a Care Order and with the parents' agreement, into the care of foster parents. Intensive marital and sexual therapy for the parents was continued on an out-patient basis and the natural mother was allowed to visit her daughter in the foster home every day, where she was encouraged by the foster mother to take over the baby's care completely. This foster mother was exceptional in her ability to tolerate the natural family's constant presence in her house and the strain of sharing the baby's affections. As the parents matured and began to resolve their problems, their daughter was gradually returned to them and a year later was with them full-time. She has remained there ever since and is making good developmental progress. It is worth mentioning that the social worker found it necessary to provide follow-up support to the foster mother after her "loss" of this baby.

For the other child discharged into care and at home at the time of follow-up, the transition had been less smooth. A Place of Safety Order had been needed to keep her at the Park Hospital and this was followed by a Care Order. Following the granting of this order, she spent 3 weeks with foster parents and then returned to her mother. This "trial-at-home" failed after 4 weeks and she subsequently spent 7 further months in a children's home. None of these placements was maintained because of the mother's extremely manipulative behaviour. At the time of follow-up she had been back with her mother for 2½ years and the Care Order had been discharged. While the mother/child relationship had certainly improved and the risk of further physical abuse greatly diminished, we were concerned over the child's emotional development. The mother remained very depressed, living alone with the child, socially isolated and in great poverty.

B. Periods in statutory care

Six other children had been discharged to the care of their parents and were living with them on follow-up but had spent periods of time in care during the follow-up interval. Four of these children had had short stays in foster homes, varying from overnight to 3 months. All these children were living with unsupported mothers and the reasons for foster placements seemed to be related to the difficulties experienced by any single parent rather than because of the previous child abuse. Thus the commonest reason for placement was that mother was ill and unable to care for the child herself. One of these four children was on a Matrimonial Supervision Order at the time he went into care and one other was on a Care Order. This last child's temporary placement with his father and grandparents was probably going to be long-term even though the mother had intended it to be only a temporary stay while she looked for a job and recuperated from a recurrent illness. His future had become the subject of a custody dispute.

The other two children discharged to the parental home and spending time in care during the follow-up interval had done so because of crises in their families and concern over their safety. Both had been made subjects of Place of Safety Orders during the follow-up interval and in both cases these orders were followed by Care Orders which were still in force at the time of follow-up. One of the two children, together with his three siblings, had spent 2 months in a children's home where the family were well-known because of placements before admission to the Park Hospital. Despite the need for continuing intensive support for this family, all concerned were convinced that the aim to keep the family together was justified and our follow-up findings endorsed this view. The second child, however, continued throughout the 7½ years since her discharge from the Park to be a cause of great concern. At the time of our follow-up, serious consideration was being given to removing her from the home. Our assessment confirmed that the anxiety over the girl's well-being was certainly justified. This child had left the Park at the age of 2 years with her parents. After spending 8 months with them she was removed on a Place of Safety Order and admitted to a children's home where she spent 10 months, visiting her parents for weekends. Following this, a period at home lasted for over 18 months until, once again in a crisis, she was placed in a children's home. After 2 months there and a 3-day stay at home she was hurriedly transferred to another children's home for 9 months. At the time of follow-up she had been back with her parents for 4½ years. However, this placement was still being described very much as "trial at home." She was one of the most disturbed children we saw during our assessment. The disturbance was not confined to her but extended throughout the family. The elder sibling, a boy, was already in a boarding school for the maladjusted. The uncommitted nature of this girl's placements was symptomatic of the ambivalence felt about whether she should be with her parents or separated from them permanently.

C. Always with parents

Twenty-two abused children (56%) had remained in the care of their parent(s) throughout the follow-up period. These children are 65% of the 34 children actually discharged to the care of their parents from the Park Hospital. Included among them are 52% of the seriously abused and 56% of the moderately abused and so the seriousness of the abuse did not appear to be influencing the long-term placement of the children with their parents. Only two of these children, a pair of twins, were subjects of Care Orders. One other child had been the subject of a Supervision Order but this had been rescinded by the time of follow-up. In some families a great deal of effort was necessary to maintain these placements, including intensive social work support, various uses of day care and sometimes even a short readmission to the Park Hospital.

V. THE SIBLINGS

Seven siblings also had at least one placement in statutory care during the follow-up interval but only one of these could be considered to have had a major placement change. She was taken into care at the same time as her abused sister and had been with her sister in the same children's home up to the time of follow-up. All the other six siblings from three families spent only short periods of time away from their parents because of family crises such as marital separation, maternal ill-health and a minor abuse incident to the index child. In addition to these statutory placements, two other siblings were in boarding schools. One of these was at a school for the maladjusted and the other at a small private school.

VI. TYPES OF PLACEMENT USED

Table 25 summarizes the different types of placement experienced by the 17 abused children who spent some time in substitute care during the follow-up interval. Of course, some children had spent time in more than one kind of placement.

Table 25   Placements used

Placement	No. of children
Temporary foster care	10
Long-term foster care, (or intended to be)	7
Residential home/nursery	11
Hospital	1

A. Foster care

Short-stay foster homes were used for ten children (26%). This includes the four living with a single parent, where the placements were used for relief in times of crisis. The other six children were placed in foster homes immediately after admission to the Park Hospital. In only two of the six cases could the foster placement be said to be part of a long-term rehabilitation plan. One was successfully carried through and the other, which involved shared care between natural and foster parents, proved unrealistic and had to be abandoned. The most severely handicapped child in the sample spent a short time with foster parents awaiting a place in an institution. It is unlikely that any consideration was given to placing him in a long-term foster home though this may well have considerably improved the quality of his life. The remaining three short-term foster placements seem to have been of the "wait and see" variety which, if circumstances had turned out differently, might have drifted into long-term placements. As it was, all three returned home only to be readmitted to care later. Two were in children's homes by the time our follow-up study was done.

Seven children were placed in long-term foster homes at some time during the follow-up interval. Three of these children had experienced foster breakdown: a proportion similar to that reported in the literature. All four of the children who had been successfully fostered had had similar placement histories: removal from their mother, followed by an assessment in a residential home prior to foster placement. In all cases the foster placement had been achieved by the time the children were just over 2 years old. These three foster families were visited and will be described in the next chapter.

In contrast to the successful placements, two of the three children who had experienced foster breakdown were at the time of placement in a group where the chance of success was low; neither had been placed until the age of four and had been in and out of care, including previous foster homes. Both were emotionally disturbed and their would-be long-term placements broke down very rapidly. The pessimistic views held by their social workers regarding further possible attempts to find them other foster homes are supported by the findings reported in the literature (Napier, 1972). The third foster placement to break down did not do so until after 4½ years and therefore would have been classified as a success in some published series!

B. Residential care

Eleven abused children (28%) and four siblings had spent some time during the follow-up period in a residential nursery or children's home. For nine of the abused and all the siblings their experience was limited to one residential establishment while the other three had all suffered multiple placements which included several children's homes each. While all admissions to residential institutions resulted from the breakdown of the previous care arrangements, it is possible to identify several ways in which the placements were being used. The four young children who found successful long-term foster placements had all spent some time in a residential nursery. With this group it had always been clearly the intention to find suitable foster parents.

Another child, together with her sister, was placed in a specific children's home because it was known the staff could provide the therapeutic help they needed before they could live in a family. This home was a voluntarily run residential nursery with 17 children under 5 years and a 1:1 staff/children ratio. The striking thing about it was that the home played a central part in the community with the local playgroup being run on the premises every day and therefore the children had regular contact with local families. The children were divided into three small family groups and there was a low staff turnover because many lived locally. Unlike other children's homes visited, there was not an institutional atmosphere. As has already been mentioned, another children's home was used to provide crisis relief for an abused child and his three siblings because the children had been there before. Thus, for six abused children and their siblings, placements in a residential nursery or home formed part of a defined and successful management plan.

For the other five children the part that a residential institution had been intended to play is less clear. All experienced other forms of being "in care" and were emotionally disturbed. At follow-up, two were living with parents and three in children's homes, having suffered previous foster placement breakdowns. The long-term plan for the least disturbed was clearly to keep her and her mother together but for the other four there seemed to be no long-term plan. There was an aura of hopelessness and helplessness surrounding these children and a feeling that their progression into delinquency was inevitable. Sadly the news reaching us about them since the end of the study reinforces this impression. The exception to this is a young boy who had thrived in the atmosphere of a small family group home in contrast to the behaviour disturbance he was displaying when living in a rejecting foster home.

The following case study is a good example of how one child became a victim of multiple home changes. We visited Brenda in an isolated children's home in a rural area. At the age of 10 she was intellectually backward and very disturbed. The staff were finding her sexually provocative behaviour difficult to cope with and felt that she was wrongly placed. She had originally been discharged from the Park at the age of 7 months to the care of her parents who were at the time living in a multi-occupancy house which contained the father's extended family. She was kept under close supervision and seen at the Park Hospital as an out-patient. Following a further bruise, she was readmitted and then discharged to foster parents while still under the age of 1 year. This placement ended abruptly when the foster father died. Following this, she was to have six more changes of placement before arriving in the children's home where we visited her nearly 10 years later. These placements included attempts at rehabilitation with natural parents, a placement with an aunt in London, rehabilitation with her father and step-mother, who also abused her, and a broken foster placement. At the time that we saw her, she had long since lost contact with her mother, her father had discontinued visiting and was asking for his daughter to be adopted!

VII. CONCLUSION

Undoubtedly the children who had found a stable home and who could feel secure about their future were those where a definitive management plan had been made before discharge from the Park Hospital and carried through with the co-operation of parents and community workers. The outcome was in many ways best for the children who went home with their parents and stayed with them throughout the follow-up period. The outcome for the children separated from their parents varied. If a decision to remove a child permanently from his parents was made during the Park Hospital admission or after a short trial at home, his chances of being found a satisfactory long-stay substitute home were high. The children for whom the prognosis was poor and the chance of a secure home low, were those where rehabilitation was tried after abuse had resulted in a period of separation. In only one case was the reunion successful and in this instance, as already described, the parents, therapists and foster parents had all worked hard on an agreed management plan. In the four other cases the child returned to care. All were to have further trials at home and for three (one with parents and two in children's homes) there was still no long-term plan at the time of follow-up.

Looking at our sample as a whole, we see that the children who were moved out of a family more than once during the follow-up interval (excluding planned short-term care), whether the family be a natural one or a substitute one, were those who showed overt behaviour disturbances on follow-up. Inevitably these were the ones who experienced further placement failures. The message is clear: to protect the child's development, each child needs a well-defined, long-term treatment plan. If after the abuse, his first family placement ends, the next family placement should be intended to be permanent. The children in our sample seemed to be more able to tolerate leaving residential care than being removed from a family. It was more important to find the right home than to be moved rapidly into any

available family placement. There are no short cuts and no easy
options: any plan of action will only succeed if it is based on accurate
knowledge of the family and an appreciation by all involved of the
special problems involved in providing care for children from abusing
families.

SUMMARY OF FINDINGS

(1)   Following the Park Hospital admission, five abused children were
       discharged into substitute care and 34 went home with the natural
       parent or parents.

(2)   Of the five in care, two remained there throughout the follow-up
       period. One had periods at home but was in care on follow-up and
       two returned to their parents and were living there on follow-up.

(3)   Of the 34 children discharged home with their parents, six were
       taken into care and were there on follow-up. Six had periods in care
       but were at home on follow-up and 22 remained with their parents
       throughout.

(4)   At the time of follow-up, the nine children living away from their
       parents were considered to be in long-term care.

(5)   Five abused children (13%) had experienced three or more major
       placement changes. None was developmentally normal.

(6)   During the follow-up interval, ten children experienced temporary
       foster placements and seven, long-term (or intended to be) foster
       placements. Eleven children spent some time in a residential home
       or nursery and one was placed in a long-stay hospital.

(7)   Children who "lost" more than one family during the follow-up
       interval were likely to show overt behaviour disturbance on follow-
       up.

IX. The children's families on follow-up

I. THE HOME INTERVIEW

Most of the information to be presented in this chapter and the next was collected during a lengthy home interview.

At the time of the follow-up assessment, 74 out of 80 children seen (93%) were living as part of a family. All these families were seen and totalled 36. Thirty-three of the families included at least one of the natural parents of the abused child. The other three were foster families caring for four of the abused children (including one set of twins)*. On follow-up there were three natural families known to us without the care of any children. Parents in two of these families were interviewed. Three other parents who had left the family home were also seen.

The families were all seen for a home interview at some time between November 1976 and July 1977; for the majority this was within a month of the main follow-up assessment at the hospital. The interviews were all conducted by the same person who visited the family home in all but three cases, where the parents were seen at the hospital instead.

The interview schedule was our own and was piloted on families who were currently receiving family therapy for the problem of child abuse. The aim was to obtain a wide range of factual data about the families since their discharge from the Park Hospital, to ask questions about the children's development, the family and marital relationships and finally to ask for impressions of the Park Hospital and memories of events at the time of abuse. We also hoped to gain some idea of the

*In one case we saw two families representing one index child: (a) the foster family of an abused child, and (b) the natural mother of this abused child who had formed a new family with a second husband and new baby.

132

family's social relationships and way of life. The aim was to make the questions as comprehensive as possible and not focus only on abuse, punishment or parent/child relationships. Obviously, we were dependent on the parents' view of things but it was rare for a parent to refuse to answer the questions or give the impression of deliberately lying. In many cases we had both family doctor's and social worker's opinions of the family's progess to confirm or contradict our own. We specifically requested an interview with both husband and wife, where appropriate, but three fathers failed to attend the interview when it came to the appointed date.

Wherever possible, even in the less *definable areas*, we tried to obtain quantifiable data. For example, instead of simply relying on impressions, the interviewer recorded exactly how many times the parent shouted at a child during the interview. When asking parents how often they lost their temper, the aim was to keep answers as precisely as possible to quantifiable categories. Questions were usually asked in the format: "Have you . . . today, within the last week, within the last month?" Parents were not asked to estimate frequency but rely only on their recent memory. The interviews were all tape-recorded and no parent refused permission for this. Interview schedules were then filled in by hand from the tapes — little was left to the interviewer's memory. Apart from the accuracy of recording, these tapes have also provided a rich source of anecdotal data which has given us much greater insight into the parents' views of the consequences of child abuse.

In addition, the interviewer's subjective professional opinions on a few areas were recorded:

(a) whether there was marital tension,
(b) whether there were problems in the parent/child relationships, and
(c) the home environment.

Originally the aim was to interview the parents while the children were around but in some cases the parents obviously preferred the children to be absent and their wishes were respected. The average length of interview was 1 hour 41 minutes and they varied from 1 hour to 2¾ hours. Only four families took longer than 2 hours to finish.

This present chapter focuses on the social and demographic data collected on the families interviewed while in the following chapter we will attempt to describe some of the more subtle aspects of life in these families. Before considering our data we will briefly review the findings and observations of other researchers who have followed up families for comparable periods of time.

II. FAMILIES IN THE LITERATURE

In Chapter II it became clear that the social and demographic characteristics in the families in our sample were often different from those of
other reported studies, and are therefore likely to continue so on
follow-up. This is especially true of the studies from outside the U.K.
However, while no direct comparison can be made, it is relevant to
consider what these studies have to show about family social characteristics on follow-up. While studies on the detailed development of
abused children are few, detailed studies of the families' progress are
even fewer.

Perhaps the sample most comparable with ours is that studied by
the NSPCC research team (Baher *et al.*, 1976). On follow-up, more than
21 months later, 20 out of the 21 abused children studied were living
with at least one natural parent. Out of the 21 of the original 25
families assessed, on follow-up it was found that only six had increased
in size in the 21-month period following referral, that most of the
mothers were using regular methods of birth control and the authors
found this a welcome change. However, the rate of unemployment had
not changed, few mothers were working and financial disorganization
was still a marked feature for nearly half the families. There was a
marked improvement in housing conditions in that 18 out of 21
families were adequately housed compared with only seven out of 25
families at the beginning of treatment. Ten out of the original 25
couples (40%) had separated by the time of writing. The families were
found to be less isolated, having more contact with their own parents
and local communities.

However, one must take into account that the conclusion to the
NSPCC's chapter on the evaluation of progress in the families is as
follows:

> "It could be suggested that with abusive families, treatment goals are in-
> evitably conservative and achievement should be seen in terms of preven-
> tion of further deterioration rather than marked improvement in family
> functioning."

Another most detailed family follow-up study was one completed in
America 2–14 years after the hospital admission of a small group of
children who were assumed to have been abused (they had all been
admitted with bony injuries) (Elmer, 1967). The main difference from
our study is that on follow-up a reassessment of the circumstances of
the injury was made to decide whether the child had been abused.
Following this, some families were assigned to a "non-abusive"

category and were added to a group of foster families who were all then compared with the "abusive" families. The mothers of the families were all given hospital and home interviews and the children were assessed medically, psychologically and psychiatrically. Nine of the 11 "abusive" mothers and 11 of the 12 "non-abusive" mothers (seven of who were foster mothers) were actually seen for interview. When looking at the demographic characteristics, Elmer found that on follow-up the 11 abusing families had an average of four children per family, and all of them were either in social class IV or V, their median monthly income was particularly low and four of them were receiving "public welfare", in most cases because of the absence of the father. As none of the non-abusive families were receiving welfare, Elmer claims that "this appears to bear out a widely held belief that child abuse occurs mainly among families on relief"! Only four families were found to be in poor housing conditions. "Several" abusive mothers were reported to have separated from husbands and all the abusive mothers were found to be far more isolated from "outside sources of companionship and help" than the non-abusive mothers.

Martin et al. (1974), in their description of abusive families on follow-up an average of 4½ years later, state that 37 out of the 58 children seen were living with biological parents, 31 of whom belonged to social classes IV and V; 14 children (24%) were with foster parents and seven (12%) with adoptive parents. In general the picture of the family background for all the abused children on follow-up was not a good one: 20 children were living in homes which were rated as "unstable" where there was "evidence of excessive disorganization, frequent unemployment, high geographic mobility, poor management and chaotic social structure," and 58% of the children had experienced parents' divorce or marital separation.

Hufton and Oates (1977), in a follow-up of children with non-organic failure-to-thrive in Australia with an average follow-up interval of 6½ years, found that 19 of the 21 children seen were with natural parents and ten families had produced more children. Nine families (43%) were dependent on welfare benefits for all or part of their income, ten families (48%) described themselves as having financial difficulties, six families (28%) described their homes as inadequate and eight families (38%) were considered overcrowded. Fifteen out of the 21 families seen (two were adoptive families) had moved house at least once. Twelve (63%) of the natural families were still intact but the authors describe the sample as having "a high degree of marital instability."

A more recent British study (Taitz, 1980) is of 47 infants "at risk", which is a less strict definition of abuse, ranging from suspected "non-accidental injury" to being considered "at risk" at birth. After a follow-up period varying from 4 months to over 5 years, Taitz found that 38 out of the 47 children (81%) were with one or both natural parents, eight were fostered (three privately) and one was in a children's home. Apart from the eight single-parent families, all the fathers but two were manual workers or unemployed manual workers. On follow-up the rate of unemployment was 32%, housing problems 33%, marital strife 42%, parental isolation 14% and criminal history 20%.

This information from the literature has a limited comparability with our own study because of differing definitions and sometimes the inclusion of substitute families. Both British studies reveal that some social problems persist years after the referral incident but the families in these samples are biased towards the lower income group. The most salutary warning comes from the NSPCC research study (Baher *et al.*, 1976) who stress that even after intensive social work help from an expert team, one can expect only limited progress.

III. THE NATURAL FAMILIES IN OUR SAMPLE

In our study the natural families will be considered separately. As stated previously, there were 33 families where at least one natural parent was caring for the children. Eighty-eight per cent of the total of 80 children seen were living in such families (this includes 77% of the abused and all but one of the siblings). In four of these 33 natural families there were only siblings or half-siblings in the home. In these four cases one abused child was dead, one was in an institution, one in foster care and one in a children's home.

Our rate of placement with at least one natural parent is almost the same as that reported by the NSPCC research study (Baher *et al.*, 1976) but is much higher than the rate (46%) given by Speight *et al.* (1979) who studied a typical sample of abused children ascertained in a hospital paediatric department.

A. Family size

Table 26 shows that on follow-up the natural families did not have large numbers of children. Only 12% had four or more children compared with the national figure for England of 29% (Davie *et al.*, 1972). During the follow-up interval, 15 children had been born to 12 families. Three of these being half-siblings to the abused children.

Table 26   Size of family

	1 child	2 children	3 children	4 children
Natural families n = 33	10	13	6	4

(These figures do not include abused children no longer living in the family.)

Just as in the NSPCC research study, in which Baher *et al.* (1976) noted considerable progress in the area of family planning, we found longer birth intervals after intervention and almost all of these 15 children were planned and very much wanted. The mean average length of birth interval between live children before admission was 2.1 years and after admission it was 3.05 years. Seventy-five per cent of the birth intervals before admission were less than 2 years in length and after discharge only 20% were that short. We feel that longer birth intervals were a crucial factor in the improvement of many of the families' circumstances. In addition to the live births, there had been seven further pregnancies, three of which resulted in planned terminations. Six couples had chosen sterilization as a means of contraception. Only seven other mothers were not taking reliable contraceptive precautions (three were women who claimed they were not having sexual intercourse, two were pregnant and only one seemed not to be bothering. The remaining couple had a long history of sub-fertility but still expressed a wish for the mother to be sterilized.)

Having unwanted children, sometimes in rapid succession, had caused great strain for many of these mothers prior to the abuse incident and one of the aims of intervention was to prevent further unplanned pregnancies. One woman was encouraged to have a termination soon after discharge from the Park Hospital. Her baby daughter had been severely battered and she had just been through the agonizing time of wondering whether this baby would be taken into care. During the hospital admission she had to work hard at forming a bond between herself and the baby and she and her husband were only just beginning to face their problems together, following many sessions of marital therapy. They were still living in a caravan and this was not the time to embark on a new pregnancy, with the first child only 8 months old. Following the termination, this couple then waited nearly 3 years before they had their second child. On follow-up, this 2½-year old child was typical of the children born later to these families in that we could not fault her development.

B. Socio-economic status

Table 27 shows the social class distribution of the 33 families, using the Registrar General's classification for occupation for the head of the household, both on admission and on follow-up. As can be seen, the social class distribution for the families as a group had hardly altered although for some individual families there had been changes.

Table 27   Social class: on admission and follow-up

	On admission n = 33	On follow-up n = 33
I + II	4	5
III	8	10
IV	8	7
V	2	1
Unsupp. mothers	5	7
Unemployed	0	1
Forces	4	2
Gaol	2	0

Two fathers had moved up the social scale by gaining better and more responsible jobs; others had been promoted although they retained the same social status. The two men who were in gaol at the time of admission were in social classes III and V on follow-up. One father had left the Forces for skilled, non-manual employment. The other changes in the figures are explained by marriages and divorces. The only father who was unemployed on follow-up was a new husband of one of the original five single mothers. Other fathers had had periods of unemployment during the follow-up interval although never longer than 4 months. Nearly three-quarters were working overtime and three had second jobs. To a certain extent this reflects the fathers' lack of interest in other things as well as the need for extra cash. A common response to the question: "What do you enjoy most in life?" was: "Work", or "Going to work." Again, the social class distribution and employment record of these families is very different from other British studies but, as stated previously, it probably reflects the population from which the sample is drawn. The 1977 unemployment rate for Oxford and the surrounding area was 4.6% (Dept of Employment Statistics Section).

All the women were asked about their employment experiences in the follow-up interval. Eleven wives were currently in part-time employment and one wife was working full-time in a factory. A further eight wives had been in employment some time during the follow-up interval. One of the single mothers was in part-time employment on follow-up and two of them had been in the past. The striking thing about these women's jobs was that they were mostly casual and unskilled with little responsibility. A large number of them were in cleaning jobs and most others were home-sales representatives. For some women this was in spite of secretarial or other training. We think that the reasons for this were both the difficulty for any woman in obtaining good, part-time employment and also that many of our sample of women were lacking in self-confidence.

The parents were all asked about their earnings. A couple of fathers refused to give information about their income but 17 fathers (65%) claimed to have an income below the average weekly pay for 1977. Few women, because of the nature of their jobs, made a significant contribution to the family's income. Only one of the two-parent families was completely dependent on Social Security benefits and only one other was receiving Family Income Supplement. For three single mothers their main source of income was Social Security benefit. The rest were receiving some payments from their ex-husbands in addition to welfare benefits. A total of nine families (27%) were in serious financial difficulties. These included two single mothers, four families where the father had a below-average income and three families with a more than adequate income. We felt that all these families' debts were the result of gross mismanagement of their whole lives and not just their financial affairs: it seemed difficult to imagine how they were ever going to extricate themselves from their financial problems. For example, one couple, where the father had a low income, were paying off a large court fee for a divorce which was causing them to run up serious rent arrears. The irony was that these parents remarried a year after their divorce without either partner ever leaving the home! Another family, with property and an extravagant life-style, had decided to sell off valuable land to pay expensive school fees for their 5-year old. For the majority of families the budgeting was done by husband and wife together. Three mothers and only one father claimed to be in sole control of budgeting. Very few parents claimed that money difficulties were the cause of marital rows.

Considering the generally low level of income in these families, their material standards of life seemed high. It may be that in some cases fathers were deliberately underestimating their total income. Half (17) had telephones compared with an estimated 75% of households in the Oxford area and 22 (67%) had cars, which is exactly the rate for households in Oxfordshire by the 1971 census. In only two families was there any outward sign of poverty. On interview and assessment both the parents' and children's standard of dress was very high. In some cases the families had very high expectations of material possessions, almost as though they felt such acquisitions demonstrated good parenting.

C. Housing

Twenty-two of the families (67%) were living in houses and the rest in flats. Another family owned a house but had been living with friends for many months while extensive renovations were being made. Overall 18% were owner-occupiers and 58% were in council accommodation compared with 50% and 24% respectively of households in Oxfordshire in the 1971 census. This low rate of home ownership probably reflects the relatively young age of families and the low incomes but in some cases it seemed to reflect a lack of initiative.

Thirty-one out of the 33 homes were visited and generally the standard of accommodation was high. For example, all the families had inside toilets and bathrooms and over half had central heating. Only the two families in temporary accommodation had to share any amenities.

Using the definition of overcrowding of 1.5 people per room — defining the kitchen as a room only if used for eating — four families (12%) were overcrowded compared with the national figure of 15% of 7-year olds in Britain in 1965 (Davie *et al.*, 1972). These families included one with four children, the family living with friends whilst their own house was renovated and two families temporarily housed in a social services' rehabilitation centre. A further eight had experienced over-crowding at some time during the follow-up interval. Only one had sub-standard accommodation at the time of follow-up compared with 20% at the time of admission. Twelve families did state that their housing was unsatisfactory, some of whom wished to change the location rather than the accommodation. Others wished to change the type of accommodation, such as the family with 3 young children living in a first-floor council flat without access to a garden or safe play area. Two other families considered their housing to be unsatisfactory but the interviewer found it very hard to understand why. One example was a mother of four young children in a beautifully furnished council house with front and rear garden and plenty of room. She wished to move because she did not like the six steps from the kitchen to the living-room!

Information was collected on the number of times the families had moved house during the follow-up period. Twenty-five (76%) had moved at least once: for the majority of these families this was a move to better accommodation. Four families had moved four or more times (12%). This mobility rate does not seem excessive considering the national norms of 64% of 7-year olds having moved house at least once and 7% having moved house more than four times (Davie *et al.*, 1972) and it is less than that reported by Martin *et al.*, (1974) where 34% had changed domicile three or more times. As the length of follow-up varies in each case, we have calculated how many families had moved on average more than once a year: six (18%) had done so. In five of these the mother was a single parent at some time during the follow-up period. A typical example was a young woman who had moved six times in less than 3 years. Her relationship with her child's father broke up soon after discharge from the Park Hospital and she went to live with her sister for a few weeks. She then moved to another town into a shared flat. This she decided was not big enough and moved into a shared house. Following a row with her fellow tenants, she moved out to a bed-sitter from where she managed to find another shared house and then, finally, she was housed by the council where she had stayed for well over a year. Her comment about this was that she "just kept moving around." Her experiences are typical of the single parent in that security of accommodation often depends on the continuity of a relationship with a partner. If not housed by the county council, single-parent families have great difficulty in securing adequate, privately rented accommodation.

D. Separations, divorces and marriages

In 10 families the parents had separated or divorced at some time during the follow-up interval. In five families this had entailed a household move for the children. At the time of follow-up, eight of these couples (24%) were still separated. These separations/divorces include one mother who married and divorced during the follow-up interval and the set of parents who divorced and remarried each other without either leaving the home. Including these two marriages, in four families the children experienced a new "marriage". The rate of marital separation seems high, although it is lower than that reported in other follow-up studies (Baher *et al.*, 1976; Martin et al., 1974). In all, at the time of follow-up, 16% of the children in the 33 "natural" families in our sample were living in a household with no male head, compared with a national figure of 6.25% of children living in a one-parent family (Wedge and Prosser, 1973).

E. Family social activities

As noted in many other studies (e.g. Baher *et al.*, 1976; Steele and Pollock, 1974), abusing parents are striking for their social isolation, their inability to get on with other people, and their lack of motivation to enjoy themselves. We felt that it was important to note these aspects of the families' existence on follow-up to give some idea of the possible influences on the children's social experiences and development.

With one or two rare exceptions, when asked about recent contact with relatives, these families did not come across as isolated people: 26 (79%) had had contact with the children's grandparents over the last month. Only five families had not had contact for more than 6 months. In two of these there had been an argument and in the others, distance somewhat prohibited contact. There was only one family who did not have contact with other relatives within the last year. However, relationships with relatives were not always congenial in spite of regular contact. For example, there was one family where the father visited the wife's mother regularly twice a week with the children, but the wife had no contact with her mother at all. In fact, 17 parents stated that their relationship with at least one of the children's grandparents was not good.

When enquiring about family social activities, we found that all but four of the families had had some sort of family outing within the last year; 69% had done something within the last month. Activities ranged from visiting relatives and friends, to pantomimes, zoos, going for walks and to the park, shopping, going to pubs with facilities for children and driving to a motorway cafe. The most frequent activity was visiting relatives. Those four families who had not done anything special included three single mothers and one family where there was a great deal of family tension and the mother was very unstable emotionally.

Holidays are far more expensive than day outings and therefore it was not surprising that the families were less likely to have had regular holidays. Sixty-nine per cent of the families had not had a holiday for at least a year, including ten families who had not had a holiday since the parents' marriage. Some families, in their answers to these questions, demonstrated a dislike of holidays. One family, for example, had been urged to take the children to the seaside by their social workers. This they had done three years before the interview. According to the parents, they did not enjoy it; it was the only holiday they had had and they did not want another one. It seemed that some of these parents found it extremely difficult to go away from home and familiar surroundings.

F. Other social activities

Fifteen of the 26 couples (58%) had been out together without the children within the last month; only four couples stated that they never went out together. When asked about regular social commitments such as membership of a club, sporting events or church-going, a third of the mothers stated that they had weekly commitments but over half had no social engagements whatsoever unless they went out with their husbands. As one mother exclaimed: "I don't go nowhere!" It was striking that most of these mothers had husbands who had regular weekly commitments. A typical answer to this question would be a list of activities and associations given by the father: "Yes, I belong to a youth club, charity organization, the Buffaloes, and a chess association." The mother meanwhile belonged to nothing and only went out with her husband to the pub. There were, however, fathers who had no social activities at all. A typical response was from one father: "No . . . Work occupies all my life!" As this was a group of families with young children, it is not surprising that family social events were much more common than social activities for the parents alone, but the lack of activities did not relate to income — rather to an attitude towards leaving the family and the home.

As noted by Baher *et al.* (1976), we have often found abusing families at the time of identification isolate themselves from the local community. This we did not find at all on follow-up. Twenty-nine families (88%) had either been to a neighbour's house or had a neighbour visiting their own house within the week prior to the interview. Only four families had little or no contact with their neighbours. Three out of these four families deliberately avoided their neighbours, including one couple who actually made the classic statement: "We keep ourselves to ourselves," stating that they had moved house to get away from the constant visits of neighbours. The other family were housed in a first-floor flat above a big business concern and were geographically isolated from neighbours.

It did seem, therefore, that most of the parents in these families were aware of the children's needs to participate in social events and meet other people. However, there was much emphasis on adults and relatives and there seemed to be fewer organized activities with other children: 22 of the families had had children visiting the house within the week prior to the interview, but many of these children came with their parents and it was really the adults who were making the visit. Seven families had not had a child visiting the home for months. Typical comments were: "No point in children coming up here — there's nothing for them", and: "I don't have any other kids in the house — got enough of my own!" Of the families where there had been recent child visitors, there still were some odd comments, such as: "They don't play with children inside the house — I don't allow it", and: "They only play with the family's children" (i.e. relatives). One family had experienced the first visit a child had ever made to the house and the mother's comment was: "I've only had one child in, ever, and that was a teacher's child."

During the actual interview, 12 out of the 30 families seen at home had at least one person calling at the house or a telephone call but the rest (60%) were totally undisturbed and, as will be described, seemed remarkably different from the foster families. It was clear that many of these parents chose an atmosphere of quiet and contented privacy rather than bustling activity.

G. Prosecutions and arrests

Other studies of child abusing families have often looked at the rate of criminality in the parents. During the interview, our parents were asked about any arrests or prosecutions during the follow-up interval. Nine parents (five fathers (13%) and four mothers (12%)) had been prosecuted during the follow-up period, two of whom (a man and a wife) had had several prosecutions and both had been in prison for non-payment of fines. Charges included drunken driving, careless driving, minor car offences such as licence expiry or faulty exhaust, shop-lifting and one case of animal cruelty. One father was arrested for assaulting his wife but she did not press charges and therefore there was no prosecution.

The high rate offences in this group of parents is however rather misleading. In only one family could it be considered that there was a history of criminality and they do not even feature in the above examples. One other family had a history of repeated minor car offences and the gaol sentences were the result of non-payment of fines. Apart from the minor car offences, the other offences (the drunken driving, shop-lifting and assault) seemed to be related to family strains and stresses. Even the case of animal cruelty was the result of unintentional neglect during a family break-up when nobody had been at home to look after the caged pets. We therefore consider that it is irresponsible to point to "criminality" in these parents without looking further into the circumstances of their prosecutions. Poor impulse control explains most of their misdeeds. It is symptomatic of these parents that they would act and speak without any forethought, that they would be unable to avoid prosecution and that they would antagonize neighbours who therefore would press charges. They may be the ones who get caught. Also, to put our information into perspective, it has recently been estimated that if conviction rates continue at the same level as they were in 1977, the lifetime prevalence rate for convictions for non-motoring offences could eventually reach 43% for men and 15% for women (Farrington, 1981).

H. Professional help

A final indication of the family's social circumstances on follow-up could be given by the number who were receiving current help from social workers, health visitors or probation officers. Eighteen families were still "open" social work cases at the time of follow-up. In all but three, the social work questionnaires confirmed that there were strong reasons for social work help, even when there had been some improvement. Of the 15 families not receiving social work help, three, according to our assessment, would have benefited from it and referrals were organized. Twenty-one families claimed that they still received visits from health visitors, eight of whom had been visited within the last month. All these families had pre-school-age children but seven other families with pre-school-age children claimed they were not being visited by health visitors. Only one family was being visited by a probation officer on follow-up but three had had such contact at some time during the follow-up period.

IV. THE FOSTER FAMILIES

Four abused children, including one set of twins, were living with foster parents at the time of the home interview. They had been with the families for 1 year 4 months, 3 years 10 months and 4 years 4 months and all the placements were considered to be permanent, both by the parents and social services department. The children all called the foster parents "Mummy" and "Daddy" or "Mum" and "Dad" although in two instances there was still some contact with the natural parents. Our assessments confirmed the success of all four placements.

The foster parents stood out in the context of a follow-up study of abusing families for their stability and easy-going personalities. They all had children of their own, but came from very different backgrounds, belonging to social classes II, III and IV respectively. The mean age of the foster mothers was 38.9 years and of the foster fathers 41.4 years compared with the much younger ages in the natural families of 28 years for the mothers and 29.5 years for the fathers. In general all three foster homes differed from the other homes visited because of their happy, noisy, bustling activity. All three families had several telephone calls during the interview and at least one visitor.

We found the foster families notably free of the problems suffered by some of the natural families. This is not surprising, considering the assessment that is made before they are accepted as foster parents for local authority social service departments. There had been no marital separation, no unemployment, no housing problems and no serious debts, even in the social class IV family who were on a very low income. One family had moved a lot (seven times in 4½ years) but that was in the nature of the father's employment. Two families were owner-occupiers and one family lived in tied housing. All three families had a car, or cars, telephone and indoor toilet and bathroom facilities, but one family did not have central heating. Only the foster family in social class IV had not had a recent family holiday, presumably because they could not afford it.

The families' contacts with grandparents, relatives, friends and neighbours were very regular. Children outside the family had visited all three homes within the week prior to the interview. They all had very regular family outings, usually visiting relatives. Two sets of parents went out together without the children every week and the other family did so every few months. Only the mother and father in social class IV did not have regular individual weekly commitments.

We will now look in greater detail at the individual foster families with particular reference to the circumstances that had led them to foster an abused child and how they tackled the difficulties this involved.

Family A: These parents, who were social class II, had five children of their own including a grown-up daughter with her own family. At the time of the interview their other children were 20 years, 15½ years, 9½ years and 5½ years old and all living at home. The parents had responded to an advertisement in the paper for a foster placement for twin girls "with a view to adoption". The family had been accepted, despite the age of the parents, because of their obvious ability to give the well-balanced care needed by the twins who had already spent over a year in a residential nursery. After an introductory period the twins had come to live in the family just after their second birthday and had been there for 1 year 4 months when we visited them at home. The twins, who had been followed up by the Park Hospital throughout, had responded to the consistent and loving care of the foster family and at the time of our assessment we were impressed by their rate of emotional and developmental progress. One of the twins was moderately neurologically handicapped but, with encouragement from her new parents, was showing determination to overcome her difficulties. Throughout the placement the foster parents had tolerated regular visits to the twins' natural mother which was becoming an increasingly difficult exercise owing to the mother's emotional instability and inappropriate behaviour. The social service department were supporting the foster parents in making an appliction to adopt the twins.

Family B: This family were social class III and had three children who were 11, 10 and 7 years older than their 4½-year old foster child. They had been a well-established fostering and child-minding family when she was placed with them as a baby. It had been hoped that the placement would be a long-term one but initially this type of commitment had not been asked of the foster parents because of the expectation that the child would grow up severely handicapped, both physically and intellectually. The challenge of caring for a handicapped child had been taken up with enthusiasm and a determination to ensure that she achieved her greatest potential. Indeed, despite severe neurological handicap, the skilled care the child received produced a far better outcome than anyone had dared hope. At one stage uninhibited and boisterous behaviour had been a major problem, calling for careful and consistent handling. At follow-up the behaviour problems had ceased and the child was happily placed and making excellent progress in a special school near her home. There was no current contact with her natural parents who had moved out of the area. The foster parents' devotion to the needs of this child had not been to the exclusion of their own children — rather they had taken a caring but professional interest in achieving the best for the child. For example, they had been quite ready to take a holiday, leaving the foster child in the care of the Park Hospital, in order to give their own children the extra attention they needed. Without this short-term relief and the sensitive support of the social worker making the placement, this fostering could well have broken down. In many ways this family resembles the professional foster parents now being recruited in many areas to care for older disturbed children (McWhinnie, 1978). Interestingly, the father was the only foster parent taking an active part in the Foster Care Association.

Family C: This family, from social class IV, was also an established foster family when the abused child was placed with them. However, this placement was unusual in that the foster mother was the natural mother's sister. The family had two children of their own — a daughter the same age as the abused child and a son about 2 years younger. At the time of the home interview they were also fostering two brothers. The abused child had been placed in a children's home following discharge from the Park Hospital. The natural mother strongly supported her sister's desire to foster the child as she and her baby had been cared for by the sister intermittently prior to the abuse. The child had been placed with the family at the age of 19 months and at the time of follow-up he had been there almost 4½ years. The placement had turned out to be extremely satisfactory for the child concerned who fulfilled all our criteria for problem-free status on follow-up. There were problems for the foster parents in their relationship with the child's natural mother but these did not spill over into their relationship with the child. The boy was not confused about his natural mother's identity and was confident that he would continue to be brought up by his aunt.

V. NATURAL PARENTS WITHOUT THEIR CHILDREN

Two of the three natural families without the care of any child were still couples while the third remained a single woman. We asked to visit these families, even though their circumstances were so different from the others, but we were requested not to approach the single mother because of her disturbed mental state (she was schizophrenic) and her inability to accept her child being in care.

The parents without children in their care whom we did meet were striking for their mental instability. It was almost impossible to hold an interview with one mother and her husband refused to be present. This woman had previously been diagnosed schizophrenic and certainly during the home visit displayed a strange obsession about neighbouring children banging on her window and throwing "conkers" at her from the trees outside. This, she thought, was happening during the interview which was held in March! Apart from this over-riding and incapacitating obsession, her thoughts about why her children were in care were quite clear: "They lost their mother's love . . . my depression."

In the second couple, the mother refused to be interviewed but talked in a bizarre way about what she wanted from life, such as new furniture throughout the house every year. Her children were in long-term care but she wanted them only to go to a convent and never be allowed to meet boys. She claimed she was a scientist although her actual employment was that of cleaning a laboratory. The father co-operated fully with the interview and showed that his only way of coping with life was to hold an absolutely rigid faith in the Bible. He attended religious meetings at least five times a week and claimed it was only his faith that kept him with his wife. This couple were bringing up the wife's younger sister who was going through a stormy and disturbed adolescence.

At the time of follow-up there were six fathers and two mothers who were considered to be permanently separated from the family. Only two of the fathers and one mother were interviewed: the rest were not contacted according to the wishes of those currently caring for the child. Both the fathers seen by us visited their child weekly. The first father had set up home with a divorced woman and her five children (including one foster child). In comparison with his wife, he seemed much more stable and responsible but admitted to incidents of quite serious physical violence. He talked about great concern for his children but felt unable to offer them a home, including the original abused child now in care and whom he wanted to release for adoption.

The second father seemed to have less involvement with his child and thought it right that she should stay with his estranged wife. The closing comments to the interviewer were: "I'd like to see her get a good father — something I will never be. It would save me a lot of money." This man was living a bachelor-type life, back with his parents and younger siblings and seemed relieved and happy to be free from family ties.

The mother whom we were able to interview was at that time in the midst of a custody dispute over her only child. She displayed signs of emotional instability but, to be fair, was going through a very distressing time. She showed serious problems about sexual identity: for example, she was taking the pill continuously to avoid ever menstruating and talked about encouraging her son to play with make-up, her bras and underwear. Her marriage had lasted only 4 months and she had consistently failed to maintain an intimate relationship with anyone.

VI. DISCUSSION

In this chapter we have concentrated on presenting traditional social and demographic data on the children's families interviewed on follow-up. For the natural families looking after their children we found many indications of improvement in the management of the family affairs. The longer birth intervals suggested improved family planning, only one family was actually in sub-standard housing compared with 20% on admission, the unemployed had found regular jobs, two fathers had settled down after leaving prison and those with a low income appeared to be managing their financial affairs better. The majority of families were definitely not socially isolated. The rate of marital breakdown in our sample approaches that reported by other follow-up studies, but marital separation cannot always be seen as a negative step in that marital disharmony had contributed to the original child abuse in many of these families. In some such cases intervention had helped the parents to separate.

Unlike some of the other studies for example, Martin et al. (1974) and Elmer (1967), we have considered foster families separately. All three families were striking for their ability to maintain a happy and stable family life and it was easy for us to understand why the placements had been so successful. Equally striking was the bizarre behaviour of the couples who were still together although their children were in long-term care. We did not doubt the wisdom of the removal of these children.

Comparisons between our sample and those from other studies and with the general population must be treated with some caution but these have been made to provide some indication of the status of our group of families on follow-up. In comparison with the Oxfordshire population, the professional groups were slightly under-represented and there was a higher than expected proportion of unsupported mothers. There was not, however, an over-representation of unskilled workers or unemployed fathers. Over half the fathers in our sample were either skilled workers or in the professional/managerial class. We did find, however, a group of eight families, including four single mothers, who were well-known to welfare agencies and who shared between them most of the social problems reported in this chapter. They were all on a very low income; they include the only unemployed father, the only example of sub-standard housing, most of the prosecutions, two of the four seriously socially isolated families and most of the families who had moved more than once a year on follow-up. All but one of them had given up the care of a child or children or had had at least one child in local authority care for more than 6 months. The rest of the sample were a very diverse group about whom it is almost impossible to make generalizations. Some did have problems such as serious debts and low income; two outwardly respectable fathers had had prosecutions and two families were very socially isolated, but as a group they were relatively free of the traditional social problems associated with child abuse. This makes us question whether the high incidence of social problems other authors quote for child abuse families are those associated with low social class and a history of dependence on welfare agencies rather than with child abuse. We are not denying that in individual families socio-economic problems can be a contributive factor towards child abuse, but there are in our inner cities many families living in inadequate housing and suffering from chronic unemployment who do not abuse their children. Likewise, in this sample, our concern over a child's welfare did not relate directly to a family's social difficulties. There were children doing very well in spite of having parents overwhelmed with social problems while other children were seriously disturbed, despite good social circumstances and an intact family. In these cases the outward veneer of respectability masked serious underlying relationship difficulties. The implications for the management of abusing families are clear: improving their social conditions alone cannot prevent recurrent abuse.

SUMMARY OF FINDINGS

(1) Seventy-four of the 80 children seen (93%) were living as part of a family. Thirty-three families included one or both natural parents and three families were foster families.

(2) Twelve per cent of the 33 natural families had four or more children (population rate 29%). During the follow-up interval, 15 children had been born to 12 families.

(3) The social class distribution had hardly altered since admission and only one father was unemployed. Sixty-five per cent of fathers claimed to have an income below the average weekly pay, but only nine families were in serious financial difficulties. This included three families with a high income. Overall the standard of material possessions was high.

(4) Sixty-seven per cent of the families lived in a house. Eighteen per cent were owner-occupiers and 58% were in council accommodation (rates for Oxfordshire: 50% and 24% respectively). Only one family lived in sub-standard housing compared with 20% on admission and 12% were over-crowded (national rate 15%). Most of the families who moved during the follow-up interval had done so to improve their housing. A small group (18%), mainly single parents, had experienced multiple moves.

(5) Twenty-four per cent of the parents were separated or divorced at the time of follow-up. On follow-up, 16% of the children were living only with their mothers (national rate of one-parent families: 6.25%).

(6) Family social activities were common for most families but there was evidence of restrictions on both the wives' individual social activities and on children's play opportunities.

(7) Nine parents had been prosecuted for minor offences during follow-up. Poor impulse control explained most of these misdeeds.

(8) Most of the 18 families who were still open social work cases at follow-up needed the help they were receiving. We considered another three to be in need of services.

(9) Four abused children, including one set of twins, were living with foster parents. All these placements were considered permanent and successful.

(10) In addition to the natural families with care of children, there were six fathers and two mothers who had become permanently separated from the original family and three natural families without care of any children. Among the latter there was striking evidence of emotional instability.

X. Parents and children at home

The preceding chapter conveyed only part of the picture presented by the families on follow-up. In this chapter we will describe some of the less tangible aspects of the families' and the children's life at home. We will consider the parents' perceptions of their own problems, behaviour and emotions regarding family life, their marriage, their view of their children and their relationship with them. We will describe the parents' accounts of the children's behaviour in the home and their ways of dealing with it. Important observations made during the home interview will be discussed. Obviously, this is subjective data and often the parents' answers to questions such as "When did X last have a temper tantrum?", depend very much on their own definitions of such behaviour. However, it was the parents' subjective view of their life at home that we particularly wished to hear about and it was possible to get them to describe fully what they meant by various terms. It was from such detailed descriptions that we learned more about their attitudes and the atmosphere in the home, and thus the chapter contains quotations from the parents as a record of their feelings. The information we have gathered on the life in these homes we hope will help readers to have a greater understanding of families where child abuse has occurred.

As the assessments used for this part of the study are so much more subjective and the decisions about what constitutes disturbance so arbitrary, a comparison with other studies is even more difficult than in the last chapter. However, it is worth briefly considering a few follow-up studies.

I. THE LITERATURE

All published studies show a high rate of psychological problems in the parents on follow-up, high rates of punitive attitudes towards the children and, even if physical abuse is not found, studies have shown that poor parent/child relationships persist. For example, the authors of the NSPCC research study (Baher *et al.*, 1976) discuss in detail the parent/child interaction as observed by their social workers 18–21 months after the beginning of therapy. They found that "the majority of mothers could not be termed even fairly accepting of the battered children"; "the mothers' attitude to discipline remained fairly harsh or inconsistent"; a third of the mothers were still rated as neglectful and "the feelings of jealousy between parents over the battered child remained a feature in over half of the intact families."

Elmer (1967), when comparing nine abusive families on follow-up with 11 non-abusive families, taking information from the mothers only, found that the abusive mothers scored high on measures of marital disharmony, with frequent separations and reconciliations. Several of the abusive mothers reported excessive drinking by the fathers. Both abusive and non-abusive mothers ranked "whipping" or "spanking" as first in their use of discipline but the non-abusive families tended to use a few types of punishment consistently while some abusive families used a broad range, which suggested to Elmer that they were desperately trying to find some way to manage their children. Elmer speculates that the similarity between the abusive and non-abusive groups is a reflection of the lower class use of corporal punishment and ridicule as reasoning was almost never used by either group. Half the abusive mothers and only one non-abusive mother showed a negative attitude both towards the child in the past and at the time of the study. Mothers' attitudes towards other children in the family were not measured. The abusive mothers showed considerably more emotional difficulties than the non-abusive mothers and several of them admitted to uncontrollable actions in the past compared with none of the non-abusive mothers.

Morse *et al.* (1970) in their follow-up of 25 children who had suffered physical abuse or gross neglect, found that parents in 18 out of 23 families exhibited emotional disturbance and/or mental retardation and on a more concrete measure, parents in 12 out of 23 families were referred for psychiatric help. The authors found that a good mother/child relationship as perceived and reported by the mothers was "the only characteristic common to the majority of children who appeared to be developing normally." In contrast, mothers of seven children who were found to be grossly disturbed reported poor mother/child relationships.

Martin *et al.* (1974) found that 29 out of 58 children assessed "were rated as currently living in a punitive environment." The median IQ of these children was ten points lower than those not living in a punitive environment, which was defined as "current excessive physical punishment (such as belt whipping and severe spanking) and/or obvious rejection or hostility toward the child." Seventy-two per cent of the natural parents were categorized as having emotional difficulties which significantly interfered with their daily functioning. Common personality traits noted were "marked dependence, social isolation, low self-esteem, low frustration tolerance and poor control of aggressive impulses" (Martin and Beezley, 1977). Twenty homes were rated as "unstable", as defined in Chapter IX, and thirty-two per cent of the children were living in such homes (Martin et al., 1974).

Children who were neglected rather than abused also have significantly disturbed parents on follow-up. Hufton and Oates (1977), in their follow-up of 21 children with non-organic failure-to-thrive, found that nine out of 13 mothers assessed described themselves as "suffering from depression", two of whom were being treated. One of the 12 fathers was a paranoid schizophrenic receiving treatment.

In the British study by Taitz (1980), described in the last chapter, it was found that "a parental history of psychiatric illness or disturbance" is the factor which most distinguishes the children who had an "unsatisfactory" outcome from those with a "satisfactory" outcome. In all, in 22 out of 47 families there was a "parental psychiatric problem."

Thus, from the limited evidence that does exist in the literature, one would anticipate finding a large number of serious family problems persisting some years after abuse has been identified.

II. THE PARENTS

The information given in this chapter will be for the 33 natural families where there were 32 mothers and 26 fathers. As already stated, there were 70 children living in these families: 30 abused children and 40 siblings.

Before considering the relationships in the families as a whole, we will describe the parents, both as individuals and as partners. As we saw in Chapter II describing the families' admission, personal problems for the parents played a large part in the process that led up to the abuse. It was therefore important to find out how they felt on follow-up. Time was given to the parents to talk about themselves, mainly after the detailed questions concerning their children, and very few did not wish to talk at length.

A. Health: physical and psychological

At the time of abuse the parents were under stress that often was associated with ill-health. Therefore on follow-up we were interested in details of this aspect of their lives. Enquiries were made about physical and psychological symptoms, medication, visits to the family doctor and referrals to psychiatrists. Information was also collected on alcohol intake, smoking and weight problems. Our main findings are summarized in Table 28.

Ill-health in the parents was classified in the same way as for the children in Chapter V. Thus a parent was considered to have had a significant health problem during the follow-up interval if he/she had had a serious acute or chronic illness or a minor chronic/recurrent illness. A total of 15 (47%) mothers and seven (30%) fathers gave a history of such health problems. Three mothers and one father were suffering from a serious physical condition at the time of follow-up. The diagnoses for the mothers were diabetes, multiple sclerosis and severe pelvic inflammatory disease. The father had chronic heart failure. The rest reported suffering from a serious acute or minor recurrent physical health problem at some time during the follow-up interval.

Table 28 Health problems in the parents

	At any time in follow-up		Current	
	Mothers	Fathers	Mothers	Fathers
Physical ill-health	15 (47%)	7 (30%)	3 (9%)	1 (4%)
Psychological problems	15 (47%)	6 (26%)	12 (38%)	3 (13%)
Regular medication			13 (41%)	1 (4%)
Heavy drinking			5 (16%)	2 (9%)
Heavy smoking			4 (13%)	6 (26%)
Weight problem			5 (16%)	3 (13%)

Mothers: $n = 32$; fathers: $n = 23$ (3 fathers not present at interview)

Many of these parents were complaining of symptoms which might well have been psychosomatic: constant headaches, back pain and tiredness. A typical response to the question about their health was from one mother: "I have a headache every day — I've got one now."

In addition to physical symptoms, 15 mothers and six fathers had suffered psychological disturbances during the follow-up period, the majority giving a history of "depression" or "nerves". Ten mothers and six fathers had been referred to a psychiatrist at some time during the follow-up interval and two mothers and two fathers had made suicide attempts. Twelve mothers (38%) and three fathers (13%) were declaring current psychological problems, including one father who was the only parent still attending a psychiatric clinic.

Thirteen mothers (41%) and one father were on regular medication at the time of follow-up. This father and eight mothers (25%) were on psychotropic drugs. According to a survey of prescriptions made during one year for a population of about 40 000 people, 9.7% of males and 21% of females were prescribed at least one psychotropic drug. However, the rates for more than five prescriptions per year were much lower: 2.5% for males and 6.9% for females. As most of the parents in our sample were on repeat prescriptions, it is in this fact that we find a difference between ours and the general population (Skegg et al., 1977). The diabetic mother was on insulin and the remainder talked of such things as migraine pills and regular analgesics for headaches.

In addition to recording the parents' perceptions of their own health, as with the children, we asked the family doctors about the parents' health and the number of times they had been seen in the previous year. As expected, not all the health problems reported by these parents were confirmed by their general practitioners. However, there was an indication that the parents attended the doctor more frequently than the general population. The average number of attendances for the women was 6.2 per year and 90% had seen their GP within the last year compared with a population rate of 74%. The men had an average of 2.4 visits a year recorded and 76% had seen their GP within the last year, compared with a population rate of 58% (H.M.S.O., 1979). The family doctors confirmed that the main reasons for attendance were psychosomatic complaints. However, before ascribing a high incidence of psychological disorder to the parents in our sample, it is worth remembering that Brown et al. (1975) found 42% of urban working class mothers who have a child less than 6 years old tend to show signs of depression to the extent that they were "judged to have suffered from a definite psychiatric disorder."

Following completion of the interviews, it became clear to the interviewer that there was a distinct group of parents (six mothers and one father: 13% of the parents seen) who at the time of home visit were considered to be suffering from serious emotional instability. All the interviews involving these parents were longer than average and elicited bizarre replies.

These parents were different from the depresssed parents or those overwhelmed by social problems. All but two had had contact with the psychiatric services. For example, the father in this category had an over-riding obsession about his "noisy neighbours." He stated categorically that he was prepared to go to prison to get rid of his neighbours. During the interview he repeatedly turned back many questions about unrelated topics to the problem with the neighbours. Yet, during the home visit there were no noises to be heard, in spite of many cautionary trips to the front door "to check". He was smoking 60-80 cigarettes a day and was extremely tense. The obsession was having an effect on the children: they were all over 4 years yet wetting the bed every night. According to their father, the noise from the neighbours was directly causing the enuresis.

A severe example among the mothers was a woman who had a strange, morbid preoccupation with death which seemed to be related to the death of her mother a few years previously. She claimed that when her pet dog died, she could not accept it and left the body in the dog basket for several weeks afterwards. She then complained at length about cattle trampling over the dog's "lovely grave." As was typical with this small group of parents, she was incoherent at times, lost her train of thought, did not finish sentences and kept on turning the questions back to the topic that was her particular interest: death.

The parents were asked about their drinking and smoking habits and whether they had a weight problem. By our definition of "more than two or three drinks every day", five mothers and two fathers admitted to being heavy drinkers. For this group the classification was quite clear: for example, one single mother said that she *only* drank "about" one bottle of wine a day and another single mother said that she usually had 6-8 whiskies in the evening. In fact, all these seven parents admitted to having, or having had, a drink problem. By the Royal College of Physicians' definition of a "heavy smoker" (1977) i.e. one who smokes 25 or more cigarettes daily, only four mothers and six fathers were found to be heavy smokers. Five mothers and three fathers had a weight problem in that they were significantly over-weight and wishing to reduce and three mothers were underweight and felt that they would like to gain weight but were unable to. As 12% of

adult males and females under 49 years in a London borough have
been shown to be moderately or severely obese, these proportions are
not significant (Baird *et al.*, 1974).

At the time of follow-up, only five mothers (16%) and 12 fathers
(52%) declared none of these health problems; 12 mothers and four
fathers currently had two or more and this included five out of seven
single mothers. As one would expect, the more ill-health the parents
had, the more disturbed we found their family life.

B. The marriage

In the literature, abusing parents have been noted for their marital instability with high rates of separation and therefore we asked a
number of questions to ascertain whether this was also true for our
sample. As we saw in the last chapter, eight marriages had broken
down by the time of follow-up but in addition to that, we asked all the
parents seen whether they had, or had had, serious marital and sexual
problems. The results of our enquiry are summarized in Table 29. Nine
parents, including only one couple, claimed to have serious current
marital problems. The wife was usually more willing to admit the difficulties and in three cases the husband did not turn up for the
interview despite it being arranged at a time convenient to him. It
appeared that fathers were more willing to admit marital problems in
the past and couples were more in agreement about past marital strife.
An example of a severe current problem is one where the father of the
family was clearly having an affair with another woman which the wife
and children knew about. This had been a firm and long-standing relationship but the father had never formally separated from his wife.
The atmosphere this created in the home was one of extreme tension

Table 29   Marital and sexual problems

	At any time in follow-up		Current	
	Mothers	Fathers	Mothers	Fathers
Marital problems	16 (50%)	10 (43%)	7 (22%)	2 (9%)
Sexual problems	14 (44%)	10 (43%)	10 (31%)	5 (22%)

Mothers: $n = 32$; fathers: $n = 23$ (3 fathers not present at interview) and the parents contradicted each other frequently. The mother said her marriage was fine and the father claimed it to be terrible and said he was not joking. The mother said that she was not satisfied with her sexual relationship and the father claimed that his was great. Throughout the interview the mother made snide remarks about "the other woman" and disclaimed any responsibility for problems in the marriage. The children in this family were amongst the most disturbed in the sample.

As with the general marital problems, when it came to discussing sexual relationships it was once again the wives who admitted to difficulties. However, five couples were in agreement that they had current sexual problems. The parents were reluctant to go into detail but the problem most often mentioned was one of excessive tiredness and loss of libido in the wife. To quote one dissatisfied husband: "It's like a monk, living with her!" One couple had actually sought professional help for their problems which they had then resolved.

It is worth noting that 13 out of 25 couples (52%) appeared to have no current problems within their marriage. They demonstrated this to the researchers in the way they shared the information about the family and their past: if they disagreed it was amicably — they could talk about their problems in the past with confidence because they had actually overcome them. The interviews with some of these couples were enjoyable. One father even arranged transport from an airport to his home, the wife greeted the interviewer with a superb lunch and the whole family waved her off on a bus into town. Meanwhile the family had talked frankly during the interview about very serious problems they had had in the past. They were even able to describe early abuse incidents which were not known about during their admission.

C. Aggression

As the families are by definition those with a problem with violence, the parents were asked about loss of temper; three fathers and eight mothers said they lost their temper more or less every day. One father confessed that he saw red "at the drop of a hat". Another said he came to blows daily with his wife but "I only hit her when she hits me!" The third father was having serious difficulty disciplining his 8-year old son and described losing control when trying to do so. The mothers who said they lost their temper every day varied from the quiet ones who seemed to have a very good relationship with their kids and who made comments like: "I do swear, but I feel it all inside really", to mothers who were having serious difficulties coping with their children, such as one woman who said: "D. fell out of his pram and I smacked him — my nerves are getting frayed. I can go berserk — bang things about — I don't beat the kids, just cry a lot."

Among the parents losing their temper daily were two of those with a drink problem, three mothers on Librium or Valium and the only father on a benzodiazipine (Norbrium). Two other mothers on tranquillizers said they lost their temper at least once a week. Once again we think we were seeing the disinhibiting effect of these drugs leading to an adult's diminished ability to control feelings of aggression (Lynch *et al.*, 1975). Five couples volunteered the information that for them marital rows involved physical violence.

III. THE CHILDREN

As a way of trying to understand the parents' relationships with their children, we asked many questions about the children's behaviour in the home, their habits and their development. It was these discussions which enabled the parents who still had problems in their relationships with their children to describe their difficulties to us.

A. Behaviour in the home: parents' reports

To encourage the parents to talk about problems they were having with their children's behaviour, we focused initially on the three activities of eating, sleeping and toilet training. In our experience with abusing families and in general child psychiatry we have found that parents' complaints about their children in these areas often indicate a more general underlying problem (Rutter, 1975). The type of behaviour complained about by parents in difficulty with their children is frequently not identified as problematic by parents who have no major relationship difficulties with their children. A study which compared children attending psychiatric clinics and those not attending found both groups to have roughly comparable rates of disorder but the clinic-attending group were much more likely to be from disrupted homes, their mothers were more likely to see themselves as "suffering from nerves" and much more likely to feel worried about their children's problems (Shepherd *et al.*, 1971). With our group of families the commonest problem the parents had with the children was that of toilet training, including enuresis. At the time of follow-up, nine out of 30 abused children (30%) and 11 out of 40 siblings (28%) were causing their parents difficulties in toileting. For 15 of the children (21%) all aged 4 or more, the complaint was of bed-wetting, together with soiling in two cases. One of these was a 10-year old abused child who was exhibiting very bizarre anal-orientated behaviour such as wiping her bottom with the dish-cloth during washing up. Another mother with very high expectations of her 18-month old complained bitterly that it was taking a very long time to potty-train him. A further five abused children had had toileting problems during the follow-up interval, but these had been resolved by the time of follow-up. To put this information into perspective, it is worth recording that one in five children at the age of 7 years still wets the bed occasionally and about one in 14 does so at the age of 10 years (Rutter, 1975).

We were interested to discover the parents' attitudes to toilet training, expecting a high proportion to have rigid ideas for their children. Eleven out of 32 mothers did expect their children to be clean and dry day and night by the time they were 2 years old. One mother even expected successful toilet training to be achieved when a child was only 12 months old, and claimed to have succeeded in this with her first daughter. Only two fathers had such high expectations of their children but, predictably, were far less likely to give any opinion. The rest of the parents who expressed their ideas either felt each child was different or had realistic general expectations — often adding that they were only going by their experience with their own children.

Ten children (five abused and five siblings) were having sleeping difficulties at the time of follow-up. With young children, interrupted nights accompanied by crying is so common as to be considered "normal". For example, in the Newsons' study of 12-month old babies in Nottingham, 35% of the mothers reported that the baby had woken in the night previous to the interview and nearly all had required attention (Newson and Newson, 1963). However, in our sample it was not the youngest group who presented problems. Indeed, all those under 2 years were said to have had no sleeping difficulties. The ten with problems were all over 2½ years and the eldest was almost 9 years old. For the two youngest children in the problem group, the difficulty was the familiar one of frequent waking and crying. For both, this had happened several times in the previous week. For two older children, the problem was that of nightmares. One boy, for example, had dreamt the night prior to the interview that someone had got into the house and killed his mother. He was screaming when his mother reached him because the killers would not let him have his mother's body. Three other children were a problem in getting to bed: all of them had finally gone to bed at 11.00 p.m. the night before the interviews.

Problems associated with eating were slightly less common: five abused and three siblings were considered to have current problems by their parents. All these children were thought not to be eating enough food. Four of the older children would take as long as $1\frac{1}{2}-2$ hours over a meal. The parents who volunteered this as a problem were obviously very concerned to get the food into the child. One mother stated that her 5-year old daughter was made to sit at her meal and had sometimes been sick over the plate. Another mother said that she smacked the hand of her 15-month old baby and made him sit in front of his food. Elsewhere she stated that the baby was still having several bottles of milk a day. A couple of the children resorted to the tactics of putting food in the mouth and keeping it shut but full. Obviously, from the comments the parents made, meal-time was the scene of a battle for these children. Some parents described similar feeding battles in the past but they had found ways round the problem. One mother told the interviewer that her 6-year old daughter had "gone on hunger strike because she didn't want to grow big because she would have to leave home if she did!" This little girl had spent 15 months in a children's home. Of the seven children who had at some time evidence of failure-to-thrive, only three were described by their parents as having had feeding difficulties.

Looking at the three problems grouped together, four abused children and three siblings had more than one problem at the time of follow-up. A total of 12 abused (40%) and 13 siblings (33%) had at least one current behaviour problem reported by their parents. However, in 17 out of 33 families, parents reported no behaviour problems at all at the follow-up interview. This group includes all the families about whom we felt no concern and where the atmosphere in the home was that of an apparently normal, happy family. For example, one interview could not begin before the children had gone to bed because of their insistence on the researcher's participation in the bed-time ritual of drinks, reading stories, cleaning teeth, etc. One of these children was severely neurologically handicapped but the atmosphere in the home was one of warmth and humour.

Another common problem encountered by parents is the temper tantrum. The parents in our sample were asked about their children's "temper tantrums" during the week prior to the interview. If they considered the child had had a tantrum, they were asked to describe the child's behaviour during it and their ways of dealing with such outbursts. Three abused children aged 8, 5 and 4, were reported to have had a temper tantrum during the day of the interview, as were five siblings who had a wide age range from 10 months to over 7 years.

In all, 32 children (46%) were reported to have had a temper tantrum within the week previous to the interview. The descriptions of the tantrums are very similar to those described by the Newsons in "Four Years Old in an Urban Community" (1968). Typical brief descriptions were: "He shouts, screams, kicks and bangs the door" and: "she pulls her hair out, bangs her head, hits and kicks." As the Newsons write: "It is characteristic of the temper tantrum that aggression is rather generalized in its expression, directed against the environment as a whole and sometimes also against the child himself." Thirty-six per cent of their sample had tantrums as often as once a week. However, it must also be remembered that our age range was wider.

Thirty-three per cent of Newson's sample were smacked for their tantrums. In our sample, 23 out of 32 children (72%) who had had a tantrum within the last week had been smacked and occasionally beaten for it. It was during the detailed descriptions of tantrums and the parents' way of dealing with them that we were alerted to some of the more worrying child-rearing practices in the families. For example, one 8-year old boy had had a temper tantrum that day, according to his parents, and did so practically every day of his life. When asked what he did, the father said that "he screams and bawls." The mother interrupted: "Even before you hit him, he screams terribly," to which the father added: "I say to him he could win an Oscar! I occasionally take the whip to him and miss and he goes screaming dramatically down the corridor and collapses in a heap." When asked what they did in response to the tantrums, the father replied: "I give them as good as they give us — I shout back!" This child had recently been referred to an educational psychologist for help with his "conduct disorder" both at home and at school. However, the parents' responses to our questions give some clue as to the aetiology of his difficult behaviour. One mother described her 6-year old son's tantrums and stated. "It's very much like Bertie was and I had Bertie put away for it, but I was younger then." She went on. "I end up smacking their legs, including the baby. They took more notice of their father because he used to smack 'em more."

Very rarely did any parent talk about diverting a child's attention or reinforcing positive behaviour, although several times children were said to have been cuddled or held tight until their outburst was over. The Newsons noted that there was a considerable class difference in the frequency rates of temper tantrums. However, with one exception, all the higher social class families in our sample had a child in the frequent temper tantrum group (i.e. at least once a week). There were often differences within families, only nine families having all their children in the frequent group.

B. Discipline

The discussion of temper tantrums naturally led on to the topic of discipline. The parents were asked some general questions: "What do you consider naughty or wrong?" "What do you do when he/she is naughty?" "What do you think you should do?" The answers to these questions brought up rather more reasonable behaviour than the angry scenes just previously described during temper tantrums. The most common childhood crime in these homes was disobedience, which the Newsons also found to be the most likely cause of punishment (Newson and Newson, 1968), followed by destructiveness, answering back, lying and stealing (only one family volunteered "stealing" and the father had served a prison sentence for this crime himself). There was a variety of other deeds catalogued by the parents as requiring punishment: the most common were acts of aggression, then bad manners such as "interrupting an adult's conversation" and then particular misdeeds such as one child "not cleaning her teeth or doing her scales." As to be expected, the parents most commonly resorted to smacking as a means of punishment: 24 out of 33 (72%) usually smacked the children but nearly all these families had other punishments in their repertoire. The next common retribution was that of excluding the child, e.g. sending him to his bedroom; then withdrawal of privileges.

Five families talked openly about "beatings". One has already been described in the section on temper tantrums. Another mother with a 5-year old, whom she had always picked on from birth, stated: "I have just given Ray two strokes of the slipper because he disobeyed me three times." She explained that she had called him three times and he had not replied. Her oldest son then popped his head round the door and showed his mother that she had completely split the slipper in two. Talking about her youngest, a 15-month old, she said: "I use my tone of voice or a good, hard smack. I hate hearing kids scream. I could be lying to you now and you wouldn't know. I don't believe in beating, like my father." Another mother who told us: "I get the belt out and send them upstairs to bed after it", frankly stated that she was certain she was doing the right thing. When asked what she thought she should do, she replied: "What I do, because that upsets them a hell of a lot!" A father, who also believed in physical punishment, stated: "They've got to learn severe discipline before they start to proper school." One mother, looking back on the beatings she had given her son before he was taken into care some years previously, said: "I really smacked him that hard that I bruised his backside or even fetched blood and I said 'If somebody don't come and take him away, you'll find a dead child in the house.' I couldn't take any more! These others don't know what a good hiding is!''

It must be stressed that not all the children who we felt were suffering from social or emotional deprivation or who were otherwise at risk were living in the families who indulged in severe punishment. Smacking and beating seem to be only one aspect of continuing child abuse. The number of smacks and shouts made during the interview were recorded. In only two families were children smacked. One was the 4½-year old girl sibling of twins who had been behaving as provocatively as she could to gain attention from her mother: she had resorted to flicking a tea-towel in her mother's face. Finally she provoked her younger sibling and made her cry, for which she was smacked. Her parents showed no interest in diverting her to play with her toys but expected her to sit quietly during the interview. Another child, a 1-year old baby sibling, was smacked for throwing his food over the floor. A more worrying incident was when a mother raised her hand to her daughter who then flinched and cowered with a very frightened expression. This mother had previously described how during a shopping trip she had taken her daughter to the ladies' toilet in order to smack her for punishment for wanting an article which the mother had said she could not have. This description of calm, cold and deliberately private punishment was more worrying than the angry outburst common to many mothers, even those who say they do not believe in smacking.

Of the total 46 children present during at least part of the interview, 16 from 11 families were shouted at in anger at least once and ten more than once. Interestingly, the frequency of shouting correlated with our anxiety about those families. One family shouted at the abused child at least nine times during the interview and at least ten times at the two siblings. Likewise, another family had a total of at least 17 shouts at the three children. With the mother's shouting and the children's persistent screaming, the interviewer left with a headache and listening to the tape afterwards was a nightmare! This was a family who had all the outward appearances of good, clean-living, hard working, middle-class citizens. Because of our concern about the mother's ability to cope with her three children, we strongly recommended the two younger children's daily attendance at a local playgroup. So extreme was this mother's desire to assuage her guilt that she had tried to avoid all substitute care for her children, with the end result of screaming chaos.

It is necessary to put this information on corporal punishment, smacking and shouting into perspective. The Newsons' study (1968) demonstrates how entrenched British attitudes are about the rightful use of corporal punishment. Any comments about diverting or reinforcing good behaviour are likely to get the pejorative label of "psychology". Seventy-five per cent of all Nottingham mothers smacked their 4-year olds at least once a week. Some of the descriptions in this book, of mothers losing control when smacking, of children looking terrified and cowering at their mother's approach, of mothers' open use of the belt or the wooden spoon on a bare bottom, or the stick, show that one should be very careful when assessing the relative importance of corporal punishment in already labelled "abusing" families. The most striking observation made by us was that in some families, if severe corporal punishment was inflicted, only one child was chosen to receive it and that seemed to be of more significance than the general rate of smacking in the home.

C. Development: parents' opinion

The parents were asked for their opinion on their child's physical and intellectual development. We intended to exclude judgements based solely on the child's behaviour but this was not always possible to achieve, especially when the parent was preoccupied with a behaviour problem. It must also be remembered that the home interview was taking place after the children's assessment at the hospital. The question about development was designed to enable the parents to give their opinion as to whether a child was advanced, normal or delayed. There emerged a group of 15 children (seven abused and eight siblings) considered to show delayed development by the researchers, but whom the parents considered advanced (three abused and three siblings) or normal (four abused and five siblings). None of the children who were growth-retarded on follow-up were perceived as under-sized by their parents. In some families, siblings were seen as advanced in direct contrast to the abused child who was somewhat delayed. Also the brightest child in a family was often perceived as advanced by the parents when they still came within the "normal" range on objective assessment.

Two abused children were identified as delayed by their parents although both were assessed by us as intellectually advanced. One, a very bright little 4-year old, was considered as delayed by his mother simply because he had been slow, according to her expectations, in being potty-trained. The other, an intelligent and delightful 5-year old, was perceived as delayed by her mother because of her inhibited behaviour at home which was likely to be a direct result of her mother's rejection. One other abused child with normal intelligence was seen as delayed because of his clumsiness.

Because of our concern about the high rate of language delay among the children we had seen, the parents were asked specifically whether they considered their children's language development to be normal. There was very little correlation between our findings and the parents' opinions. Usually this was because the parents had failed to notice even gross language delay but occasionally it was because of unrealistically high expectations of the rate at which language should be acquired. This information from the parents provided further illustration of how their relationship with a child could affect their perception of his/her development and how often they were unable to appreciate both the child's difficulties and his strengths.

IV. PARENT/CHILD RELATIONSHIP: PARENTS' VIEW

Apart from the open acts of aggression and visible signs of child abuse, we were concerned to obtain information from the parents about their feelings for their children. A number of questions, both direct and indirect, were devised with this aim in mind. Direct questions were asked, such as: "How do you get on with X?" and: "Is this different from before?" Parents were then asked to describe what they especially liked or disliked about their children and to describe both their good and bad points. They were also asked to sum up each child in one word or one sentence. It was in the more indirect questions that problems in relationships were highlighted.

Firstly, we found some parents overtly declaring feelings of not wanting their child or not loving him the way they would wish. Sometimes the parents even made comments of rejection about children who were already in long-term care. For five out of 70 children still at home, five mothers and one father made very rejecting remarks. All these five children had been abused. Comments were: "I don't want to cuddle her." "I push Daniel away from me — I don't like physical contact — he's too clingy." Of a mentally handicapped child, the mother stated: "I resent her pretty face." And the father: "I would rather she were in a wheel-chair. Life would have been easier without her." Another mother said: "I feel as if he's not my child. I wanted to hurt him so much and he wasn't even naughty! It feels as though I didn't give birth to him." Then, finally, a single mother commented on her 5-year old: "I resent her existence: she cramps my life-style."

Obviously, some of the underlying bonding failure in these cases continued, even though physical abuse stopped. We felt great concern about the emotional development of all these five children although not all of them were showing symptoms from this lack of maternal warmth. For example, a 5-year old girl whose mother, when asked to sum her up in one sentence, said: "Nothing really", was one of the nine abused children who were doing well in all areas of development and was a delightful child to be with. She seemed to be seeking and successfully finding emotional warmth from her stepfather and other adults in her life such as her teacher, an aunt and a friend of her mother's. The mother constantly complained that her daughter spent more time in her friend's household than her own . Only two of these five children's names were on the social services "At Risk" register at the time of follow-up and three of them were living in homes where the general standard of parenting was extremely good. It was only when these parents talked about their other children that the scapegoating of the one child was highlighted.

To move on from extreme examples of rejection, we then found numerous illustrations of how difficult the parents found their children. As few parents experience no difficulties with their children, we must be careful about the interpretation of some of these comments but we have tried to concentrate on those children where the negative comments outweigh the positive ones. Fifteen mothers and three fathers claimed serious difficulties with 23 children (11 abused and 12 siblings). This included the five mentioned above. These difficulties ranged from a general dislike of all the children to insightful understanding of relationship difficulties with a particular child. For example, one mother was finding difficulty coping with all her children. "It's very trying that I'm the only person who exists for them — all of them!" Although she had a very stable and long-term relationship with her co-habitee, she was unable to use his support. Another mother (a single parent) said: "I don't think I've got a relationship with my children like other people — sitting down to talk an' that." Other mothers talked about feelings of rejection: "We don't get on at all well. I can't stand her screaming, her defiance, her lies." (This child was still being abused.) Of another daughter she said: "I feel I could do the same to her as I did to Tanya." Of a young 2-year old sibling, one mother said: "I find it a struggle to get on with Lucy. She's spiteful, a little devil. I find it easy to dislike her." One mother of a 5-year old girl sibling said: "She's very prickly. We're two people who rub each other up the wrong way. It'll be better when she leaves home."

V. INTERVIEWER'S OBSERVATIONS OF THE FAMILY

In addition to information given directly by the parents, the interviewer obviously formed an impression of what the family were like at home. In most families there was an opportunity to see parents and children together although the children may not have been there throughout the interview. The interviewer had transported some families to the follow-up assessment at the Park Hospital and this provided further opportunity to form an impression of the family relationships. By going into the home, the interviewer was able to gain a valuable insight into the effect the home environment could be having on the child.

A. Parent/child interaction

Originally it was not planned to make systematic observations of parent/child interactions apart from the aggressive outbursts already described. However, for those families where the children were present, certain impressions were formed and recorded.

One of the over-riding general observations was that a number of these children were exceptionally quiet and controlled during the interview or extremely independent for their age in that they made few, if any, demands of their parents' attention for over an hour. For example, a 4-year old girl left the interview at the beginning and went to play downstairs out of earshot. When she returned much later she had prepared herself a meal which she then took away to eat. Another 3-year old boy sat totally still and silently on his father's lap throughout an hour-long interview, only making very occasional whispered comments to his father. These compliant children were a great contrast to those children in more relaxed families who were able to play independently but made more frequent and often boisterous interruptions which were dealt with quickly and positively by their parents. In retrospect, considering the young age of many of the children, the interviews were remarkably easy to conduct. Often the compliant behaviour at home was in great contrast to the behaviour reported outside the home — the same children being described as aggressive and disruptive at school. An extreme example is an 11-year old lad who sat on his father's lap with a very worried expression throughout the interview and yet was attending a school for the maladjusted because of his extreme antisocial behaviour in the classroom.

A few children produced unusual and worrying behaviour. For example, one compliant 3-year old wept silently for some time when she knew that the interviewer was about to leave. The mother commented: "Don't worry, she's always doing it."

Occasionally it appeared to be that the abused child continued to be the odd-one-out. For example, a 6-year old boy was the only child absent from the sitting-room during the interview. It took his parents longer than an hour to notice his absence with: "Where's Simon then?" and he came in very timidly, wringing his hands. He sat for a while quietly observing his siblings at play, only to return to his bedroom to play by himself later on.

B. Child care in the home

Having collected together impressions and observations during the home interview and at other times, we felt a general concern about the quality of the home environment in 13 households containing 29 children. The concern was not necessarily connected with the warmth of the parent/child relationship, rather in some families with the general poor quality of the child care and in others with the serious lack of opportunities in the home for normal social development. In only one or two cases were there diffuse relationship problems producing an overwhelming atmosphere of hostility.

The following five examples illustrate the types of families who gave us concern and the range of problems we encountered:

(1) One 4½-year old little girl lived with her mother in temporary accommodation. The mother admitted to drinking at least a bottle of wine a day and talked about numerous people and places where she sent her daughter while she pursued her active social life. In spite of this, the child seemed to have little contact with other children. Shortly after the follow-up assessment, this mother disappeared to the States, only to return a few months later having neglected a number of medical appointments for her daughter who had a serious eye defect.

(2) Another single mother had a great deal of warmth for her child. However, there were signs of serious neglect such as the child being brought home by a policeman first thing in the morning. He had to wake the mother who was still in bed asleep, unaware that her son had even left the house! She sent him to playgroup in a taxi, alone, and was seldom there to fetch him in the evening.

(3) A third family, despite living in a social services rehabilitation centre, kept a very dirty and sordid home. Their baby daughter's development was surprisingly normal but the mother had such a flat and peculiar affect

that there was serious concern that the family would not survive much longer, especially as the mother was pregnant. The father, throughout the interview, kept returning to describe his violent temper which he thought stemmed from his childhood when he was kept in a cellar by his grandmother who used to stick pins into a straw dog and say: "Nigel die!" He had then gone to live with his father who regularly beat him. Both parents had taken repeated overdoses and made attempts on their lives by self-injury. We felt they had a low threshold for aggression which even a normal child would have put to the test. In fact, after the second child was born, it was severely battered and rendered mentally handicapped.

(4) In a fourth family we were concerned that the strained, tense and unpleasant atmosphere in the home was having an effect on the children. The mother was suffering a severe degree of multiple sclerosis, a totally dissatisfying marriage and family life. The parents described frequent scenes of the wife abusing her daughter and swearing, only to be followed by the husband thrashing his wife for abusing the child. There were already signs of severe emotional disturbance in two out of the three children and both had very high scores of maladjustment on the teachers' questionnaires. The third daughter, who at the time of follow-up was least affected, took an overdose several years later.

(5) A more subtle form of deprivation was seen in an upper social class family. When challenged by the researchers that she might actually think more of her horses than her children, the mother replied: "No, . . . about the same I should think." The children's lives had to fit in with the horses' requirements and on the day of the follow-up asessment they would have gone without food all day, had not the interviewer insisted on buying some sandwiches.

Not every child in these 13 families was showing evidence of social and emotional deprivation. In fact, seven out of the 29 children in these households were doing well on all aspects of the follow-up assessment and showed no overt signs of emotional disturbance. One thing that they had in common was that they were extremely likeable children.

Because of our concern about these 13 families, we were interested to see how many of them had children whose names were included on the social services "At Risk" register. Ten families had at least the name of the abused child on the register but in only three families were siblings included. For one family this meant that the only member to be included on the register was the abused child in permanent care, away from the household! The three families who did not have a child's name on the register were receiving very regular social work help. Thus we were relieved to find that all these 13 families were considered by the social services department to have some priority.

VI. DISCUSSION

As found in the few studies from the literature, parents who have abused their children in the past often continue to have individual psychological and marital problems. The mothers especially in our group so frequently described recurrent minor complaints such as headaches, that it seemed a substantial number were still under some sort of stress at the time of follow-up. Very few mothers suffered from no personal medical or psychological problems on follow-up and over a third were suffering from two or more problems. It must be remembered that these parents were being given much time and encouragement to talk about such difficulties but it is interesting that so many of them subjectively felt that they were suffering. The low rate of serious ill-health in our parents on follow-up is the main aspect in which there seems to have been marked improvement.

On the other hand, the parents had considerably improved as couples and some of the least stable marriages had ended during the follow-up interval. Some marital problems did remain and the interviewer witnessed a few obviously very unhappy marriages. Almost a third of mothers were still claiming to have sexual problems but these varied in their importance and impact on the marriage as a whole. The marriages which the parents claimed to be bad did not all have the children with declared behaviour problems and all but two had at least one child who featured in the children who did well who are described in the next chapter. In only two out of the eight declared bad marriages was it obvious to the interviewer that the children were suffering emotionally.

The parents were, in general, being very open about all their personal problems and in no case did the interviewer detect that the marriage was at serious risk where the parents were not disclosing the information. However, it is worth noting that for three of the bad marriages the fathers did not turn up for the pre-arranged interview. Usually the parents still wished to discuss with the interviewer their own problems and gain some attention for themselves. One or two were still desperate to obtain the interviewer's sympathy and understanding of the problems they were suffering prior to the abuse incident.

As has been described, a few of the families were still fairly frequently violent and demonstrated that hitting out at those closest to them was their way of dealing with anger and frustration. This was not simply a cultural matter as it did not only feature in the lower class families: rather the families with current problems of violence were those with the very disturbed parents and the very poor marriages. Although most of the children in these families were no longer being abused, the violent and disturbed conditions which contributed to the original abuse still existed.

For those who have to make an assessment of a child's safety in the home, it is worth noting that it was only through comprehensive questioning about all the children in the family, and parents' attitudes to many aspects of child-rearing that the potential risk to some individual children was made clear. Usually it was when answers were compared with those made on other children in the family that one child stood out as being treated or perceived differently. Also, when given enough time to talk about themselves and their family, these parents were all prepared to describe honestly their feelings for their children.

As some parents obviously had very distorted views of the child's development, it was extremely useful for us to demonstrate the child's particular skills and weaknesses to the parents. For example, with one boy who was exceptionally clumsy, but bright, when this was demonstrated as a specific problem and when the parents were given simple commonsense methods of dealing with his clumsiness and helping him to improve, their whole relationship with the child altered and he became for them a far less "difficult" child. Other parents, when they realized how well their abused child was performing compared to the expected for their age, went away glowing with pride and renewed enthusiasm to make up for the problems in the past. Much guilt for past actions was allayed when we could demonstrate to the parents their children's obvious achievements.

It is quite clear from this chapter that a few of the families continued to have very serious relationship problems, years after the abuse incident, but perhaps it is encouraging that all but one of them were receiving current social work services. Obviously for some families an actual abuse incident is only part of a long-term problem and even the unique services which the Park Hospital could provide could not help all. But this chapter has concentrated on the problems and yet again we end with the emphasis that over half of these families were striking for their stability and the interviewer had the strong sensation that the parents had matured considerably since the time of crisis and admission to the Park Hospital. Most of the parents openly described the problems in the past but felt they had overcome them. Of the families seen, only one or two showed any reluctance to take part in the project. Considering the researchers were from the Park Hospital and concerned with the problem of child abuse, it was interesting how willingly parents did discuss their problems with their children. Those who were still having serious problems and not receiving help were told of the interviewer's concern and readily agreed to receiving further services. They were not, on the whole, the suspicious, threatened people we had met previously. Most of the parents stated fervently that they wished to participate in the study to help all other families who might at some time find themselves in the same predicament.

SUMMARY OF FINDINGS

(Data from 33 families: 70 children, 32 mothers and the 23 fathers interviewed.)

(1)   Fifteen (47%) mothers and seven (30%) fathers had a history of a significant health problem during the follow-up interval. Three mothers and one father were suffering from a serious physical condition at the time of follow-up.

(2)   Fifteen mothers and six fathers gave a history of psychological disturbance during the follow-up interval. For 12 (38%) mothers and three (13%) fathers the problem was a current one. For six mothers and one father there was evidence of severe emotional instability during the home interview.

(3)   The parents had attended their family doctors more frequently than the general population. Many of their complaints were psychosomatic in nature.

(4)   The more ill-health suffered by the parents, the more disturbed we found the family life.

(5)   Forty-eight per cent of the couples admitted current marital or sexual problems. The mothers were more willing to discuss these difficulties than were the fathers.

(6)   Eight mothers and three fathers mentioned they lost their tempers at least once every day. Five couples admitted that marital rows involved physical violence.

(7)   Twelve (40%) abused and 13 (33%) siblings were reported by their parents to have behaviour problems associated with eating and/or sleeping and/or toilet training. Four abused and three siblings had problems in more than one of these areas. Seventeen (52%) families reported no such problems in any of their children. The lack of reported problems correlated well with a good home atmosphere.

(8)   Thirty-two (46%) children were reported to have had at least one

temper tantrum during the week prior to the interview. Seventy-two per cent of the children had been smacked for their tantrums (cf. 33% in Newsons' study).

(9)   Seventy-two per cent of the parents used smacking as the commonest form of punishment. In five families there was open talk of beatings.

(10)   Fifteen children (seven abused, eight siblings) showed developmental delay that was not appreciated by the parents. On the other hand, there were three children identifed as "behind" by the parents who were of at least average ability.

(11)   Parents made very rejecting remarks to the interviewer about five abused children living at home.

(12)   The researchers felt general concern about the quality of the home environment in 13 households containing 29 children.

XI. The children who did well

In this book we have described in detail the status of 40 abused children followed up a mean of 4 years after discharge. Data have also been presented on 41 siblings living in the same families. Throughout it has been apparent that not all the children studied were growing up neurologically and intellectually handicapped or maladjusted. Some were obviously making excellent progress and were doing well, even when judged by the standards one would apply to a population of children being seen for example in child health clinics or normal schools. In this chapter we will describe the characteristics of these children who were problem-free at follow-up, look at differences between them and those with persistent problems and finally attempt to identify factors that were commonly associated with a problem-free status.

I. DEFINING "PROBLEM-FREE"

In the literature, studies on the development of the abused child, while giving high rates of subsequent handicap, tell us little about the abused child who survives and would be considered "normal" in all areas of his development. In reading the studies we find passing references to such children. For example, Morse et al. (1970) state that the only children in their sample to be judged within normal limits intellectually and emotionally had all lived continuously with their parents since the original diagnosis. Martin and Rodeheffer (1976) describe a small group of abused children (eight out of the sample of 58 studied in 1974 by Martin et al.) who were high achievers academically with IQ's one or more standard deviations above the mean. Martin postulates that there may be a significant bias in children who survive the

177

abusive environment, the more intelligent being able to perceive and meet parental expectations while duller children unable to do so are at greater risk of recurrent abuse, removal from home and foster breakdown.

Like these authors, we are interested in looking in further detail at the "survivors" in our sample. When defining "problem-free", we decided to restrict ourselves to objective measures which could be applied to the children as individuals. Therefore we did not consider evidence of positive change in the parents and improvement in their relationship with their child to be necessary before considering the child himself to be doing well. We concentrated on the child's own health, growth, development and behaviour. To qualify for the "problem-free" group, a child had to be healthy (no serious chronic ill-health), neurologically intact (no serious or moderate neurological impairment), well grown (height and weight over third centile), intellectually normal (normal developmental assessment; IQ over 75) and show no evidence of behavioural disturbance (not maladjusted on the B.S.A.G. questionnaire or deviant on Rutter's teacher's questionnaire — see Chapter VI). While no formal measure of behaviour was included for the pre-school child, it is unlikely that a young child with a severe behaviour problem would have been judged to be completely developmentally normal on the Sheridan assessment (see Chapter VI) because of interference of the behaviour in the testing.

In developing our criteria for "problem-free" status it was not our intention to equate directly such a status with effective intervention. As we have stated before, the main focus of our study was the description of the long-term problems experienced by abused children, not evaluation of intervention. It is clear for example that those children suffering permanent neurological handicap could not be classified as "problem-free" whatever their progress and however successful the intervention with their family.

II. RESULTS

All the 40* abused children and 41 siblings followed up by us were classified into the two categories "problem-free" or "with problems" at follow-up. On three children follow-up data were incomplete. One abused child had died; he obviously should be considered as having an unsatisfactory outcome. The data collections were incomplete on the other two (an abused child and her sibling) because of the mother's reluctance for us to approach the school. For analysis of the data these

*The dead child is included in the data in this chapter.

two have also been assigned to the group with problems as we were informed that they would have been labelled "maladjusted" by their teachers.

Out of the total of 81 children studied, 30 (37%) fulfilled all our criteria for "problem-free". This includes nine (23%) abused children and 21 (51%) siblings. The mean average age at the time of assessment was 5.3 years in the problem-free group and 5.9 years in the group with problems. Among the abused, equal proportions of boys (25%) and girls (21%) were in the problem-free group. Slightly more female siblings did well (57%) than males (45%). Table 30 shows the problem status at follow-up for the abused and sibling groups.

Table 30   Status at follow-up (81 children)

	Problem-free	With problems
Abused n = 40	9	31
Siblings n = 41	21	20

The difference between the two groups is statistically significant ($p = 0.014$ Fisher Exact Test: 2 tailed) and Table 31 shows that this difference is largely owing to the higher incidence of neurological problems among the abused children.

Table 31   Children with problems at follow-up (51 children)

	Health only	Growth only	Neurological and/or other problems	Intellectual and/or behavioural problems without neurological deficit
Abused n = 31	1	1	11	18
Siblings n = 20	—	—	3	17

Eleven were identified as having neurological handicap, though it must be remembered that such impairment was not always the direct result of abuse (Chapter V). Only two of the neurologically handicapped (one abused and one sibling) did not have other associated problems. Only three children had isolated problems of serious chronic ill-health (the haemophiliac child) or growth failure. Over half of the abused and the majority of the siblings who failed to reach the problem-free group did so because of developmental delay, intellectual retardation or behaviour problems which were not associated with neurological handicap. Such problems were considered together because the measures used for individuals differed according to their age, making more detailed analysis too complex. It was of course not uncommon for a child to have both developmental and behavioural problems.

When trying to identify factors associated with a problem-free status, because the numbers in our study are so small, it was only possible to consider one main variable at a time. Although we analysed many variables, we have selected for report only those which showed a significant difference between the "problem-free" and "with problems" groups or those variables which are interesting in that they did not show the difference we might have expected from earlier work. Initially the abused children and siblings will be considered separately.

III. THE ABUSED CHILDREN

A. Perinatal factors

The first factor looked at was abnormal labour or delivery which we once again defined as any labour lasting more than 24 hours, premature delivery (before 37 weeks) and any operative delivery (excluding easy lift-out forceps) (Lynch, 1975).

Among the group with problems, the incidence of complications in labour and delivery was significantly higher ($p = 0.023$ Fisher Exact Test: 1 tailed). Seventeen (55%) had experienced an abnormal labour or delivery compared with only one of the nine children in the problem-free group. None of the problem-free group had been born before 37 weeks' gestation but three had been small-for-dates at term. Among the group with problems, 12 babies were prematurely born, of whom four were also small-for-dates. One baby was small-for-dates at term (Table 32). Thus prematurity was associated with problems at follow-up ($p = 0.025$; Fisher Exact Test: 1 tailed) while just being small-for-dates was not. Only one of the problem-free group had required admission to the Special Care Unit. She was a severely ill, full-term baby. Fifteen of those with problems at follow-up had been admitted,

Table 32 Prematurity/small-for-dates

Status at follow-up	Pre-term Normal for dates	Pre-term/ Small for dates	Full-term Small for dates	Full-term Normal for dates
Problem-free n = 9	—	—	3	6
With problems n = 31	8 (26%)	4 (13%)	1	18

including all those who were pre-term and/or small-for-dates, and three additional full-term babies.

There is evidence in the child development literature of the compounding effect of an adverse home environment and perinatal problems. Werner *et al.* (1967), in their study of 670 live births in Kauai (Hawaii) in 1955, clearly illustrated that while the mental and social development of all the children when seen at 2 years of age had been affected by the quality of their home, the effect was especially pronounced for those who had suffered severe perinatal stress. Drillien's (1964) longitudinal study of premature children (birth weight below 5½ lbs) found that: "The effect of low birth weight is seen to be most marked in children who have had the added disadvantage of an adverse home background and a poor genetic endowment of intelligence." The effect of the standard of maternal care on weight and height at ages 2 years and 4 years was found to be most pronounced in the small prematures (under 4½ lbs) and while all birth weight groups (controls and prematures) showed a rise in behaviour disturbance when there had been environmental stress, the small prematures were again affected most.

B. Ill-health

When looking at the health problems among the children after the neonatal period and before the abuse incident, we found a high rate in both groups. As many as five out of the nine problem-free group suffered from a significant health problem as defined in Chapter V compared with 15 out of the 31 in the group with problems.

The occurrence of health problems in the mothers between the birth of the abused child and the time of the identifying injury is shown in Table 33. Both physical and psychiatric illnesses are included.

Table 33   Early health problems: mothers of 40 children

Status at follow-up	None	Physical	Psychiatric	Both
Problem-free n = 9	1	1	6	1
With problems n = 31	14	3	7	7

Only one mother of the nine problem-free children did not have a health problem and seven of the nine at the time of admission gave a recent history of psychiatric or emotional illness compared with 14 of the 31 (45%) in the group with problems. Superficially the high incidence of psychiatrically ill mothers would seem to be incompatible with a good outcome yet it may be that if the main precipitating factor is the mother's temporary disturbance, the child has a reasonable chance of surviving unscathed, the prognosis being less good when the abuse is associated with developmental difficulties in the child or long-standing social problems.

C. The abuse

It might be expected that those who did well had not been victims of recurrent abuse; however, four problem-free children were included among the 17 children who had suffered definite abuse prior to the actual referral incident.

Using the classification of severity of abuse given in Chapter II, serious injury did not necessarily mean the child would have problems at follow-up; four of the nine children judged to have done well had suffered serious abuse. This included two with serious head injuries, one having survived an intracranial bleed and the other multiple fractures of the skull.

The sample of abused children seen in follow-up had been a young group at the time of abuse with 63% under the age of 1 year at the time of admission to the Park Hospital. One would expect the young age of a child to influence the outcome in two possible ways: the younger child is at increased risk of the assault producing long-term neurological damage but on the other hand he will have been exposed to abnormal child-rearing for a relatively short period of time. Thus, although at least six of the infants in our sample identified under the age of 1 year suffered injuries that resulted in moderate or severe neurological handicap, overall a higher proportion of those presenting under the age of 1 year did well (seven out of 25) compared with those presenting over 1 year (two out of 15). None of the ten children admitted over the age of 2 years was considered to be problem-free on follow-up (see Table 34).

Table 34   Age at admission

Status at follow-up	Admitted under 1 year	Admitted between 1-2 year	Admitted over age 2 years
Problem-free n = 9	7	2	—
With problems n = 31	18	3	10

D. Developmental problems on admission

At the time of identification of the abuse incident resulting in admission to the Park Hospital, seven children showed evidence of growth retardation. One was found among the nine children who were problem-free on follow-up, while six had problems, three of whom had failed to do well because of continuing failure to thrive, among other reasons.

The identification of developmental delay or behavioural problems in an abused child during the initial hospital stay did not preclude him from doing well at follow-up (see Table 35). However, only one of the problem-free group exhibited both developmental delay and behavioural disturbance while 14 (45%) of the children not doing so well at follow-up had shown both problems.

Table 35   History of developmental problems on admission

Status at follow-up	None	Developmental delay	Behaviour problems	Both
Problem-free n = 9	4	2	2	1
With problems n = 31	10	2	5	14

While this difference is not statistically significant, it does indicate the trend that one might expect ($p = 0.067$; Fisher Exact Test: 1 tailed); the more developmental and behaviour problems a child has accumulated by the time his abuse comes to notice, the more likely he is to continue to have problems in the future.

E. Intelligence

There were 26 abused children over the age of 3 years with IQ scores over 75 (see Chapter VI). These children were not excluded from the problem-free group on the grounds of low intelligence but 19 were excluded for other reasons: growth, health, neurology and behaviour. The remaining seven in the problem-free group included the only two with IQ's in the superior group (IQ 110+) and three of the four with IQ's in the good/average group (75–100). Table 36 shows that those children with IQ's over 110 were statistically more likely to be judged to be problem-free at follow-up than those with IQ's between 110 and 75 ($p = 0.003$; Fisher Exact Test: 2 tailed).

Table 36   Effect of IQ on problems at follow-up (IQ 75 + only)

Status at follow-up	IQ 110+	IQ 75 - 109
Problem-free $n = 7$	5	2
With problems $n = 19$	1	18

This finding could be seen to support Martin and Rodeheffer's (1976) hypothesis that intelligence can facilitate survival in an abusive environment.

F. Legal sanctions and placements

Three of the children who were problem-free on follow-up had been the subjects of statutory sanctions; two were on Place of Safety Orders during the Park admission, one returning home on a Care Order and the other on a Supervision Order. The third child was received into voluntary care straight from the Park Hospital, parental rights being taken subsequently. By the time of follow-up the Supervision Order had been rescinded while the legal status of the other two children remained unchanged. Among the children with problems, 65% had at some time been subjects of statutory sanctions and the legal status had changed for nine (29%) during the follow-up interval but in only one case was this because of the rescission of an order. While statistical differences cannot be shown, there is a noticeable trend towards increased legal activity surrounding the children with problems. However, the need for early legal sanctions did not prevent a child from doing well at follow-up (see Table 37).

Table 37   Legal sanctions

Status at follow-up	Some legal action taken	No legal action taken
Problem-free $n = 9$	3	6
With problems $n = 31$	20	11

At the time of follow-up, not all the children in the problem-free group were living with both natural parents. One was with her mother and co-habitee, one with a lone mother and another with his father and grandparents. One child was in long-term care and had been with foster parents since he was a baby. In the group with problems, there was a similar variety of placements but eight were in permanent care, of whom only three had found long-term substitute families.

During the follow-up interval, three problem-free children had experienced placements away from natural parents. Only one of these involved a major placement change. However, 12 of the 14 children with problems at follow-up who had had placements away from parents had had major placement changes (see Table 38). This

Table 38   Major placement changes

Status at follow-up	None	1 or 2	3 or more
Problem-free $n = 9$	8	1	—
With problems $n = 31$	19	7	5

demonstrates the expected tendency for the children who did well to have had fewer upheavals in their lives than those who exhibited problems at follow-up.

G. At risk register

It seemed reasonable to take the inclusion of a child's name on the social services "At Risk" register as an index of current social worker concern for the child's well-being. Sixty-five per cent of the children in the group with problems had their names on an "At Risk" register at the time of follow-up. Two of the nine problem-free children also had their names included — one was at home on a Care Order and the other's name was removed a few months after the assessment. Neither of these children was at risk of abuse although one was in danger of being kidnapped by one of his warring parents.

IV. THE SIBLINGS

When considering the siblings it must be remembered that some of them are from the same family and therefore not every sibling is a totally independent item, unlike the abused children. When we compared the problem-free siblings with the rest, the statistically significant differences that we found for the abused children were not observed. One explanation is that, for example, abnormal delivery or prematurity are such low frequency events amongst the siblings that no significant difference would show in our small numbers. Table 39 demonstrates this problem.

Table 39   Abnormal labour/delivery in siblings

Status at follow-up	Abnormal labour or delivery	Normal labour + delivery
Problem-free $n = 21$	1	20
With problems $n = 20$	2	18

The difference between the two outcome groups for the occurrence of superior intelligence is also less marked for the siblings (see Table 40) ($p = 0.23$; Fisher Exact Test: 2 tailed).

Table 40   Effect of IQ on outcome in siblings (IQ 75 + only)

Status at follow-up	IQ 110+	IQ 75 - 109
Problem-free n = 14	5	9
With problems n = 12	1	11

While most of those in the superior and above average range of intelligence had no problems, neither did 45% of those with IQ's between 100–75. This may be because of the greater tolerance of the parents towards the siblings or because the siblings had less disadvantages to contend with than their abused brothers and sisters. The only difference between the problem-free siblings and those in the group with problems which approached any significance was the timing of their birth: 73% of those born after intervention were doing well compared with 38% of those who had already been born at the time of the original Park Hospital admission and were living in the family at its most disturbed time (p = 0.066; Fisher Exact Test: 2 tailed). We hope that this shows the benefits of intervention reflecting on the care of children born subsequently.

V. THE FAMILIES

The 33 natural families with care of 70 children were examined in an attempt to identify characteristics that might have influenced the problems experienced by the children. (The ten children in care and the one dead child were excluded.)

Overall there was a tendency, which was more marked among the abused than the siblings, for a child in a family with only one or two children to be doing better than those from a larger family. Nevertheless, the four families with four children all had at least one sibling who was doing well.

The social class distribution between the children with problems and those without differs very little. The only difference worth noting was that nine out of the 11 children living with single mothers had problems. This included four siblings and five abused children. Likewise, the amount of the parents' current earned income seemed to have little effect on the children's outcome. Similar proportions of children from all income brackets came into both the groups with and without problems. However, only one sibling of the total of six children living with parents receiving social security benefit was problem-free. Whether or not the mother was in employment had no direct influence on the incidence of problems.

Very few of the children in our sample lived in over-crowded or un-satisfactory housing conditions and when they did, it did not preclude them from doing well. Nor did the children who had moved house with their family more than once a year all have problems.

The descriptions of the families' social activities in Chapter IX show that few were socially isolated. Even those that were had some children who were doing well. This may well have been because the children had opportunities at playgroups and school for socialization.

In order to relate the children's status on follow-up to difficulties being experienced by the parents, we identified a group of parents for whom there was objective evidence of disturbance. We included parents with a current chronic and serious physical illness, parents who had had more than a brief contact with a psychiatrist during the follow-up interval and parents who had divorced or who had had prolonged separations from their partner. This applied to 18 families with 38 children living with them (17 abused and 21 siblings). In spite of the parents' problems, which may well have affected their child-rearing practices, 39% of their children were doing well — almost the same proportion as those doing well from the more stable families (41%) (see Table 41).

Table 41   Children's status on follow-up related to parents' problems

Status at follow-up	Parents with difficulties (18 families) (38 children)	Parents without difficulties (15 families) (32 children)	Total (33 families) (70 children)
Problem-free	15	13	28
With problems	23	19	42

In summary it was not possible from our data to define those parents or families whose children were more likely to do well or who were certain to be experiencing problems on follow-up. This was probably because many of the families had children in both groups. Indeed we found that 23 (70%) of the 33 families studied had at least one problem-free child. This is very encouraging as it shows that the majority of the parents did have the ability to rear a child successfully, despite past and present problems.

VI. OUR IMPRESSIONS OF THE CHILDREN WHO DID WELL

When we were with the children who did well, we felt we were observing the contrasting type of behaviour from that often associated with abused children and described by us in Chapter VII. These children had a striking ability to enjoy themselves, laughing and making us laugh. They had self-confidence and were able to make their wishes known without being difficult. They were, like the normal group of children assessed developmentally (Chapter VI), spontaneous and not at all withdrawn. They asked questions and made comments on what was happening. Their behaviour was not precocious but appropriate for their age and intelligence level. Their school question-naires confirmed that their ability to get on with people extended to their peer group.

We found all these children likeable; they were able to interact ap-propriately with other children and adults. This was not a superficial impression as on further examination of their biographies, we found that they had indeed been able to form good and lasting relationships. For some children these had developed within the family while for others, secure relationships had been established with adults outside the nuclear family. One example was where a father had developed a very close relationship with his son, spending much time with him in the evenings and at weekends. This man was determined to compensate for his earlier neglect when he had regularly left his depressed wife to cope alone with a fretful baby and had failed to intervene when the abuse started. It was this father who brought the child for a follow-up assessment at the Park Hospital, showing delight when it became obvious that the child was now developmentally normal with above average intelligence. He insisted that he was as much to blame as his wife for the earlier abuse and repeated that he was determined to make it up to both wife and child.

Another example is the only abused child in long-term care who was doing well. He had established a strong relationship with his foster parents and foster siblings. This new nuclear family gave him the con-fidence to cope with the uncertainty of his continuing unsatisfactory relationship with his natural mother and her new husband without developing behavioural disturbance. This child was full of normal, boisterous, imaginative and boyish activity without being uncontrollable or hostile like some of the children from abusing families. He was very fortunate that his closest relationship was with his foster father who formed an ideal example and he was realistically looking forward to following his "father's" footsteps into agricultural work.

In contrast to this, another child performed equally well despite continuing and overt rejection by her mother with whom she lived. Looking back into her biography, we find that at the age of 2 years she had attended a small local day care centre where a strong mutual attachment had been formed between her and a member of staff. She visited this woman's home and lived there on several occasions when her mother was admitted to hospital. This bond had given the child confidence and ability to go on to make other adult friends outside the home. At school she was a popular child to teach and was achieving her full academic potential. She had many friends of her own age and elected to spend much of her spare time with another family. During her assessment she charmed everyone with a ready smile and quiet wit. She was not too compliant and obviously had a strong will of her own.

We observed that there were two types of parent who allowed their children the opportunity to form an attachment to an adult outside the home. Firstly, there were those who had gained more insight into their relationship with their child and were able to accept intellectually that other adults could probably offer the child an emotional warmth that was lacking from them. Prior to intervention, many of these parents had been rejecting and yet possessive.

For example, a mother who was emerging from a life-time of psychiatric disturbance, welcomed the interest of the local playgroup, recognizing that they could provide her daughter with opportunities which she and her husband found difficult to organize. The playgroup leader had picked up the child's superior ability and was giving her special care and compensating for the parents' lack of drive and their social isolation.

The other type of parent was from a typical social problem family and only too happy for their child to spend as much time outside the home as possible. For these children it is often a matter of chance whether they form a good relationship with another adult or not. In some families we saw this happening with one child while a sibling was well on the way to a delinquent adolescence.

It is difficult to know whether secure relationships had helped to produce likeable qualities in these children, or whether their more likeable personalities had enabled them to initiate the good relationships. Whatever had happened in the past, by the time we saw these children they were well on the way to being life's "winners", in dramatic contrast to the few children at the other end of the scale who, on account of their own maladjusted behaviour and the responses this evoked, were rapidly losing any chance of a happy life.

> "For unto every one that hath, shall be given and he shall have abundance: but from him that hath not, shall be taken away even that which he hath." *(Matthew* 25:29)

VII. DISCUSSION

The examination of factors associated with problem-free status on follow-up gives us some idea of the profile of a child likely to have a chance of surviving the abusive experience without obvious physical, developmental or emotional handicap. We have seen a definite trend for the children who were problem-free at follow-up to have been identified as abused when they were young but to have escaped long-term neurological deficit. They were unlikely to have experienced perinatal problems or to have accumulated both developmental and behavioural abnormalities before intervention. Following intervention, although they may have been the subject of legal proceedings, these were unlikely to have been protracted or recurrent and placement changes were few. One possible protective factor identified among the abused children was the possession of above average intelligence.

Among the siblings it is more difficult to draw conclusions from our data about the characteristics of those likely to do well. An important factor seems to be the timing of their birth in relation to intervention in the family. The children born after the identification of abuse were doing better than those who were already living in the family at the time of abuse, even though they had escaped physical assault. The reasons why the differences observed in the abused group do not hold out for the siblings are complex but we can speculate that as they have not been the identified abused child, they have fewer disadvantages to fight against, in addition to having had a less traumatic start in life. They may therefore have less need for the protective factor of higher intelligence.

When we leave our objective data and consider the impressions these children made on us, it is our hypothesis that the children who did well and were problem-free, had successfully passed the developmental hurdle of basic trust (Erikson, 1965) and were therefore able to form good relationships and, having learned appropriate behaviour, presented as friendly, normal, likeable children. Therefore, it seems to us that one of the paramount aims of intervention for the abused child must be to provide the experience and opportunities for him to form secure relationships with people he can trust.

XII. Observations and ideas

In this book we have described in detail a few families whom we came to know very well for a brief moment. We were taking still pictures from the fast moving films of these children's rapidly changing lives. However, what we were observing was clearly the consequence of what had passed before and will surely influence that yet to come. The children's biographies have continued to unfold since our assessments and further information has filtered through to us up to the time of writing which has confirmed the need to view the consequences of abuse as a developmental process. Some families have continued to go from strength to strength, moving further away from the stereotype of "a typical abusing family"; some have produced and are successfully rearing further children. In contrast to this, one notorious problem family battered their new baby. Now, with all her three children in long-term care, the mother is pregnant again. In another hostile and disturbed family the eldest daughter, in a desperate plea for help, has taken an overdose. We hope her attempt to gain acknowledgement of the extent of the problems within the family will be more successful than ours. In other families, biographies have been jolted by events apparently unconnected with abuse, a tragic example being the totally unexpected death of a young father in the sample. Our understanding of the consequences of abuse would be still greater if we could return at intervals to capture more moments in these children's lives, following them up until they themselves become parents.

It should have become obvious to the reader by now that there is no magic formula that can guarantee the optimum outcome for a given abused child. For each case, once the abuse has occurred, the definition of successful outcome will vary. The goals set for a seriously neurologically handicapped baby will have to differ from those set for an older, intelligent, mildly injured but seriously rejected child. Our book therefore can only help by influencing the philosophy and general practice in the care of abused children — we cannot recommend a defined set of procedures to be followed.

Our study was looking at the consequences of child abuse for a few children who had received intensive intervention. While this resulted in some excellent long-term therapeutic arrangements, it was also possible to identify short-comings. With hindsight we will try to use these observations to draw conclusions about the sort of approaches which we feel could improve the abused child's later development. Some specific examples have already been given earlier in the book. It is our intention here to add some further ideas and make more general observations of how existing services could become more effective.

It will be argued that we cannot draw general conclusions from the results of our sample because the families we studied were not typical abusing families. We would like to contest this and claim that our study provides a wider and more realistic view of the consequences of child abuse because, unlike the traditional follow-up studies, it did not draw index cases solely from the lower socio-economic groups nor did we have high numbers of children lost to follow-up. Our sample includes families from the lower social classes, multi-problem families and a few with a history of petty crime. In addition we have one or two professional families and other fathers who are high salary earners. Such people do abuse their children but are still rarely recognized because of the difficulty of admitting that the problem exists among those who could easily be our colleagues or friends. The findings discussed in the previous chapter serve to demonstrate that after the identification of abuse, the children with more privileged parents are not necessarily those with fewer problems. All the multi-problem families had at least one child doing well on our very strict criteria.

We will present our general observations and ideas about practice from the viewpoints of the three main groups of individuals involved: the children, the parents and the professionals.

I. THE CHILDREN

Throughout our investigations we gained the impression that all too often the children's needs as individuals were being ignored while the available time and effort were expended rather diffusely in improving the well-being of the family as a whole. As we have already observed, there was a danger of this occurring even during the initial Park Hospital admission, where the need for detailed assessments on the children could be overshadowed by the desire to keep a family in therapy. In the home it is even easier to forget to look at all the children as individuals and to fail to up-date knowledge of each child's particular needs. Where follow-up of a family consists of traditional social work visiting, this classic mistake is frequently made.

For example, within our sample at follow-up, a hostile middle-class mother was being visited very regularly by a diligent social worker during the day while her elder (abused) child was at school. The mother was expected to talk about her problems in her relationship with the children, which she hardly acknowledged, and the relevant child was seldom seen. This child, we found, had particular problems in school which the teacher was making huge efforts to help her overcome. But no contact had been made between the social worker and the school and the teacher was really in the dark as to what was happening to the child at home. Meanwhile, the social worker had only a mental picture of the child she was discussing, much of which relied on the mother's distorted views. Because of this client's blatant hostility, the health visitor had departed from the case, despite there being a younger child at home, and the social worker was simply thankful to be allowed into the home. The abused child had a serious visual defect, the treatment of which had been neglected by the parents, and she had learning difficulties and serious behaviour problems with her peers. Obtaining help for these handicaps should surely have taken priority over getting the mother to "accept" social work visits.

Even when a family welcomes continuing home visits and the children are safe from further inflicted injury, detailed developmental assessments may reveal specific problems requiring intervention. For example, 3-year old twins were being successfully rehabilitated with their natural parents. A Care Order was still in force and social workers were visiting regularly. Just prior to our assessment, "great progress" had been recorded by the social workers and their visiting had been cut from once a week to once a fortnight. We were not sure exactly what this "progress" was, but the children had certainly been safe from physical injury for well over 18 months. The family was to all intents and purposes now a normal, if somewhat materialistic, diligent, upper working class family and an interview with the parents would not have identified the family as needing help. However, because of the mother's difficulty in caring for very young children, the twins were seriously retarded in their language development and their behaviour was becoming such that they would have been quickly rejected at any local playgroup. It was only when the children were looked at as individuals that the extent of their developmental problems became apparent. This case, like all others, needed continuing monitoring not only for injuries and parent/child relationships, but for the children's growth, neurology, intellectual, social and emotional development. Any case review system must plan to incorporate all these elements.

The message naturally follows on from the conclusions drawn earlier (Lynch and Ounsted, 1976) about the need for a comprehensive developmental assessment for all abused children at the time of identification. Once the abuse has been detected and presumably stopped, the child's development still needs to be monitored; specific help will be required for any defect detected and will take far more time and skill than simply keeping the child safe from physical injury. One thing is certain: we cannot rely on social work services alone to fulfil this function. Even intensive, highly skilled social work help from the NSPCC special unit found that progress was seriously limited in some cases until follow-up individual therapy for the child was incorporated into their treatment plans (Trowell and Castle, 1981).

The high rate of continuing visual and neurological problems also shows that thorough paediatric assessments of these children should continue for some time after the abuse. We find that social workers do not always realize the importance of the child's medical and developmental follow-up. They may be unaware of any medical appointments and therefore unable to ensure that the child obtains the services he needs. The medical staff for their part must be aware of the child's emotional and developmental needs and encourage parents to avail themselves of help offered by the health service. Medical and social work professions must co-operate in ensuring that children keep appointments and get the appropriate therapy.

Some of the children had such strikingly disturbed, hostile and negative behaviour that not only was it impossible to assess their intellectual potential but also their lives were becoming seriously disrupted. Unless long-term therapy includes help for disturbed behaviour, the effects of any other intervention will be lost as the children develop first into delinquent and hostile teenagers and then into the violent parents of a future generation of abused children.

For some families, to break the cycle of deprivation and violence, it may be necessary to include in the treatment plan behaviour or play-therapy programmes specifically aimed at the children. A 7-year old boy who was always the odd-one-out will demonstrate the need for this:

Simon came to notice because he was seriously abused by his father, but this was only the culmination of a series of minor injuries and he had also suffered from prolonged and unrecognized failure to thrive. Intensive therapy for the whole family radically improved relationships and the child was not being abused on follow-up. However, the child was sensitive enough to recognize that he was the odd-one-out. The father openly talked about how it was still more difficult to get on with him and, while the other children clamoured round the house and successfully demanded their parents' attention, Simon tended to withdraw into his own shell, fearing rejection. The parents were gradually trying to change their interactions with him and were able to discuss the problem but meanwhile, Simon was expressing all his anger, hostility and disappointment at school. His teacher wrote thus: "Simon is a difficult child to comment on because he says very little in class. However, he does disrupt other children by taking their things or disturbing their work . . . He does try to annoy other children by constant chattering or stealing. He is often the centre of mischief in the playground."

Unless this child received individual help and therapy to improve his social relationships, then he would proceed to destroy any friendships made and expect not to be liked, getting into deeper and deeper trouble. These problems would not disappear if the child were to be uprooted and taken into long-term care. Firstly, the chances of finding a foster couple who would be able to tolerate his testing-out and his parents' difficult and demanding behaviour, would be very low. Secondly, the parents would not withdraw from Simon's life completely, leaving him very confused (see Jenkins, 1969) and probably would reasonably demand a "trial at home" which would exacerbate Simon's feelings of rejection.

However, despite the parental attitudes, there were many positive features in Simon's home and he had a good and close relationship with his siblings. The best hope for Simon would be to leave him at home but at the same time find help outside the home from an adult who could become a significant figure in the child's life, helping him feel wanted, recognizing his talents and boosting his self esteem. Simon would then be able to find an identity for himself and improve his image among his peers. As it will be recalled, we described several children in Chapter XI where we felt just such relationship with an adult outside the family had significantly contributed to their successful outcome.

If a child begins to make a good relationship with an adult, this could be explored and promoted and incorporated as part of the long-term therapy. All too often such relationships are dismissed as being by the way. For example, one of our most unhappy and disturbed children had formed an excellent relationship with his primary school teacher and a member of the school kitchen staff, but case discussions centred on the child's difficult behaviour in his children's home and relationships with the staff there. If the child had been asked, he would have told them that those adults at his school were not at all by the way but central to his well-being.

When looking at the successful progress of some of our under-5's, it was quite clearly the help the child was receiving from a play-group, day nursery or nursery school that was significantly changing the child's attitude and behaviour. We feel that day-care is too often used just as a place of safety and the resources available are not fully tapped or incorporated into the family treatment plan. For example, we know children who are picked up by transport at the beginning of the day, taken to nursery and returned home at the end of the afternoon while the mother has neither met the nursery nurse caring for her child nor has any idea of the day's activities. In contrast to this, where the mother is encouraged to attend frequently, not only has she the opportunity to learn more about interacting with children but also it becomes possible to break through her social isolation.

Much of what we have written about the abused child also applies to the siblings. Their high rate of minor neurological problems, behavioural and developmental problems and maladjustment at school all point to the subtle, long-lasting effects of the family environment on all children in the family. Policies regarding siblings of abused children seem to have an all or nothing quality about them. In our study we have come across all children within one family being considered "at risk", sometimes in spite of the good development and obvious survival of the siblings. In other families, siblings have been taken into care simply because other children in the family have been abused. At the other extreme, unharmed siblings are almost ignored and attention focuses on the abused child even though the siblings could have serious developmental and emotional problems.

II. THE PARENTS

When working with parents in abusing families, it should be remembered that not so very long ago most of them were themselves abused or deprived children. Therefore they share many of the behaviour characteristics of the older children in our sample: hostility, aggressiveness, low self-esteem, inability to trust and poor communication skills. For the parents, the danger of a family-focused approach is that they will only be considered as mothers and fathers and not as separate adults in their own right. Such an attitude will reinforce the inability many of these young men and women have in identifying themselves as individuals with control over their own behaviour. Whatever the likely outcome for a child, whether rehabilitation at home or long-term care, the parents' needs must be taken into account and opportunities for individual and marital therapy be available. Group therapy too must not focus entirely on parenting. Much of what the parents themselves said drew our attention to their needs and it was quite clear that whatever was done for the child, if they were ignored, they could sabotage any progress. To help avoid this, counselling could be made available for the individual parents even years after the abuse incident.

Ironically, abusing parents care very much about being seen as good parents. Very few can state categorically that they do not want their child with them because to claim to want them seems to be proof that they are good parents. Unlike the foster parents in our sample, the natural parents were less able to look objectively at the good and bad in their children and laugh at their faults. They wanted their children to be all good so that they could love them more. Not one of the parents interviewed (apart from a father who had left his wife) had an indifference towards their children — a "don't care" attitude. They wanted deeply to love them, even though sometimes they were seriously rejecting them. This upset them terribly. All too often a statement that they care about their children is taken as proof that the parents want to look after them. On the contrary, it may be one indication that they are prepared to accept whatever is best for a child, if it is explained with confidence by someone whose authority they respect. If a child is in long-term care and it is hoped will stay there, the parents will still benefit from long-term support and follow-up, otherwise we have observed that their desire to be a good parent can get channelled into one of two directions: either persistently requesting the child's return or by having yet another child.

At the time of follow-up we found that some parents still wanted to talk about their feelings and experiences at the time of abuse. One or two had only described in detail to their social workers what had happened years after the incident. It seemed that it was only when they were stronger, had progressed and had formed a really trusting relationship that they felt able to do this. At the home interview we had given all the parents the opportunity to discuss the time of their admission to the Park Hospital and to talk about child abuse. They all had different ways of dealing with this. Some refused to discuss the battering incident whereas others wished to describe their problems leading up to the abuse, to get the interviewer to understand fully their predicament at the time. In contrast, others denied the abuse at follow-up even though at the time of admission some of these parents had actually sought help because they said they had abused. What parents found they wished to avoid most of all was the emotive label "battering". One mother was talking about the injuries which she said she had inflicted on her baby: "I did that to Susannah, but I'm not a baby batterer." Another mother, when describing her serious ill-health and trying to cope with twins, said: "It wasn't baby battering — anyone could have done it." One or two parents talked about sensations of "depersonalization" during the abuse incidents. For example, a young mother who had caused intracranial bleeding in her young baby, said: "It wasn't me who did it. It was this monster who walked out of me and went and did it." The emotional anguish some of these parents were having to cope with was summed up by one young woman who pointed to her handicapped daughter in the distance and said: "I have to look at her every day, see her handicap and know that I caused it. Imagine having to live with that!" In general we felt that the better adjusted parents were those who had accepted what had happened, were ashamed of it, but regarded it as the past and were there to get on with the future. Those parents dwelling on what they had done, trying to seek sympathy and understanding, seemed to have much further to go. An example of a better adjusted mother was one whose husband had been angry that we wished to see the later-born sibling for follow-up assessment. His comment was that it was "just like Big Brother." Her retort was that she had nothing to hide, she wanted to prove what a good mother she could be and that all the bad things were well in the past.

Some parents did proceed to the thorny topic of "what do we tell the child?" in response to such questions as "Why was I at the Park Hospital, Mummy?" There are no easy answers to this question but it would seem that there is appearing a need for counselling services for abused children grown up, rather like those available for adopted children. We have recently had the experience of a young woman, who was seriously physically and sexually abused as a young girl, wanting to read her notes to understand fully what had happened to her as a child at the time when she is planning to become a wife and a mother.

The parents in our sample continued during the follow-up interval to have relatively high rates of health problems and minor psychosomatic complaints for which they consulted their family doctor. Potentially this makes him a key figure in a family's follow-up, but only if there is co-operation and communication between him, the health visitor and the social worker. The true significance of the parents' complaints may then become apparent and may well give warning of increased stress within the family. The effect of even minor health problems on any parent's ability to relate to a child should not be underestimated. For example, even dysmenorrhoea or toothache can effectively prevent a mother from enjoying being with her baby. In such a case , a social worker's efforts are best directed to ensuring that the mother sees her doctor or keeps a dentist's appointment.

Likewise, in our efforts to provide the long-term emotional support for the parents, we must not overlook their need for practical help and advice which may continue for some time after resolution of the acute crises. For example, the family's social isolation means they have few, if any, friends or relatives to turn to for help. Most normal families welcome short respites from constant child care and have friends or relatives on whom they can call, who readily and naturally take a child off the mother's hands for a few hours or days. Many abusing families will need, at least initially, professional help in finding and trusting substitute care especially as they find separation from their children difficult. Under these circumstances the use of short-term care should not be seen as a failure by parents or therapist. Certainly at the time of our follow-up assessment we felt that some families and children would benefit from planned relief from each other. One small boy was a predictable aggravation to his mother during school holidays when he and his three siblings were home all day. The suggestion of two weeks with foster parents in a seaside town during the summer holiday was eagerly received by both the child and his parents.

Throughout this section we have written of the parents as if both are always equally considered. In practice, however, it is very easy for the father to become excluded and for professionals following up a family to focus solely on the mother. Very understandably, social work carried out during working hours predominantly involves the mother; groups are held during the day for mothers, and in paediatric clinics, both in the hospital and the community, it is the usual practice for the children to be brought by the mother alone. This behaviour is often not questioned even when the father is unemployed. Not infrequently fathers both collude with and resent this approach, requiring an explicit invitation before they will be home for a social worker's visit or attend for an assessment. The mothers for their part may seek to continue their husband's exclusion, not wishing to share the attention with him. By talking to the fathers at the time of follow-up, it became clear that some had felt excluded even during the initial Park Hospital admission. One father, who had spent most nights away from the unit because of the need to be at work early in the morning, described how much he had resented all the extra care and attention his wife and child were getting and how this had driven him into the nearest pub! Later in the study period it was becoming acceptable for fathers to seek and be granted leave of absence from their jobs in order to participate in the therapeutic programme more fully. To ensure that fathers remain involved during follow-up entails a more flexible approach to appointments and home visits. Professionals may have to be prepared to see families in the evenings and at weekends. One of the most successful groups run at the Park Hospital was held for fathers by a Consultant early every Sunday evening.

We hope that we have been able to show that each parent, like each child, must be assessed as an individual and be provided with access to long-term support. Because it is often easier to identify with an adult than a child, we must beware of putting the needs of a parent before the best interests of a child. At the same time it must be recognized that ignoring parental needs may result in continual attempts to obstruct plans for the child.

III. THE PROFESSIONALS

We are using the term "professionals" to cover the many disciplines who at some time in their working life are involved in child abuse cases. For some, such as the health visitor and social worker, child abuse is becoming an increasing part of their work-load. Others, like teachers, are less likely to come into regular contact with child abuse. However, it has been made obvious in this book that abused children and their families require at some time or other special help from a very wide range of disciplines.

It seems important to us that all these different professions acquire a background knowledge of the implications of child abuse against which they can provide their specialist skills. This approach will only succeed when there is an efficient coordinator available to the families and the professionals.

As with any researchers using case-notes for obtaining data, we frequently felt frustrated by the absence of clear documentation. This is not simply an academic point as there were occasions when important decisions about a child's future were made by professionals relying on their predecessor's written accounts. Where the recording was inadequate, the current workers risked making the wrong decisions or found themselves unable to convince their seniors that there was sufficient evidence for intervention. If good base-line data are available, then there is a yard-stick against which to measure the family's progress. As we have emphasized before, this should always include growth measurements and developmental assessments of the children.

The findings in our book clearly show that when making decisions, it is necessary to look beyond the severity of the injury. Without a comprehensive assessment it is likely that several of the severely injured babies in our sample, who were rapidly and successfully returned to their parents, would have spent considerable periods of time in care and there would have been less certainty about recommending permanent separation for a child who had been only mildly injured. We were also disturbed to find during the follow-up period almost an obsession about injuries from some professional helpers who constantly asked whether there were further inflicted injuries but did not ask how the child was developing. As already cited, this blinkered attitude led to the neglect of handicap and a specific learning disorder in one child. In another 8-year old girl it was causing her even greater psychological distress as she knew why she was being medically examined regularly at school. Ironically, the detection of bruises in this case never led to effective intervention but rather resulted (in the child's eyes) in further scapegoating and negative attention. We hope that this book will go some way towards preventing such a narrow attitude by showing that often the inflicted injury plays a relatively minor role in long-term outcome and that the absence of recurrent injuries in no way guarantees the well-being of the children in the family.

Another reason for developmental problems being overlooked was the all too human need to avert one's gaze from something one does not want to see. It is often hard to come to terms with the fact that the family one has devoted so much time to has not been "cured". This was brought home to us personally when we compared some of the study children with the group of children recruited as controls for our developmental assessment. We also encountered an administrative pressure for there to be a "through-put" of families in order to keep the system going. It was expected that once improvement had been detected, then families and children would quickly be crossed off the books. It was our experience that withdrawal from these cases always had to be very carefully planned well in advance. What has been striking to us is that those families who seemed to be facing the future most successfully were those who had asked the staff at the Park Hospital always to remain in the background, "just in case."

Given the very varied experiences of the children in our sample, we are even more aware of the difficulty in predicting outcome and making prompt and correct decisions about the future. And yet, we found a worrying group of cases where there was a lack of conviction about deciding whether to keep a child with his parents or to keep him in care. This meant that decisions were constantly being changed and the child subjected to many upheavals. We are not trying to say that decisions should never be changed but once this has happened, the decision should not be reversed yet again. Indeed, one or two of our more successful long-term placements were made after a very brief, well supervised but unsuccessful attempt at rehabilitation. The parents in these cases were seen to be given a chance and later on, when our decisions were questioned, we had the evidence and confidence to withstand pressure to try again. There were a few very unhappy children in our sample who were direct victims of this "try again" policy and seemed to have moved in and out of care at the whim of their parents.

IV. CONCLUSION

For the children in our study the consequences of child abuse varied greatly from children living happily with their parents to those abandoned in institutions. We felt strongly that for some the consequences could have been better, especially if more individual and intensive long-term therapy had been provided. However, even for those whom we found to be happy, well-adjusted and living at home, there is no way of predicting their future ability as parents. This leaves us in a dilemma: on the one hand wishing to keep in touch with the children to make help easily available when needed; on the other hand wanting to avoid the label of deviance and unnecessary intrusion into their lives. The way forward for us seems to be further development of screening programmes at the time of birth when vulnerable parents can be given appropriate help before any serious damage, physical or emotional, has been inflicted on the baby (Ounsted *et al.*, 1982). Our ultimate aim must be prevention.

References

(Numbers in square brackets indicate where the reference is referred to in the text.)

Als, H., Tronick, E., Adamson, L. and Brazelton, T. (1976). The Behaviour of the Full-term but Underweight Newborn Infant. *Developmental Medicine and Child Neurology* 18, 590-602.

[49]

Arthur, G. (1952). The Arthur Adaptation of the Leiter International Performance Scale. Western Psychological Services, California.

[88]

Baher, E., Hyman, C., Jones, C., Jones, R., Kerr, A. and Mitchell, R. (1976). At Risk: An Account of the Work of the Battered Child Research Dept., N.S.P.C.C. Routledge & Kegan Paul, London.

[7, 18, 21, 22, 35, 37, 39, 42, 43, 82, 83, 100, 134, 136, 137, 142, 143, 154]

Baird, I.M., Silverstone, J.T., Grimshaw, J.J. *et al.* (1974). Prevalence of Obesity in a London Borough. *Practitioner* 212, 706-714.

[159]

Baldwin, J.A. and Oliver, J.E. (1975). Epidemiology and Family Characteristics of Severely Abused Children. *British Journal of Preventive and Social Medicine* 29, 205-221.

[21]

Beswick, K., Lynch, M.A. and Roberts, J. (1976). Child Abuse and General Practice. *British Medical Journal* 2, 800-802.

[14]

Birrell, R.G. and Birrell, J.H.W. (1968). The Maltreatment Syndrome in Children: A Hospital Survey. *Medical Journal of Australia* 2, No.23, 1023-1029.

[1, 2, 4, 60]

Blager, F. and Martin, H. (1976). Speech and Language of Abused Children. *In* "The Abused Child" (Martin, H., ed.) Ballinger, Cambridge, Mass.

[83]

Bohman, M. (1970). "Adopted Children and their Families." Proprius, Stockholm.

[118]

Brown, G.W., Bhrolchain, M.N. and Harris, T. (1975). Social Class and Psychiatric Disturbance Among Women in an Urban Population. *Sociology*, 225-254.

[157]

Brown, J.K. and Thistlethwaite, D. (1976). Cerebral Palsy and the Low Birth Weight Infant. Presented at 10th International Study Group on Child Neurology and Cerebral Palsy, Oxford.

[49]

Caffey, J. (1972). The Theory and Practice of Shaking Infants. *American Journal of Diseases of Children* 124, 161-169.

[63]

Canning, R. (1974). School Experiences of Foster Children. *Child Welfare* L 111, 582-587.

[118]

Castle, R.L. and Kerr, A.M. (1972). A Study of Suspected Child Abuse. N.S.P.C.C. Battered Child Research Dept., 1 Riding House Street, London.

[6, 18, 43, 48]

Chamberlain, R.N. and Simpson, R.N. (1979). "The Prevalence of Illness in Childhood." Pitman Medical, Tunbridge Wells.

[72, 74-75]

Cooper, N.A. and Lynch, M.A. (1979). Lost to Follow-up: A Study of Non-attendance at a General Paediatric Out-patient Clinic. *Archives of Disease in Childhood* 55, 765-769.

[75, 79]

Creighton, S.J. and Owtram, P.J. (1977). Child Victims of Physical Abuse. A Report on the Findings of N.S.P.C.C. Special Unit's Registers. N.S.P.C.C., London.

[18, 32, 41, 43, 44, 48]

Davie, R. Butler, N. and Goldstein, H. (1972). "From Birth to Seven. A Report of the National Child Development Study." Longman Group, Ltd., London.

[136, 140, 141]

Davies, P.A., Robinson, R.J., Scopes, J.W., Tizard, J.P.M. and Wigglesworth, J.S. (1972). Clinics in Developmental Medicine Nos. 44/45: Medical Care of Newborn Babies, S.I.MP. Heinemann Medical, London. Lippincott, Philadelphia.

[49]

D.H.S.S. (1974). Non-Accidental Injury to Children. Letter: L.A.S.S.L. (74) 13.

[32, 42]

D.H.S.S. and Home Office (1976). Non-Accidental Injury to Children: The Police and Case Conferences. Letter: L.A.S.S.L. (76) 26.

[42]

Deschamps, G. (1979). Problems Associated with the Adoption of Abused Children. In "Medical Aspects of Adoption and Foster Care" (S. Wolkind, ed.) Clinics in Developmental Medicine No.70 S.I.M.P. with Heinemann Medical, London; Lippincott, Philadelphia.

[119]

Doll, E. (1965). Vineland Social Maturity Scale. American Guidance Service Inc., Minnesota.

[88]

Douglas, J.W.B., Ross, J.M. and Simpson, H.R. (1968). "All our Future: A Longitudinal Study of Secondary Education." Peter Davies, London.

[112]

Drillien, C.M. (1964). "The Growth and Development of the Prematurely Born Infant." Livingstone, Edinburgh and London.

[181]

Dunn, L.M. (1965). "Expanded Manual for the Peabody Picture Vocabularly Test." American Guidance Service Inc., Minnesota.

[88]

Ebbin, A.J., Gollub, M.H., Stein, A.M. and Wilson, M.G. (1969). Battered Child Syndrome at the Los Angeles County General Hospital. American Journal of Diseases of Children 118, 660-667.

[6, 50]

Elmer, E. (1967). "Children in Jeopardy: A Study of Abused Minors and their Families". University of Pittsburgh Press, Pittsburgh.

[115, 134-135, 150, 154]

Elmer, E. and Gregg, G.S. (1967). Developmental Characteristics of Abused Children. Pediatrics 40, 596-602.

[1, 6, 48, 50-51, 56, 60, 63, 79, 81, 82]

Elmer, E. (1977). A Follow-up Study of Traumatized Children. *Pediatrics* **59**, 273-279.

[2, 5, 100, 116]

Erikson, E.H. (1965). "Childhood and Society." Penguin Books, Harmondsworth, England.

[192]

Farrington, D.P. (1981). The Prevalence of Convictions. *British Journal of Criminology* **21**, No.2, 173-175.

[145]

Freeman, R. (1977). The Questionnaire as a Research Tool. *In* "Child Abuse Prediction, Prevention and Follow-up" (A.W. Franklin, ed). Churchill Livingstone, Edinburgh, London and New York.

[3]

Friedman, S.B. and Morse, C.W. (1974). Child Abuse: A Five-Year Follow-up of Early Case Finding in the Emergency Dept. *Pediatrics* **54**, No.4, 404-410.

[4]

Galdston, R. (1965). Observations on Children who have been Physically Abused and their Parents. *American Journal of Psychiatry* **122**, 440-443.

[98]

George, V. (1970). "Foster Care: Theory and Practice." Routledge and Kegan Paul, London.

[117]

Gil, D.G. (1969). Physical Abuse of Children: Findings and Implications of a Nationwide Survey, *Pediatrics* **44** No.5, Part 2, 857-864.

[3]

Gil, D.G. (1970). "Violence Against Children." Harvard University Press, Cambridge, Mass.

[82]

Goldfarb, W. (1945). Effects of Psychological Deprivation in Infancy and Subsequent Stimulation. *American Journal of Psychiatry* **102**, 18-33.

[116]

Gray, J.A. (1977). Drug Effects on Fear and Frustration. *In* "Handbook of Psychopharmacology," Vol. 8 (L. Iverson, S. Iverson, S. Snyder, eds). Plenum Press, New York.

[16]

Gray, J. and Kempe, R. (1976). The Abused Child at Time of Injury *In* "The Abused Child" (H.P. Martin, ed.). Ballinger, Cambridge, Mass.

[98-99]

Green, A.H., Gaines, R.W. and Sandgrund, A. (1974). Psychological Sequelae of Child Abuse and Neglect. Paper presented at 127th Annual Meeting of American Psychiatric Association, Detroit, Michigan.

[2]

Greengard, J. (1964). The Battered Child Syndrome. *Medical Science (Philadelphia)* **15**, 82-91.

[50]

Gregg, G.S. and Elmer, E. (1969). Infant Injuries: Accident or Abuse? *Pediatrics* **44**, 434-439.

[50, 80, 81]

Hall, M.H. (1975). A View From the Emergency and Accident Department. *In* "Concerning Child Abuse" (A.W. Franklin, ed.). Churchill Livingstone, Edinburgh, London and New York.

[3]

Hallett, C. and Stevenson, O. (1980). "Child Abuse: Aspects of Inter-professional Co-operation." George Allen and Unwin, London.

[32]

Harcourt, B. and Hopkins, D. (1971). Ophthalmic Manifestations of the Battered Baby Syndrome. *British Medical Journal* **3**, 398-401.

[62]

H.M.S.O. (1979). Morbidity Statistics from General Practice, 1971-1972. Second National Study on Medical and Population Subjects, No.36. H.M.S.O., London.

[75, 157]

Hoggett, B. (1977). "Social Work and Law: Parents and Children." Sweet and Maxwell, London.

[30]

Holman, R.R. and Kanwar, S. (1975). Early Life of the Battered Child. *Archives of Disease in Childhood* **50**, 78-80.

[60-61]

Howells, J.G. (1974). "Remember Maria." Butterworth and Co. Ltd, London.

[3]

Hufton, I.W. and Oates, R.K. (1977). Non-Organic Failure to Thrive: A Long-Term Follow-Up. *Pediatrics* **59**, No.1, 73-77.

[101, 109, 135, 155]

Illingworth, C.M. (1977). Paediatric Accident and Emergency: Medical or Surgical? *Public Health* **91**, 147-149.

[75]

Jenkins, R. (1969). Long-Term Fostering. *Case Conference* **15**, 9, 349-353.

[118, 197]

Johnson, B. and Morse, H. (1968). "The Battered Child: A Study of Children with Inflicted Injuries." Denver Department of Welfare, Denver.

[51, 79]

Kadushin, A. (1970). "Adopting Older Children." Columbia University Press, New York.

[118]

Kempe, C.H., Silverman, F.N., Steele, B.F., Droegemuller, W. Silver, H.K. (1962). The Battered Child Syndrome. *Journal of the American Medical Association* **181**, 17-24.

[62]

Kempe, C.H. (1968). Some Problems Encountered by Welfare Departments in the Management of the Battered Child Syndrome. *In* "The Battered Child" (R.E. Helfer, C.H. Kempe eds). University of Chicago Press, Chicago.

[39]

Kempe, R. (1976). Related Aspects in Child Psychiatry (Section 3: Arresting or Freezing the Developmental Process by Helfer, R.E., McKinney, J.P., Kempe, R.). *In* "Child Abuse and Neglect: The Family and the Community" (R.E. Helfer and C.H. Kempe, eds). Ballinger, Cambridge, Mass.

[83]

Klaus, M.H. and Kennell, J.H. (1976). "Maternal-Infant Bonding." C.V. Mosby Co., St Louis.

[49]

Klein, M. and Stern, S. (1971). Low Birth Weight and the Battered Child Syndrome. *American Journal of Diseases of Children* **122**, 15-18.

[48, 60]

Koel, B.S. (1969). Failure to Thrive and Fatal Injury as a Continuum. *American Journal of Diseases of Children* **118**, 565-567.

[50]

Kraus, J. (1971). Predicting Success of Foster Placements for School-age Children. *Social Work* **16**, 63-72.

[117]

Krieger, I. (1974). Food Restriction as a Form of Child Abuse in Ten Cases of Psychosocial Deprivation Dwarfism. *Clinical Pediatrics* **13**, 127-133.

[57]

Loadman, A.E. and McRae, K.N. (1977). The Deprived Child in Adoption. *Developmental Medicine and Child Neurology* **19**, 213-223.

[119]

Lynch, M.A. (1975). Ill-health and Child Abuse. *Lancet* **2**, 317-319.

[22, 34, 61, 180]

Lynch, M.A. (1976). Child Abuse — The Critical Path. *The Journal of Maternal and Child Health* **July 1976**, 25-29.

[15, 62]

Lynch, M.A., Lindsay, J. and Ounsted, C. (1975). Tranquillizers Causing Aggression. *British Medical Journal* **1**, 266.

[16, 161]

Lynch, M.A. and Ounsted, C. (1976). Residential Therapy: A Place of Safety *In* "Child Abuse and Neglect: The Family and the Community" (R.E. Helfer, C.H. Kempe, eds). Ballinger, Cambridge, Mass.

[15, 196]

Lynch, M.A. and Roberts, J., (1977). Predicting Child Abuse: Signs of Bonding Failure in the Maternity Hospital. *British Medical Journal* **1**, 624-626.

[49, 61]

MacCarthy, D. (1979). Psychological Effects on Growth. *Maternal and Child Health* **4**, 306-311.

[57]

Martin, H. (1972). The Child and his Development. *In* "Helping the Battered Child and his Family" (C.H. Kempe, R.E. Helfer, eds). Lippincott, Philadelphia and Toronto.

[6, 50, 62, 80, 82]

Martin, H., Beezley, P., Conway, E. and Kempe, C.H. (1974). The Development of Abused Children. *Advances in Pediatrics* **21**, 25-73.

[1, 4, 6, 48, 50-51, 56, 62-63, 67-68, 82, 83, 116-117, 135, 141, 142, 150, 154-155, 177-178]

Martin, H. (1976). Which Children Get Abused: High Risk Factors in the Child *In* "The Abused Child: A Multi-disciplinary Approach to Developmental Issues and Treatment" (H. Martin, ed). Ballinger, Cambridge, Mass.

[61]

Martin, H. and Rodeheffer, M. (1976). Learning and Intelligence. *In* "The Abused Child" (H. Martin, ed). Ballinger, Cambridge, Mass.

[81, 82, 177, 184]

Martin, H. and Beezley, P. (1977). Behavioral Observations of Abused Children. *Developmental Medicine and Child Neurology* 19, 373-387.

[100, 116-117, 155]

Martin, H. (1979). Child Abuse and Child Development. *Child Abuse and Neglect* 3, 415-421.

[101]

McRae, K.N., Ferguson, A. and Lederman, R.S. (1973). The Battered Child Syndrome. *C.M.A. Journal* 108, 859-866.

[1, 4, 48, 115]

McWhinnie, A. (1978). Professional Fostering. *Adoption and Fostering* 94 (4), 32-40.

[148]

Morris, M.G., Gould, R.W. and Matthews, P.J. (1964). Towards Prevention of Child Abuse. *Children* II, 55-60.

[98]

Morse, C.W., Sahler, O.J.Z. and Friedman, S.B. (1970). A Three Year Follow-Up Study of Abused and Neglected Children. *American Journal of Diseases of Children* 120, 439-446.

[1, 6, 51, 63, 81-82, 115, 154, 177]

Mushin, A.S. (1971). Ocular Damage in the Battered Baby Syndrome. *British Medical Journal* 3, 402-404.

[62]

Napier, H. (1972). Success and Failure in Foster Care. *British Journal of Social Work* 2, 2, 187-204.

[117, 128]

Newson, J. and Newson, E. (1963). "Patterns of Infant Care in an Urban Community." Penguin Books, Harmondsworth, England.

[162]

Newson, J. and Newson, E. (1968). "Four Years Old in an Urban Community." Penguin Books, Harmondsworth, England.

[164, 165, 166-167, 176]

N.S.P.C.C. Casework and Development Dept. (1975). Registers of Suspected Non-Accidental Injury. A Report on registers maintained in Leeds and Manchester by N.S.P.C.C. Special Units. N.S.P.C.C. London.

[6, 18, 37, 41, 48, 49]

N.S.P.C.C. (1969). *See* Skinner, A.E. and Castle, R.L.

N.S.P.C.C. (1972). *See* Castle, R.L. and Kerr, A.M.

N.S.P.C.C. (1976). *See* Baher, E., Hyman, C. *et al.*

N.S.P.C.C. (1977). *See* Creighton, S.J. and Owtram, P.J.

Oates, R.K. and Hufton, I.W. (1977). The Spectrum of Failure to Thrive and Child Abuse: A Follow-up Study. *Child Abuse and Neglect* 1, 119-124.

[50]

Ounsted, C. (1972). Biographical Science: An Essay on Developmental Medicine. *In* "Psychiatric Aspects of Medical Practice" (B. Mandelbrote and M.C. Gelder, eds). Staples Press, London.

[84, 98]

Ounsted, C., Oppenheimer, R. and Lindsay, J. (1974). Aspects of Bonding Failure: The Psychology and Psychotherapeutic Treatment of Families of Battered Children. *Developmental Medicine and Child Neurology* 16, 447-456.

[17, 62]

Ounsted, C. (1975). Gaze Aversion and Child Abuse. *World Medicine* 10, (17) 27.

[2, 19]

Ounsted, C., Gordon, M., Roberts, J. and Milligan, B. (1982). The Fourth Goal of Perinatal Medicine. *British Medical Journal* 284, 879-882.

[15, 204]

Paine, R.S. and Oppé, T.E. (1966). Neurological Examination of Children. Clinics in Developmental Medicine, Nos. 21/22, S.I.M.P. Heinemann, London.

[65, 77]

Parker, R.A. (1966). "Decision in Child Care: A Study of Prediction in Fostering." George Allen and Unwin, London.

[117]

Pierson, M. and Deschamps, G. (1976). L'adoption des enfants maltraités. *Journées Parisiennes de Pédiatrie* 28, 426-431.

[119]

Prosser, H. (1976). "Perspectives on Residential Care." N.F.E.R. Windsor, Berks.

[120]

Prosser, H. (1978). "Perspectives on Foster Care." N.F.E.R., Windsor, Berks.

[117]

Reinhart, J.B. and Elmer, E. (1964). The Abused Child: Mandatory Reporting Legislation. *J.A.M.A.* 188, 358-362.

[34]

Roberts, J., Beswick, K., Leverton, B. and Lynch, M.A. (1977). Prevention of Child Abuse: Group Therapy for Mothers and Children. *Practitioner* 219, 111-115

[14, 79]

Roberts, J. and Hawton, K. (1980). Child Abuse and Attempted Suicide. *British Journal of Psychiatry* 137, 319-323.

[22]

Rodeheffer, M. and Martin, H. (1976). Special Problems in Developmental Assessment of Abused Children. *In* "The Abused Child" (H. Martin, ed). Ballinger, Cambridge, Mass.

[99, 103]

Rutter, M., (1967). A Children's Behaviour Questionnaire for Completion by Teachers: Preliminary Findings. *Journal of Child Psychology and Psychiatry* 8, 1-11.

[107, 109]

Rutter, M., Tizard, J. and Whitmore, K. (1970). "Education, Health and Behaviour." Longman, London.

[70, 112]

Rutter, M., Graham, P. and Yule, W. (1970). A Neuropsychiatric Study in Childhood. Clinics in Developmental Medicine 35/36. S.I.M.P. Heinemann, London

[70]

Rutter, M. (1975). "Helping Troubled Children." Penguin Books Ltd., Harmondsworth, England.

[161, 162]

Sandgrund, A., Gaines, R.W. and Green, A.H., (1974). Child Abuse and Mental Retardation: A Problem of Cause and Effect. *American Journal of Mental Deficiency.* **79**, 327-330.

[61, 80-81]

Seashore, H. (1951). Differences between Verbal and Performance I.Q.'s on the Wechsler Intelligence Scale for Children. *Journal of Consultant Psychology* **15**, 62-67.

[89]

Seglow, J., Pringle, M.L.K. and Wedge, P. (1972). "Growing up Adopted." N.F.E.R., Windsor, Berks, England.

[118]

Shaw, M. and Lebens, K. (1978). "Substitute Family Care: A Regional Study. 2. What shall we do with the Children?" A.B.A.F.A. London.

[120]

Shepherd, M., Oppenheim, B. and Mitchell, S. (1971). "Childhood Behaviour and Mental Health." University of London Press.

[161]

Sheridan, M.D. (1975). "Children's Developmental Progress from Birth to Five Years: The Stycar Sequences." N.F.E.R., Windsor, Berks.

[83, 96]

Sibert, J.R., Maddocks, G.B. and Brown, B.M. (1981). Childhood Accidents: An Endemic of Epidemic Proportions. *Archives of Diseases of Childhood* **56**, 225-227.

[75]

Skegg, D.C.G., Doll, R. and Perry, J. (1977). Use of Medicines in General Practice. *British Medical Journal* **1**, 1561-1563.

[157]

Skinner, A.E. and Castle, R.L. (1969). 78 Battered Children: A Retrospective Study. N.S.P.C.C. Battered Child Research Dept. London.

[18, 37, 43, 49]

Smith, S.M., Hanson, R. and Noble, S. (1973). Parents of Battered Babies: A Controlled Study. *British Medical Journal* **4**, 388-391

[21, 22]

Smith, S.M. and Hanson, R. (1974). 134 Battered Children: A Medical and Psychological Study. *British Medical Journal* **3**, 666-670.

[48, 50, 60, 62, 80, 83]

216   References

Speight, A.N.P., Bridson, J.M. and Cooper, C.E. (1979). Follow-up Survey of
Cases of Child Abuse Seen at Newcastle General Hospital 1974-1975. *Child
Abuse and Neglect* 3, 555-563.

[37, 45-46, 117, 118, 120, 136]

Steele, B.F. and Pollock, C.F. (1968). (2nd Edition: 1974). A Psychiatric Study
of Parents who Abuse Infants and Small Children. *In* "The Battered Child"
(R.E. Helfer and C.H. Kempe, eds). University of Chicago Press, Chicago and
London.

[22, 60, 142]

Stott, D.H. (1974). "Bristol Social Adjustment Guides Manual. The Social
Adjustment of Children." 5th Edition. Hodder and Stoughton, London.

[107, 108, 110]

Stutsman, R. (1931). "Guide for Administering Merrill-Palmer Scale of Mental
Tests." Harcourt, Brace and Wald, Inc.

[88]

Sunday Times Magazine (1977). 1st May. p.33.

[3]

Sussman, A. and Cohen, S.J. (1975). "Reporting Child Abuse and Neglect:
Guidelines for Legislation." Ballinger, Cambridge, Mass.

[31, 34]

Taitz, L.S. (1980). Effects on Growth and Development of Social,
Psychological and Environmental Factors. *Child Abuse and Neglect* 4,
55-65.

[135-136, 155]

Tardieu, A. (1860). Études médico-légal sur les sévices et mauvais traitements
exercés sur des enfants. *Annales de Hygiène Publique et de Médicine Légale*
13, 361-398.

[98]

Thoburn, J. (1979). Good Enough Care? A Study of Children Who Went Home
on Trial. *Child Abuse and Neglect* 3, 73-80.

[36]

Tizard, B. (1977). "Adoption: A Second Chance." Open Books, London.

[119-120]

Touwen, B.C.L. and Prechtl, H.F.R. (1970). The Neurological Examination of
the Child with Minor Nerve Dysfunction. Clinics in Developmental Medicine
No.38 S.I.M.P. Heinemann, London.

[65, 77]

Trowell, J. and Castle, R.L. (1981). Treating Abused Children. *Child Abuse and Neglect* 5, 187-192.

[196]

Wechsler, D. (1963). "Wechsler Pre-school and Primary Scale of Intelligence Manual." Psychological Corporation, New York.

[88]

Wechsler, D. (1976). Wechsler Intelligence Scale for Children Manual (Revised). N.F.E.R. Publishing Company. Imprint of Humanities Press Inc., Atlantic Highlands, N.J. 07716.

[88]

Wedge, P. and Prosser, H. (1973). "Born to Fail?" Arrow Books, London.

[142]

Werner, E., Simonian, K., Bierman, J.M. and French, F.E. (1967). Cumulative Effect of Perinatal Complications and Deprived Environment on Physical, Intellectual and Social Development of Pre-school Children. *Pediatrics* 39, 490-505.

[181]

Weston, J.T. (1968). The Pathology of Child Abuse. *In* "The Battered Child" (R.E. Helfer and C.H. Kempe, eds). University of Chicago Press, Chicago and London.

[49]

Wilford, M., McBain, P., Angell, N., Tarlin, S. *et al.* (1979). English Child Protection Legislation and Procedure: An Aid or a Hindrance to the Abused Child and the Family? *Child Abuse and Neglect* 3, 315-321.

[31]

Wolkind, S. (1977). Women Who Have Been in Care: Psychological and Social Status During Pregnancy. *Journal of Child Psychology and Psychiatry* 18, 179-182

[120]

Wolkind, S., Kruk, S. and Hall, F. (To be published). The Family Research Unit's Study of Women From Broken Homes. What Conclusions Should we Draw?

[120]

Index

219